LOCOMOTION PAPERS   LP136

THE
ELY & ST IVES
RAILWAY

by
Peter Paye

THE OAKWOOD PRESS

© Oakwood Press & Peter Paye 2014

First edition published 1982
Second revised edition published 2014

British Library Cataloguing in Publication Data
A Record for this book is available from the British Library
ISBN 978 0 85361 732 7

Typeset by Oakwood Graphics.
Repro by PKmediaworks, Cranborne, Dorset.
Printed by Gomer Press, Llandysul, Ceredigion.

All rights reserved. No part of this book may be reproduced or transmitted in any form or by any means, electronic or mechanical, including photocopying, recording or by any information storage and retrieval system, without permission from the Publisher in writing.

Note
Much of the rolling stock used on the Ely & St Ives Railway was also used on many other ex-Great Eastern Railway branches. For this reason the plans published in the author's earlier titles have not been repeated in this volume.

By the same author and published by Oakwood Press:

The Snape Branch (2005), The Hadleigh Branch (2006), The Jersey Eastern Railway (2007), The Framlingham Branch (2008), The Wisbech & Upwell Tramway (2009), The Bishop's Stortford, Dunmow and Braintree Branch (2010), The Mellis & Eye Railway (2012), The Aldeburgh Branch (2012), The Hayling Railway (2013)

Title page: 'J15' class 0-6-0 No. 65457 departing from Wilburton with a train loaded with sugar beet in the autumn of 1958. During the sugar beet season October to January, Wilburton and neighbouring Stretham and Haddenham dealt with a large volume of this traffic but for the other nine months of the year very little traffic was generated and weeks went by without a train calling save to drop off an occasional wagon of coal and pick up the empty vehicle once the coal merchant had emptied the contents. Most of the sugar beet from the branch stations was sent to the Ely processing factory.   *Dr I.C. Allen*

Front cover: 'J15' class 0-6-0 No. 65457 trundles across Grunty Fen, between Stretham and Wilburton with the up branch goods train, consisting of a covered van, nine open wagons, mostly loaded with sugar beet and a brake van in the autumn of 1957.   *Dr I.C. Allen*

Rear cover, top: Haddenham station with 'J17' class 0-6-0 No. 65583 entering with an Ely to St Ives freight working. The small station building hosted a booking office, waiting room and staff room and in this 1957 view facing towards Ely, 27 years after the withdrawal of passenger services, the station phone was still available for use by the public. The goods yard in the background is occupied by two open wagons and a covered van, whilst the 480 ft-long down reception siding partially covered in weeds is in the foreground.   *Dr I.C. Allen*

Rear cover: Pre-Grouping Railway Clearing House map showing the Ely & St Ives Railway and environs.   *Oakwood Press Collection*

Published by The Oakwood Press (Usk), P.O. Box 13, Usk, Mon., NP15 1YS.
E-mail: sales@oakwoodpress.co.uk
Website: www.oakwoodpress.co.uk

Contents

	Introduction	5
Chapter One	A Railway from Ely to Sutton	6
Chapter Two	Extension to St Ives	16
Chapter Three	Great Eastern Takeover	26
Chapter Four	Grouping and Nationalization	45
Chapter Five	The Route Described	61
Chapter Six	Permanent Way, Signalling and Staff	95
Chapter Seven	Timetables and Traffic	115
Chapter Eight	Locomotives and Rolling Stock	139
Appendix One	Lengths of Platforms and Sidings	171
Appendix Two	Level Crossings	172
Appendix Three	Bridges	174
	Acknowledgements	175
	Bibliography	175
	Index	176

'J17' class 0-6-0 No. 65532 negotiates the deep cutting on the approach to Bluntisham with the weekdays-only St Ives to Ely goods train consisting of five covered vans and tailed by a brake van in 1957. The 3¾ milepost from St Ives is to the lower right. After the closure of the central section of the line from Bluntisham to Sutton in 1958, a truncated goods service was maintained between St Ives and Bluntisham as the mill provided considerable traffic to the railway. However, as tonnages reduced it was considered uneconomic to keep the short section open and when the contract between BR and the traders expired, the traffic was withdrawn and the line to Bluntisham from Needingworth Junction closed on and from 5th October, 1964. *Dr I.C. Allen*

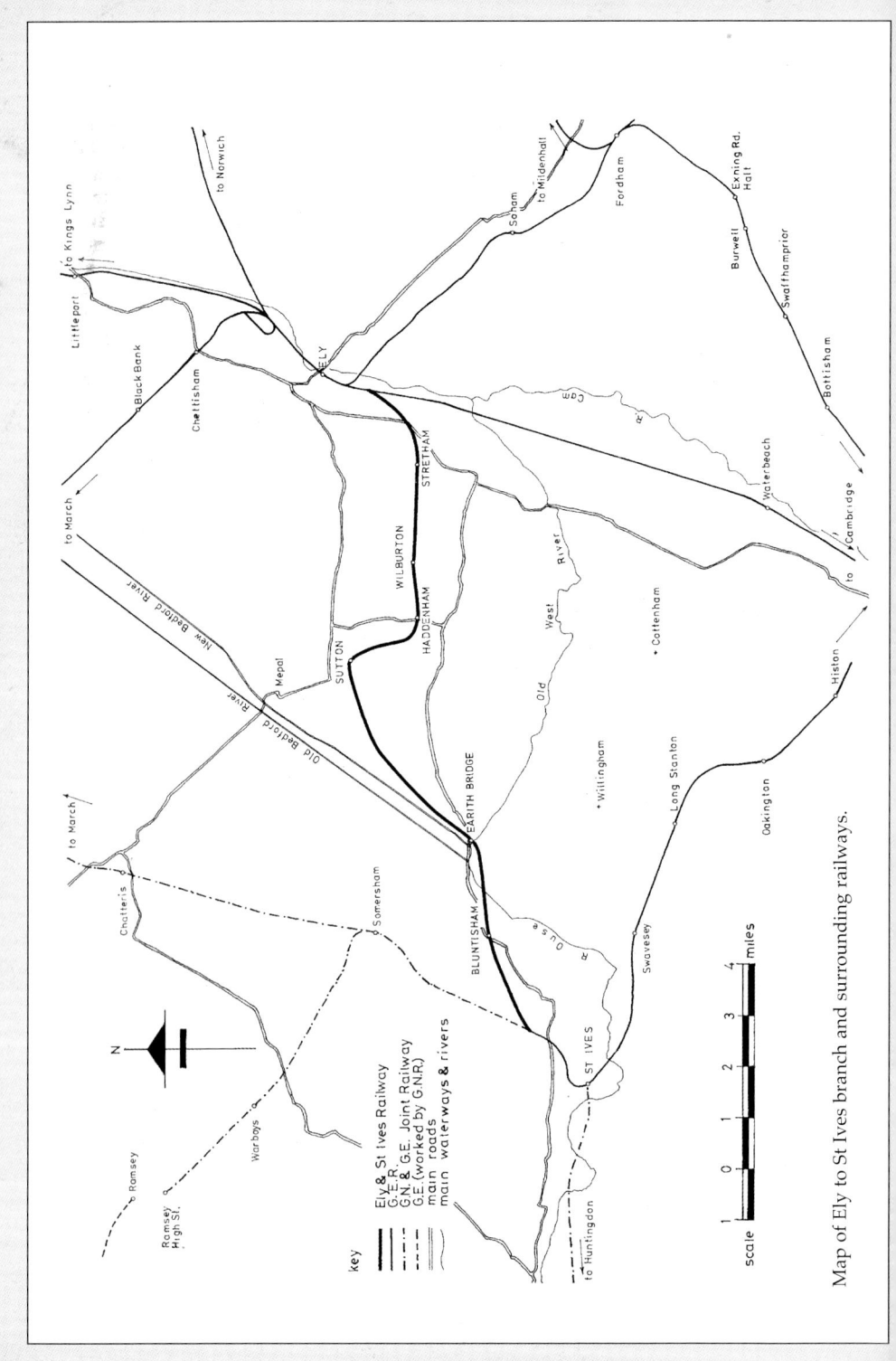

Map of Ely to St Ives branch and surrounding railways.

Introduction

Travellers enduring the ride between Cambridge and Ely on elderly Great Eastern Railway (GER) coaching stock or later London & North Eastern Railway (LNER) replacements in the late 19th and early 20th century, often complained of the monotony of the landscape through which they passed. This vast tract of treeless alluvial black fields, famed for the cultivation of root crops and stretching in each direction to the horizon, was part of the southern area of the fens. A Highland gamekeeper journeying by train near Ely on his first visit to southern England, awestruck by the sense of space remarked, 'whichever way I look there is nothing to interfere with the view'. The fens were not, however, uniformly flat for there were several fen islands where higher land allowed settlements to develop above the flood plain. The magnificent Ely Cathedral was established on one such island and the edifice majestically appearing out of the mist on a dank winter morn or against the blue sky of a summer day or the sunset of an autumn evening was a joy to behold after the seemingly endless flat terrain. With all eyes on the splendid building little attention was paid to the single-track railway, which meandered away to the west from the main line, a mile or so south of the city. This line following a winding course between fen islands and largely avoiding any earthworks served a number of communities, but most were on the higher land, and thus some distance from the stations. After crossing the Old and New Bedford rivers by a substantial viaduct near Earith, the branch railway emerged to join up with the Cambridge to March line a little north of the town of St Ives.

The Ely, Haddenham & Sutton Railway (EHSR), engendered by local businessmen and farmers, was opened in 1866 and worked from the outset by the Great Eastern Railway. With the threat of infiltration into the locality by other embryonic railways it became imperative to counteract such competition and the EHSR with GER backing finally extended to St Ives in 1878. The re-titled Ely & St Ives Railway (ESIR) remained nominally independent until it was incorporated into the GER in 1898. Built essentially as a farmers line to get crops and cattle to and from local markets, passenger traffic was always of a secondary nature. In the years to World War I both passenger and freight traffic prospered but with the ever-encroaching development of motor transport, and in particular local bus services from the early 1920s, a service of only a few trains a day could not compete and led to severe loss of trade. Except for the towns of Sutton and Haddenham, the branch stations often went months without booking a passenger, and inevitably the wholly uneconomic passenger train service was withdrawn in 1931. Freight traffic continued to thrive, especially between June and October, when much fruit traffic was dispatched and then, from the mid-1920s, from October to January when every goods yard was full with wagons being loaded with sugar beet for forwarding to the sugar processing factories at Wissington, Ely and Peterborough. World War II brought additional military traffic and the line was used on occasions as a diversionary route for freight trains from the Midlands. Peacetime and the end of fuel rationing sounded the death knell and the central section of the route from Bluntisham to Sutton was closed in 1958 to leave truncated sections at each end. As road transport went from strength to strength so the operation of these short sections of line for dwindling traffic became totally uneconomical and the Ely to Sutton section closed in July 1964 with St Ives to Bluntisham succumbing in October of the same year.

Relatively unknown to many, the line was an essential link in the evolution of the fenland settlements before the coming of the internal combustion engine. The full fascinating story of the Ely to St Ives Railway from opening to closure is told within; details have been checked with available documents, but apologies are offered for any errors, which might have occurred.

Chapter One

A Railway from Ely to Sutton

The Fens, extending from Lincolnshire in the north to Cambridgeshire in the south and taking in parts of Huntingdonshire, Norfolk and Northamptonshire, provide some 680,000 acres of the richest farmland in Britain. Whilst the silt fens of the north are uniformly flat, the peat fens of Cambridgeshire contain many former islands, some rising to over 100 feet above sea level. Fenland settlements such as Ely, Sutton, Wilburton and Haddenham were established on these pockets of high land and from these ridges Hereward the Wake fought the Norman invaders. From Roman times, however, waterways and causeways had been utilized as routes between settlements but the area was always isolated from the surrounding counties and East Anglia, and few strangers ventured into the dank lands.

In the 17th century the value of the fens for cultivation was realised and the Earl of Bedford and others contracted Sir Cornelius Vermuyden, a Dutch engineer, to drain the land. Despite fervent local opposition to the scheme, Vermuyden subsequently diverted the waters of the River Ouse from its original winding course into a cut or drain 21 miles long from Earith to Denver. In the absence of local manpower Scottish and Dutch prisoners of war were utilized and the work was completed in 1637. Unfortunately further flooding occurred and later a second channel was cut half a mile to the east and parallel to the former cut. The new channel became the Hundred Foot Drain or New Bedford River whilst the old channel became the Old Bedford River.

Further drainage followed as small dykes and cuts were made, and the land drained using wind, and later steam power. Windmills were at one time located at Mepal, Haddenham and Sutton, whilst at Stretham the steam pump engine installed in 1831 was utilized until 1940. Smallholdings and farms were quickly established on the newly acquired soil and those not engaged on the land became peat cutters, fishermen, fowlers and boatmen. Road systems in the area were slow to materialize and barge and punt traffic remained far cheaper for the conveyance of goods than horse and waggon. Unfortunately water transport proved far too slow for perishable crops grown in the fens and goods often rotted before arrival at markets. The arrival of the few turnpike roads made little difference and it was not until the advent of the railway that improvements were made.

The Eastern Counties Railway (ECR) striking north from Cambridge en route to Brandon reached the cathedral city and capital of the fens at Ely in 1845. In the same year the Ely & Huntingdon Railway was authorized but because of monetary difficulties only the short section, 4 miles 48 chains in length, from St Ives to Godmanchester was constructed and this opened to traffic on 17th August, 1847, the same day as the ECR opened its line from Chesterton Junction, north of Cambridge to St Ives. Lack of finance caused the abandonment of the Ely to St Ives section but the East Anglian Railway, which acquired the Ely & Huntingdon, resurrected the scheme and obtained an Act of Parliament in July 1849 to build the railway. The authorized time for construction was allowed to lapse, however, and the idea was subsequently shelved.

The failure of another scheme to link Ely and Bedford by rail and the reluctance of the ECR to assist with the promotion of any branch or cross-country line left matters in abeyance. The merger of the ECR with the Eastern Union and other East

Anglian railways to form the Great Eastern Railway with effect from 1st August, 1862 changed the policy regarding official encouragement for local branch lines.

Thus in the autumn of 1863 two prominent landowners, Oliver Claude Pell of the Manor House, Wilburton and Frederick Camps of the neighbouring village of Haddenham, succeeded in encouraging enough support from other local landowners in the area to promote the building of a railway linking Ely with Sutton. The initial route proposed was along the fenland island ridge from Ely via Witchford direct to the town of Sutton. The leading exponents of the railway, however, living in Wilburton and Haddenham, villages on the parallel fenland ridge two miles to the south, opposed such plans and subsequently the routing of the proposed line ran a mile or so south of Ely before turning to the west across low lying fenland below the ridges and some ½ to 1½ miles from Wilburton and Haddenham. Having served these villages the route of the proposed line then turned directly north-west to terminate about half a mile from Sutton. By keeping to the lower ground the promoters maintained the railway on fairly level gradients obviating steep descents and ascents to and from the fenland ridge to the valley bottom. The necessary plans were presented to the Parliamentary Private Bill office on 23rd December, 1863 with copies to the Clerk of the Peace for the Isle of Ely and the various parish councils on the proposed route on 30th December.

The proposed Ely, Haddenham & Sutton Railway was the subject of discussion by the GER Directors at the meeting on 4th February, 1864. The gathering was of the opinion the line would not harmonize with the GER system, and was considered to have little reasonable prospect of being remunerative. The GER authorities, however, had no intention of objecting to the Parliamentary Bill outright, only with a number of clauses. A further scheme to extend the line beyond Sutton to Somersham on the St Ives to March line however hardened the attitude of the GER Board. Sinclair, the GER Engineer was requested to investigate whether the extension would jeopardize the main line company's intended link up with the Lancashire & Yorkshire Railway and the GER (Northern Junction) scheme. Following Sinclair's report the GER offered the EHSR financial assistance equal to a third of the capital required for the railway on condition that they withdrew the Bill for the Somersham extension from Parliament. The Bill was subsequently withdrawn leaving the GER free to negotiate on the future working of the Ely to Sutton line. On 16th March, 1864 a deputation consisting of Oliver Claude Pell, Mr Wheeler and John Sutherland Valentine, the Engineer, attended the meeting of the GER Traffic Committee to solicit a proportion of payment towards the construction of the new line. They were courteously received but learned that the GER was promoting a line right through the heart of the district and until the fate of the Bill before Parliament was known the company could not commit itself or provide financial aid for the Ely to Sutton scheme. The GER authorities later agreed to immediate finances being made available provided they were represented on the local company Board. The company was also prepared to work the line for 50 per cent of the gross receipts, if construction was to the satisfaction of the GER Engineer. No opposition was received and the Bill passed both Houses to become law.

For some time infrastructure at Ely station had left much to be desired and complaints were many. To counteract the criticism and in anticipation of another railway using the facilities a contract was awarded on 28th April, 1864 to Freeman & Sons of Ely for alterations and repairs at a cost of £1,720.

The Ely, Haddenham & Sutton Railway Act 1864 (27 & 28 Vict. cap. lxxxvi) which received the Royal Assent on 23rd June, 1864 authorized the building of a railway

ANNO VICESIMO SEPTIMO & VICESIMO OCTAVO

VICTORIÆ REGINÆ.

****

Cap. lxxxvi.

An Act to authorize the Construction of a Railway from *Ely,* through *Haddenham,* to *Sutton,* in *Cambridgeshire.* [23d *June* 1864.]

WHEREAS the making of a Railway in the *Isle of Ely* from the *Great Eastern* Railway at *Ely,* through *Haddenham,* to *Sutton* would be attended with local and public Advantage, and the Persons herein-after named, with others, are willing, at their own Expense, to construct the same: And whereas Plans and Sections of the said Railway showing the Line and Levels thereof, with a Book of Reference to the Plans containing the Names of the Owners and Lessees or reputed Owners and Lessees and of the Occupiers of the Lands through which the said Railway will pass, have been deposited with the Clerk of the Peace for the *Isle of Ely*: And whereas it is expedient that the *Great Eastern* Railway Company should be authorized to contribute Funds towards the Construction of the said Railway, and to enter into Arrangements with respect to the Working, Use, and Management of the said Railway, and that the Company hereby incorporated should be authorized to use a Portion of the *Great Eastern* Railway; but inasmuch as the Purposes aforesaid cannot be accomplished without the Authority of

[*Local.*] 12 D Parliament,

Front page of the Ely, Haddenham & Sutton Railway Act of 23rd June, 1864.

entirely in the Isle of Ely commencing in the parish of Ely St Mary by a junction with the GER near Ely station, 200 yards north of the (then) 71¼ mile post from London, and passing through the parish of Streatham [sic], hamlet of Thetford, extra-parochial place of Grunty Fen and parishes of Wilburton, Haddenham, Sutton, Wentworth and Witcham and terminating in a field called Parsonage Close in the parish of Sutton, belonging to the Dean and Chapter of Ely and occupied by J. Hawkins. The company was authorized to install a level crossing at Streatham, in the hamlet of Little Thetford, where the railway crossed the London to Lynn turnpike road, No. 16 on the deposited plans, and also public roads, Nos. 15 and 83, in the extra-parochial place of Grunty Fen. Three years were allowed for the purchase of the necessary land and five years for the completion of the works. To finance the construction of the railway the EHSR was authorized to raise £36,000 in £10 shares with borrowing powers for £12,000 when the whole of the £36,000 was subscribed for and half actually paid up. The GER was authorized by clause 14 of the statute to subscribe £12,000 towards the undertaking. Clause 31 of the Act allowed the EHSR running powers over the GER from the junction into Ely station, together with the use of sidings and other facilities, whilst clause 34 permitted the EHSR and GER to enter into an agreement which included the provision of rolling stock, and management of the working and maintenance of the railway.

The original Directors of the EHSR were Oliver Claude Pell of the Manor House, Wilburton, Cambridgeshire, Chairman and James Cropley and Frederick Camps of Haddenham together with Lightly Simpson of 25 Gower Street, Bedford Square, London WC and William Henry Shaw of 1 Great George Street, Westminster, London SW representing the GER. The Secretary of the company was T.P. Bond of 2 Dartmouth Street, Great Queen Street, London SW, whilst John Sutherland Valentine of 11 Park Street, Westminster, London SW was appointed Engineer and James Wheeler of 4 Victoria Street, Westminster, London SW, Solicitor. Valentine was already Engineer of the Lynn & Hunstanton and West Norfolk Junction Railways. The contract for the construction and works was awarded to W.S. Simpson of Park Farm, Ely who tendered at £48,000. Lightly Simpson and Valentine recommended the contractor despite his poor work on the construction of the West Norfolk Junction Railway and the Ware, Hadham & Buntingford Railway in Hertfordshire.

During the autumn of 1864 Valentine surveyed the route of the proposed railway and negotiated with landowners for the required land. Good progress was made and in the New Year the contractor was given possession of the land from the junction with the GER, a mile south of Ely as far as Stretham. By March 1865 surveys were completed through to Sutton and two-thirds of the required land had been purchased. Some of the landowners of the remaining required property delayed completion of purchase by demanding a higher price for the land. W.S. Simpson and his men in the meantime made good progress with preliminary works from the junction and by mid-February were preparing to lay half a mile of permanent way and complete the fencing-off of a further two miles of the formation.

The initial lethargic local interest shown in the railway was dispelled by the start of construction work. At a meeting held in the Ship Inn, Sutton on 8th February, 1865 and chaired by William Cole of Mepal a 'lively enthusiasm' was shown in the line and as a result of the anticipated improvements to the area agriculture, several farmers and local gentry added their names to the share list.

Valentine reported on 11th March, 1865 that all the necessary surveys were completed and 6 miles 5 furlongs of land required for the railway had been purchased. The remaining 2 miles was expected to be in the hands of the company by April. One mile of line was formed and fenced in and the contractor was laying half a mile of track to carry ballast and soil to and from the incomplete section. The Engineer optimistically hoped the line would open for traffic later in the year.

Satisfactory negotiations were concluded with landowners in the Sutton area by May, when all the remaining land required for the railway was purchased. The contractor continued to make good progress aided by fine weather and 200 or so men were employed on the earthworks with a further 50 on buildings and other ancillary items. The site of Wilburton station was reached in June, by which time Stretham and Wilburton stations and associated houses were also under construction. Work had also commenced on the building of the overbridge to carry the road over the railway west of Haddenham station. At the end of the month Simpson commenced the section of formation forward from Haddenham working in a northerly direction towards Sutton. The edge of the high ridge was left and the peaty fenland required the adoption of a different method of construction and consolidation of the trackbed.

A freak storm in the area in July 1865 caused considerable damage when part of the formation of the railway was washed away near Stretham. The weather during the following months improved, and the contractor's men quickly made good the damage and continued construction at a steady rate. By August 1865 the railway was almost completed as far as Haddenham and the Engineer advised the Directors and proprietors that the permanent way was laid to within half a mile of the junction, south of Ely. Between Haddenham and Sutton earthworks were completed as far as the boundary drain and negotiations were in progress over the purchase of additional land in the parish of Sutton. The station buildings at Stretham, Wilburton and Haddenham were in a forward state but work on Sutton station was delayed until the completion of the harvest as many local navvies had temporarily left the employ of the contractor to gather in the crops.

With the railway nearing completion the Directors thought the time for expansion was opportune. The plan for extending the railway beyond Sutton to St Ives or Somersham was resurrected in the summer of 1865 when the local Directors hoped to forward a Bill for the 1865/6 session of Parliament. After consultation with the GER Board it was felt that the time was inopportune for such proposals and the idea was shelved.

At the end of September a boy was arrested by GER police and charged with willfully placing permanent way chairs on rails in a manner likely to cause the derailment of a train. The case was dismissed when the lad was discovered to be only seven years of age. In October 1865 the area from Sutton to Ely was hit by the cattle plague when hundreds of animals were slaughtered. At one stage the local navvies were blamed for carrying and spreading the disease in the district. The outbreak was so widespread that within weeks wiser thoughts prevailed and the workmen were allowed free movement.

The *Cambridge Chronicle* for 2nd December, 1865 reported that work had started on the station at Sutton and that it was expected the Ely to Sutton line would open on 1st January, 1866. It concluded, 'We hope the rumours are correct for there are not many villages with the population of Sutton that have been so long shut out from railway communication'. The rumours, however, proved unfounded for much work remained to be completed.

Early in the New Year the EHSR Directors secured a working agreement with the GER with the main line company providing locomotives and rolling stock to operate the train services and personnel to staff the stations for 50 per cent of the gross receipts. The GER by entering this agreement maintained complete control of traffic between the physical junction of the two railways south of Ely and Ely station. This clause was inserted to prevent the EHSR from entering into an agreement with any rival railway company of the GER.

The Secretary of the EHSR initially notified the Board of Trade (BoT) on 2nd January, 1866 that the railway was ready for inspection and that the company proposed to operate a passenger train service between Ely and Sutton. The second notification was sent on 15th March and the date for inspection was tentatively arranged for the end of the month, which unfortunately coincided with another outbreak of cattle plague in the area. Captain H.W. Tyler, however, duly arrived on Wednesday 28th March to conduct the official inspection and travelled over the line accompanied by GER officials and EHSR Directors. The inspector found that the single line offered for inspection was 6 miles 53.40 chains in length, running from a junction with the GER a mile south of Ely to a station near Sutton. The steepest gradient was 1 in 110 and the sharpest curve at the junction was of 20 chains radius. The train was stopped at various points to enable Tyler to make a closer inspection of the infrastructure and it was noted the permanent way was similar to that on the West Norfolk Railway between Heacham and Wells, which was of no surprise as Valentine was also Engineer of the Norfolk company. The fencing of the new line to Sutton was principally post and rail, but in some places was formed of hedgerows. Tyler considered that a considerable part of the fencing was of insufficient height to afford proper protection and at the stations consisted of three-rail fencing only. He required the railway company to improve and heighten the fencing where necessary and for the hedges to be carefully made up where growth was thin, to prevent animals trespassing on the line. Corner pieces at the sides of many of the occupational and public crossing gates also required strengthening. The inspector found the permanent way, and six culverts were satisfactorily constructed. The one overbridge of 25 ft 5 in. skew span had brick abutments in mortar and arch of brickwork in Roman cement and appeared to be standing well. A signal box had been erected at the junction with the GER main line south of Ely and the points from the double track main line to the single branch line were worked from this box. Tyler required the interlocking of these points with the signals.

During the inspection at Stretham the inspector found the platform canopy support columns to be only 5 ft from the edge of the platform and required them to be set back to a distance of 6 ft from the edge with a deeper beam spanning between the columns to support the roof. The inspector disapproved of two pairs of facing points in the main single line on the approach to Sutton and requested the removal of one of them with alternative arrangements for the lead into a siding, whilst the other leading to the loop line was to be interlocked and equipped with a switch indicator. Tyler received no information from the GER authorities regarding the method of working the line or which points were to be locked at the intermediate stations. He criticized the lack of distant signals but on being informed by Valentine that the line was to be worked by one engine only, instructed that distant signals be erected on the approach to the junction at Ely and on the approach to Sutton station only. The inspector noted that the GER had yet to provide a certificate regarding the method of operating the single line. Tyler was adamant that an engine turntable was required at Sutton and desired the GER to provide a new turntable at Ely as the existing one was inconveniently sited and of insufficient length for the size of engines to be used on the line.

Returning from Sutton the inspector queried the unauthorized level crossing near Stretham at 1 mile 22 chains and in his report stipulated the re-routing of the road from the south to the north of the railway to eliminate the crossing. Because of the incompleteness of the works, the unauthorized level crossing and the numerous alterations, Captain Tyler refused to sanction the opening of the railway with the proviso that the position would be reviewed within a month. However the *Cambridge Chronicle* of 31st March, reporting the visit of the inspector, misled its readers saying that 'with the exception of a few minor matters the line was pronounced satisfactory' and 'was expected to open in a few days for passenger traffic'. At the end of March the railway company sold 18 horses, which had been used on construction work hauling contractor's wagons.

The Directors immediately asked Valentine to rectify the shortcomings mentioned by the inspector and he quickly conferred with both Simpson and the local GER Engineer. The formal opening of the railway was arranged for 6th April, 1866 when the local directors and GER officers, who had stayed in Ely overnight, travelled by special train, hauled by Gooch 2-2-2 tender locomotive No. 276. The train was met at all stations by the recently appointed station masters, who had taken up residence a few days earlier. On 7th April both the EHSR and GER officially notified the BoT that the line was to be worked by the Train Staff and Ticket method of operation, in accordance with the provisions of the working agreement between the two companies and approved by the BoT on 22nd February. On the same day the Secretary of the local railway also notified that the EHSR intended to close the unauthorized level crossing by making a road on the north side of the railway from the Cambridge to Ely turnpike leading from Little Thetford to Grunty Fen, within three months. They also intended to provide a turntable at Sutton within the same period. The GER authorities wrote later in the month advising that the points at Stretham, Wilburton and Haddenham station sidings were to be kept locked for the main single line. Valentine said that the contractor had moved the platform fences back at Stretham and Wilburton and replaced the canopy beams by support brackets at the former station.

Captain H.W. Tyler was obviously satisfied with the speedy progress of the remedial work for he authorized the opening of the line to all traffic on 7th April, 1866, a decision which was passed on to the GER and EHSR Directors two days later, with the added proviso that the authority was subject to the satisfactory completion of the outstanding work. On 11th April the report of the BoT inspector was noted and it was confirmed arrangements would be made to open the line to passenger and goods traffic on 16th April, 1866. The working agreement with the GER was for a period of 10 years from the opening date.

The railway was duly opened to the public on Monday 16th April, 1866 with little enthusiasm shown by the local populace. The *Cambridge Chronicle* thought the line would 'prove a great asset to the inhabitants of the district, especially Sutton where hitherto the nearest station to the town had been Ely or Chatteris'. Much to the surprise of the villagers at Sutton, Wilburton, Haddenham and Sutton, no market tickets were issued to Ely and cheap Parliamentary fares were only available on one up train, the 8.10 am from Sutton. A letter to the *Cambridge Independent Press* and published on 28th April, 1866 complained of the prohibitive fare of 2s. 0d. from Sutton to Ely and back, which represented a fifth of the average agricultural workers weekly wage in the fens at that time. The writer also requested market day tickets at Parliamentary or half-Parliamentary rates as available on other GER lines in the Ely area.

The facilities available on the new line for goods traffic left much to be desired and farmers, growers and railway staff were soon complaining of the lack of equipment.

A RAILWAY FROM ELY TO SUTTON 13

On 9th May, 1866 the goods manager requested the urgent provision of a fixed crane and weighing machine at both Sutton and Haddenham and weighing machines at Wilburton and Stretham. Valentine concurred with the request but considered that as the cranes and weighing machines formed part of the working plant of the line, the GER should provide them. The GER Traffic Committee begged to differ with Valentine and whilst agreeing the provision of the equipment recommended that the order be passed to the EHSR Directors to supply. After the opening of the line several farmers continued to press for adequate compensation for the compulsory purchase of their land. In one instance the railway company offered £9 for a small plot near Wilburton against the farmer's claim of £25. Early in June 1866 the parties came to a compromise and the farmer received £12.

The railway quickly fulfilled its purpose as passenger and freight traffic from Sutton and the rich agricultural fenland was transported with ease to Ely and thence to markets at Cambridge, Ipswich, Peterborough and London. As a result road carrier services reduced in frequency and instead acted as feeders to and from the branch stations. For some time, however, the GER Traffic Committee was concerned with the high costs of operating a number of new branch lines and after due investigation authorized (on 20th June, 1866), a series of measures to reduce train mileage. On the Ely to Sutton line it was found that the branch engine only ran 48 miles each day. It was therefore decided as far as practicable to send the engine to Cambridge and back as often as required working goods traffic, thereby obviating the need of a Peterborough-based locomotive to work south of Ely.

On Monday 16th July, 1866 a train killed a horse on one of the many occupational crossings between Haddenham and Sutton. The locomotive, 'Jenny Lind' class 2-4-0 No. 107, sustained damage requiring repairs at Cambridge. Reporting the incident the *Cambridge Chronicle* commented 'as this crossing is much used in season and there is no crossing keeper there, we fear other accidents will occur unless the engine driver is instructed to use his whistle long and loud as he gets round the curve from Haddenham station'. Two days later on 18th July Moseley, the General Manager, reported that the EHSR had not provided cranes and weighing machines at stations as required. It was duly recommended that the GER would supply the equipment and charge the Sutton company with the cost.

On 7th August, 1866 yet another accident occurred when the 8.10 am Sutton to Ely train formed of three 4-wheel coaches, brake van No. 118, composite No. 206 and third No. 83, hauled by 'Jenny Lind' class 2-2-2 No. 107 (again) running tender first, with the tender off sister locomotive No. 103, became derailed all vehicles at Ely Sutton Branch Junction. The coupling between the engine and tender fractured and the latter swung to the left and fell on its side taking with it the fireman, who sustained serious injuries. Fortunately none of the 40 or so passengers suffered injury. The locomotive sustained damage to the smokebox door, lifeguard irons, sandpipes, springs, handrails, footsteps, lagging strap and feedpipes, whilst the tender was a casualty with broken head and side lamps. In evidence at a subsequent inquiry driver James Beaumont, who had 10 years' footplate experience including one year on passenger trains, stated he approached the junction at a slow speed of 8 mph, 'more slowly than usual, as there were no wagons to pick up at the intermediate stations and the train was running on time'. The signalman at Ely Sutton Branch Junction, Daniel Hall, had inspected the points a quarter of an hour before the train arrived at 8.33 am and noted that despite the slow approach the vehicles were oscillating considerably. George MacAllan, the Cambridge District motive power superintendent, travelled to the site of the incident with the accident breakdown van and established that the trailing wheels of locomotive No. 107 had left the rails at the heel of the points and dragged the carriages off the road to the right, whilst the tender had fallen on its side to the left, with the unfortunate fireman underneath. Samuel Johnson, the GER locomotive superintendent, who had summoned MacAllen to Stratford on 7th August for a first-hand report, visited the site of the incident the following day and stated there was nothing in the appearance of the road or on the engine to show that anything was faulty, and confirmed from evidence that the train was being driven at a slower speed than normal.

On 28th September, 1866, the EHSR Directors reported to the shareholders their disappointment at the low receipts, which had been adversely affected by the serious and lengthy outbreak of cattle plague in the area. Receipts from the opening of the line to 30th June, 1866 amounted to:

	£.	s.	d.
Passenger	161	8	11
Parcels	5	14	8
Goods	199	1	1
Total	366	4	8

The following day, 29th September, Simpson requested payment of £68 7s. 0d. for the provision of the turntable at Sutton, while at the GER Traffic Committee meeting on 24th October, 1866 Gamble, a GER Director, drew attention to the fact that the work of supplying cranes and weighing machines to EHSR stations was in progress. No formal undertaking had been given by the local company to offer payment for their supply and installation. The Secretary advised that a letter had been sent to Bond, the local secretary, that costs would be charged against the EHSR and that instructions had been issued to deduct the amount from traffic receipts. As a precaution against future disputes concerning the cost of equipment, the law clerk and Swarbrick, the Deputy General Manager, were asked to investigate whether the owning or operating company should be liable for payment. By 7th November Swarbrick reported he had met with Shaw, the law clerk and agreed that cranes, weighing machines, turntables and other materials attached to the freehold of the EHSR, and indeed other lines worked by the GER, should be provided by the owning company and not the GER. On the same day it was reported that lamps were required in front of Haddenham station and the EHSR Engineer had stated that if plain posts were ordered then his company would bear the costs. If, however, the lamps were portable then the GER should be liable for the costs. On 19th August, 1867 the contract for the building of a shed for corn storage at Wilburton was awarded to Mr Waters of Haddenham who tendered at £150, the building being completed the following year at a cost of £197.

Receipts for the second half-year of operation to 30th June, 1867 showed an 8.4 per cent reduction from the previous period, although a 1½ per cent dividend was paid to shareholders.

Six months ending	31st December, 1866			30th June, 1867		
	£	s.	d.	£	s.	d.
Passenger	429	19	1	370	18	5
Horses	38	0	6	22	3	1
Goods	808	17	5	777	1	2
Total	1276	17	0	1170	2	8

Having taken over a number of small lines the GER was seeking economies and by closing five stations in 1866 had effected a saving of £85 in the first quarter of 1867. Further small stations earning poor receipts were investigated, especially where there was the possibility of traffic finding its way to adjacent stations. Unbeknown to the EHSR Directors and shareholders, investigations were carried out at Stretham, where the nearest station to the east was Ely 2¾ miles distant and to the west Wilburton, a distance of two miles, with view to closure. The station was a borderline case with annual earnings of £457 11s. 9d. for 1866, but on 10th May, 1867 the decision was taken not to close, a factor being the adjacent level crossing. Had the station closed the crossing would still have to be manned at an annual cost of £50.

By the end of June 1867 £49,679 8s. 6d. had been expended on the building of the railway and associated work. Expenditure on the line to 30th June, 1868 had increased by £288 3s. 4d. and reached £49,967 11s. 10d. whilst receipts for six months ending were 4.5 per cent above the previous June returns. Early in the New Year it was revealed that the earnings of the 6¾ mile-long branch from Ely to Sutton in 1867 were £2,539, equal to £377 per mile. The first half-yearly returns for 1868 increased by 7.2 per cent and the shareholders received a 2 per cent dividend, whilst receipts to 31st December increased by a further £165. Passenger receipts, however, remained almost static, with most of the increase coming from goods traffic.

Since the opening of the railway, concern was expressed about the late delivery of mail to Sutton and matters came to a head in February 1868. The *Cambridge Chronicle* took up the fight and on the 8th reported, 'There is great inconvenience from the late delivery of letters in the village. The first train leaves Sutton at 8.10 am and the delivery of letters does not commence until 9.00 am, so any person requiring letters before leaving on the train cannot do so'. It iterated that Haddenham and Littleport, both equidistant from Ely received their letters 1½ hours earlier and asked the General Post Office to improve the service to Sutton. Many at the time thought the mail was sent by the branch train but it was in fact sent by mail cart on the road from Ely and a call was made to transfer the delivery of mail to rail.

In May 1868 the GER authorities notified the EHSR Board that in 1867 the line had worked at a deficit of £1,211. In view of the financial collapse of the main line company in 1866, the GER was in no position to sustain such conditions and required an increase over and above the existing 50 per cent gross receipts for working expenses. The local Directors were unhappy with such proposals bearing in mind the steady increase in traffic on the line was producing a dividend, which any increase in working expenses would dissolve. The EHSR Directors duly notified the GER that they had entered into the original agreement for a period of 10 years from 16th April, 1866 and refused to re-enter negotiations.

Chapter Two

Extension to St Ives

The continuation of the railway to the west and south of Sutton was still in the minds of developers and on 28th November, 1868 plans were announced both for the Haddenham, Willingham & Longstanton Railway and the Sutton, Mepal and Somersham Railway. The former commenced in the parish of Haddenham in the Isle of Ely, in the County of Cambridge, from a junction with the EHSR at a point 100 yards from the western end of the platform at Haddenham and terminated in the parish of All Saints, Longstanton in the County of Cambridge at a junction with the St Ives to Cambridge branch of the GER at a point measured 200 yards or thereabouts from the south-east end of the passenger platform at Longstanton station. The railway was to pass through Haddenham, Hilrow and Aldreth in the Isle of Ely, County of Cambridge and Willingham, Rampton and Longstanton in the County of Cambridge. The second proposal, the Sutton, Mepal & Somersham Railway, commenced in the parish of Sutton in the Isle of Ely, County of Cambridge by a junction with the EHSR at a point 30 yards or thereabouts measured along the railway in a southerly direction from the passenger platform at Sutton station and terminated in the parish of Somersham in the County of Huntingdon by a junction with the St Ives and March line of the GER, at a point 100 yards or thereabouts measured along the branch in a northerly direction from the northern end of Somersham station. The proposed line passed through Sutton, Witcham and Mepal in the Isle of Ely, County of Cambridge and Colne and Somersham in the County of Huntingdon. The *Cambridge Chronicle* commenting on the proposed schemes prophesied, 'whether these extensions will succeed we are not prepared to say, but it is certain the Sutton line should be extended to the St Ives line'. The GER Directors discussed the proposal at their meeting on 10th December, 1868 and noting that Oliver Pell was the leading sponsor of the Somersham scheme deferred further discussion until more information was available. The undertaking sought running powers over the GER and EHSR and the Bill was presented to the Parliamentary Bill Office at the end of the year. On 7th August, 1868 Messrs Salisbury & Turner represented the GER on the EHSR Board.

On 1st February, 1869 the promoters of the Haddenham, Willingham & Longstanton scheme reported they had made the requisite deposit of £1,750 to the Bank of England and on the same day Edwin Cross, Solicitor for the Bill and D. Oldfield, the Engineer, with others attended before an examiner of the House of Commons to confirm that the standing orders had been complied with. Ten days later the GER Board agreed for Edwin Cross to attend a meeting and elaborate on the proposal for the Haddenham to Longstanton scheme, when it was revealed the new line was 6½ miles in length. However, to reach St Ives required running powers over the GER for 5½ miles from Longstanton. Further approaches were made and on 24th February it was agreed a deputation could meet with the GER Traffic Committee on 27th of the month. There the promoters asked for financial assistance and other help with the scheme but were informed the Directors were not prepared to offer terms for working the line but would not oppose the passage of the Bill through Parliament. In the meantime the Sutton, Mepal & Somersham Railway scheme failed to get its Bill past the Parliamentary deadline.

At the half-yearly meeting of the EHSR held on Thursday 25th March, 1869, the Directors and proprietors initially agreed to petition against the Longstanton Bill and called for the withdrawal of the 'obnoxious provision' regarding the running powers included in the document. Oliver Pell, as a Director of the EHSR and a leading advocate for the new line, however, calmed the situation and proposed the resolution not to impede the progress of the Haddenham, Willingham & Longstanton Railway Bill, provided the promoters confined running powers to Sutton station. The motion was carried by seven votes to five but Valentine objected and demanded a full poll and the meeting was adjourned for that purpose. The reconvened meeting was held on 1st April, 1869 at the Lamb Hotel, Ely when the vote was cast. After a delay of two hours the motion was carried by 46 votes for to five against. The previous day Oliver Pell had addressed a public meeting of the Haddenham and Longstanton line at the Three Kings Inn at Haddenham. He expounded at great length on the advantages the district had received from the building of the Ely to Sutton line and how much more could be achieved by aborting the proposed scheme and extending the railway direct to St Ives. By 22nd April the GER Directors learned that the Haddenham to Longstanton Bill had passed the Lords and instructions were issued to immediately oppose the scheme in the Commons.

Despite the combined opposition, the Haddenham, Willingham & Longstanton Railway Act (32 and 33 Vict. cap. cxlvi) duly received the Royal Assent on 26th July, 1869. This authorized the building of a railway six miles, four furlongs and nine chains in length commencing in the parish of Haddenham, in the Isle of Ely, in the County of Cambridge, by a junction with the Ely, Haddenham & Sutton Railway, and terminating in the parish of Longstanton, in the County of Cambridge by a junction with the St Ives and Cambridge branch of the Great Eastern Railway. To finance the building of line the company was authorized to raise £40,000 in £10 shares with borrowing powers of £13,333, once the authorized capital had been subscribed and half of the amount paid up. Clause 29 of the statute required the company not to make the junction at Longstanton nearer than five chains from the end of the station buildings nearest to the junction without the consent of the GER, whilst clause 30 permitted the provision of a level crossing over No. 54 public road in the parish of Willingham. Any works required when the railway passed over the level of the fens known as the Bedford Level had to be agreed and completed to the satisfaction of the Bedford Level Corporation, whilst clauses 32 and 33 subjected the company to payment of drainage taxes and to preserve the right of drainage over the fens. Three years were allowed for the compulsory purchase of land and five years for the completion of works. The initial Directors of the company were Albert Pell MP of the Carlton Club, London SW, Oliver Claude Pell of the Manor House, Wilburton, Frederick Camps of Haddenham, Read Camps and George Biddall. Oliver Pell and Frederick Camps were Directors of the EHSR.

In the meantime Messrs Valentine and Bond had attended the GER Traffic Committee meeting on 13th July to raise the issue of apportionment of EHSR traffic receipts. After lengthy discussion it was agreed to refer outstanding issues to the Railway Clearing House (RCH). The matter lingered on some months despite repeated requests for a reply. Finally in response to a letter of 18th November, 1869, Mr Dawson of the RCH responded on 22nd of the month. He considered the two main points in contention:

1. Whether on passenger traffic between GE stations south of Ely Junction and stations on the Ely, Haddenham and Sutton Railway, which is carried via Ely station and the Ely, Haddenham and Sutton Railway are or are not entitled when the through fares are composed of two local fares from Ely to the Ely local fare to the respective EHSR stations to or from which through passengers may be conveyed.

[32 & 33 VICT.] *The Haddenham, Willingham, and Longstanton Railway Act,* 1869. **[Ch. cxlvi.]**

CHAP. cxlvi.

An Act for making a Railway from the Ely, Haddenham, and Sutton Railway at Haddenham to the Great Eastern Railway at Longstanton ; and for other purposes.

A.D. 1869.

[26th July 1869.]

WHEREAS the making and maintaining of a railway from the Ely, Haddenham, and Sutton Railway at Haddenham to the Great Eastern Railway at Longstanton would be of public and local advantage :

And whereas the persons herein-after named, with others, are willing at their own expense to carry the undertaking into execution if authorized so to do, and are desirous of being incorporated into a Company for that purpose :

And whereas plans and sections of the proposed railway, showing the line and levels thereof, and the lands which may be taken for the purposes of this Act, and also books of reference to the plans containing the names of the owners or reputed owners, lessees or reputed lessees, and occupiers of the lands, have been deposited with the respective clerks of the peace for the Isle of Ely and the county of Cambridge, and those plans, sections, and books of reference are in this Act referred to as the deposited plans, sections, and books of reference :

And whereas the objects of this Act cannot be effected without the authority of Parliament :

May it therefore please Your Majesty that it may be enacted ; and be it enacted by the Queen's most Excellent Majesty, by and with the advice and consent of the Lords Spiritual and Temporal, and Commons, in this present Parliament assembled, and by the authority of the same, as follows :

1. This Act may be cited for all purposes as "The Haddenham, Willingham, and Longstanton Railway Act, 1869." — Short title.

2. "The Companies Clauses Consolidation Act, 1845," and Part I. (relating to cancellation and surrender of shares) and Part III. — General Acts herein named incorporated.

[*Local.*—*146.*] A 1

2. Whether the through traffic and also the foreign traffic by the EHSR are entitled to a share of the receipts accruing to the portion of line between Ely Junction and Ely station.

In answering I am of the opinion that all traffic sent from or to any station of the Ely, Haddenham and Sutton Railway to or from any station on or beyond the GER, then the EHSR is entitled to a share of the receipts less the working expenses which accrue to the portion of the line between Ely station and Ely Junction. As regards the principle of the division of receipts from the passenger traffic between the EHSR stations and the stations on the GER south of Ely, the Railway Clearing House Regulations provide and the practice is that, where the through fares are composed of local fares each company receives in the division of the through fares its local fare and I am of the opinion this principle should rule.

The subject was discussed at the GER Traffic Committee meeting on 29th November, when a letter from Valentine asking for any outstanding monies was considered. Both items of correspondence were sent to the law clerk for action.

On the Ely to Sutton line the local GER officials were concerned that the telegraph installation between stations on the branch was incomplete. The Electric Telegraph Co. was asked to investigate and on 19th January, 1870 it was estimated that the cost of completion to Sutton would be £87. Later in the same year the GER General Manager reported that facilities at Sutton were incomplete. At the Way & Works Committee meeting on 6th July it was announced that costs for completion would be £26, and it was agreed to seek the sanction of the EHSR Directors before proceeding with the work. The expenditure was readily agreed but on 12th October when the work was nearing completion Bond, the EHSR Secretary, advised the GER authorities that their contractor was ready to redecorate and repaint the station buildings and the GER works would impede the redecoration. Before allowing the work to proceed it was agreed the General Manager and Engineer would arrange a meeting with Bond to rectify the situation.

For many months farmers and landowners had complained of the lack of facilities at EHSR station goods yards. The GER goods manager was also in receipt of correspondence and after consultation with local station masters agreed that 1 ton capacity fixed cranes were required at Wilburton, Haddenham and Sutton as a matter of urgency. The application was passed to the Way & Works Committee who agreed the provision of the necessary equipment on 10th May, 1871, subject to the expenditure being borne by the local company. Despite the apparent urgency it was 2nd July, 1873 before the cost of the cranes was estimated at £50 each. Because of the excessive price the GER General Manager was instructed to reach an agreement with the EHSR Directors regarding the sharing of expenses. This was readily agreed and the cranes were installed in the autumn of the same year, but were removed at an early date as they were considered unnecessary for the little traffic requiring craneage! At this time the Directors of the EHSR were Oliver Claude Pell, Frederick Camps and J.S. Valentine, with G.W. Currie and Lightly Simpson representing the interests of the GER. T.P. Bond was Secretary.

On 24th September, 1873 it was revealed during an annual review of prices for gas consumption at GER stations, including London termini, that the charges made at Haddenham of £5 10s. 0d. per annum were the cheapest on the system, despite the fact the charge was 8s. 4d. per thousand cubic feet. At the opposite end of the scale annual charges at Witham station, on the Liverpool Street to Norwich main line, were £100 at 6s. 8d. per thousand cubic feet.

Plans were formulated and agreed on 7th October, 1874 for the sinking of a well at Sutton to improve the water supply at a cost of £55. After a further survey the EHSR

Engineer reported on 2nd December that it would be impossible to obtain supplies so readily as the area was located over a subsoil of blue clay. The GER Engineer disagreed with the findings and requested permission to sink a shaft at a cost of £25, provided the local company paid all costs. The matter dragged on into the New Year and on 27th January, 1875, the GER and EHSR Engineers were instructed to hold a joint site meeting. This was duly arranged and subsequently on 2nd April, 1875 the Way & Works Committee sanctioned the sinking of the well at a cost of £25.

Haddenham station gas supplies were again the subject of a report in April 1875 when the charges remained fixed with the local gas company at 8s. 4d. per thousand cubic feet, whilst the following month it was revealed annual charges for the previous year had increased to £6 2s. 6d.

The Great Northern Railway (GNR) had for some years contemplated an extension from their Cambridge branch at Shepreth to March by-passing the University City and striking north paralleling the GER St Ives to March line. One of the proposed routes was via Earith Bridge, where the line was to cross the Great Ouse on its way to the ultimate goal of Lincoln. At the time relations between the GER and GNR were not on the best of terms and the proposed move caused alarm at Bishopsgate. Charles Parkes, Chairman of the GER, actually pursued the proposal for an extension of the Ely to Sutton line on to St Ives to prevent the GNR from building their competitive route through GER territory.

The idea for the extension beyond Sutton to St Ives had been initially revived as early as 1872, as the failure of the local schemes brought doubts as to the future role of the EHSR. It was evident to the GER authorities that the steady increase in traffic at Sutton, Haddenham, Wilburton and Stretham, although satisfactory in the short term, could not be sustained. The proposal by the GNR to infiltrate the GER territory concentrated the mind and finally settled the issue beyond doubt. Plans for the extension to St Ives were drawn up and prepared for presentation to Parliament in the 1876 session. The GER Chairman had discussed the matter with various local dignitaries and on 14th July, 1875 suggested the Board visit the district. John Valentine was requested by the EHSR Directors to resurvey the 1864 route as quickly as possible and prepare drawings for the viaduct to carry the railway over the River Ouse. On 29th September, 1875 Valentine submitted his estimates for the building of the extension totalling £62,928 12s. 6d.

The plans for the extension were finalized by 10th November, 1875 and were submitted to the Private Bill Office of Parliament. Copies were also submitted to the Clerks of the Peace for the County of Cambridge at Cambridge, the Isle of Ely at Wisbech, County of Cambridge, and Huntingdonshire at Huntingdon on 30th November. No objections to the proposals were received and the Bill had a smooth passage through both Houses. In the meantime the GER Directors agreed revised working arrangements for the Ely to Sutton line and approved the extension Bill on 15th December, 1875, the GER proprietors approving on 28th January, 1876. The contract reiterated much of the agreement made between the EHSR and GER in 1866 and confirmed the GER would work the original section of line as hitherto providing rolling stock and staff to operate the line as well as maintaining the assets and way and works to the same standards as those on the main lines of the company. In the event of dispute between the EHSR and GER the matter was to be subject to arbitration with the General Manager of the Great Western Railway, or failing him, the General Manager of the London and North Western Railway acting as umpire. The GER would charge the EHSR interest at 5 per cent per annum on all monies expended on works. Part II of the schedule required the EHSR to fully consult with the GER on the building of the extension line between Sutton and St Ives, whilst part III stipulated that from and after completion of the extension, the railway was to be considered as one unit and worked in perpetuity by the GER. The GER was then to work the original railway and the extension railway and pay the whole of the expenses in connection with the management, working and maintenance of the line, receiving in return the full gross earnings. For its part the EHSR would receive out of the gross receipts a toll or sum equal to 5 per cent per annum on the share capital actually issued for the construction of the extension, together with a payment of 2 per cent per annum on the £38,000 capital expended on the original railway for the first two years, and then at a rate of 4 per cent per annum in perpetuity. Part IV granted powers for the GER to lease the EHSR original and extension railways on terms set out in part III of the schedule.

The Ely, Haddenham & Sutton Railway Extension Act (39 Vict. cap. vi) dated 7th April, 1876 authorized the construction of a railway 8 miles 3 furlongs 8 chains and 30 links in length, commencing in the parish of Sutton in the Isle of Ely, in the County of Cambridge by a junction with the existing railway of the company, 16 chains or thereabouts from the existing terminus and passing through the parishes of Sutton, Haddenham and Bluntisham-with-Earith and terminating in the parish of Holywell-cum-Needingworth in the County of Huntingdon by a junction with the St Ives and March railway of the Great Eastern Railway, 9 chains 30 links north of the 74 milepost from London. Level crossings were authorized over public road No. 18 in the parish of Haddenham, public road No. 2 in the parish of Willingham and public road No. 11 in the parish of Holywell-cum-Needingworth. To finance the work the company was authorized to raise £60,000 in £10 shares and borrow £20,000 when all the capital had been subscribed for and half paid up. Three years were allowed for the compulsory purchase of the land and five years for the completion of works.

The Act also specified certain requirements regarding the crossing of the River Ouse. The consent of the Bedford Level Corporation was to be obtained before any work was carried out on the great level of the fens known as the Bedford Level and especially with the bridges, culverts or embankments near or over the Ouse. Any land taken for the railway on this section was subject to drainage tax, whilst the rights of drainage were to be reserved by the Bedford Level Corporation. In carrying the railway over the Great Ouse the company was required to erect a substantial bridge with two spans or openings of a clear width of 60 ft each, measured at right angles across the river. Piers, piles and other supports were to be parallel to the sides of the river and erected to allow a towpath 6 ft wide to be maintained alongside the river whilst the spans of the bridge or viaduct were to be at least 8 ft above the high water level. The bridge over the West River near Earith was required to have a 30 ft span, measured at right angles, the structure having at least 7 ft clearance above the high water level, whilst allowing for a 6 ft wide tow path alongside the waterway. The company was empowered by clause 13 of the statute to provide means of clearing any ice that may be formed against the bridges in winter, so as to maintain the free flow of water under the structures. Finally the Act confirmed and made binding the contract agreement made between the EHSR and the GER on 15th December, 1875 and by clause 29 authorized the company to change its name from the Ely, Haddenham and Sutton Railway to the Ely and St Ives Railway when the extension line was opened to traffic.

The Directors at their meeting on 11th April, 1876 requested Valentine to finalize the surveying of the route of the authorized railway without delay and within a month the Engineer had made arrangements with the Bedford Level Commissioners regarding the viaduct to carry the railway over the River Ouse. Most of the finances for the extension were raised by the GER.

[39 VICT.] *The Ely, Haddenham, and Sutton Railway* [Ch. vi.]
Extension Act, 1876.

CHAPTER vi.

An Act to authorise the Ely, Haddenham, and Sutton Railway Company to extend their authorised Railway to the Saint Ives and March Railway of the Great Eastern Railway; to change their name; and for other purposes.

A.D. 1876.

[7th April 1876.]

WHEREAS by "The Ely, Haddenham, and Sutton Railway Act, 1864," in this Act called "the Act of 1864," the Ely, Haddenham, and Sutton Railway Company, in this Act called "the Company," were authorised to construct a railway in the Isle of Ely from the Great Eastern Railway, near Ely, to Sutton, and to enter into working agreements with the Great Eastern Railway Company:

27 & 28 Vict. c. lxxxvi.

And whereas the said railway has been completed and opened for traffic and is now worked by the Great Eastern Railway Company, and the extension thereof to join the Saint Ives and March Railway of the Great Eastern Railway Company would be of public and local advantage, and it is expedient that the Company should be empowered to construct the said extension, and that the agreement between the Company and the Great Eastern Railway Company which is set forth in the schedule to this Act should be confirmed:

And whereas it is expedient that the name of the Company should be changed:

And whereas plans and sections showing the lines and levels of the railway authorised by this Act, and also books of reference containing the names of the owners and lessees, or reputed owners and lessees, and of the occupiers of the lands required or which may be taken for the purposes of this Act, were duly deposited with the clerks of the peace for the Isle of Ely and for the counties of Cambridge and Huntingdon, and are herein-after respectively referred to as the deposited plans, sections, and books of reference:

And whereas the purposes of this Act cannot be effected without the authority of Parliament:

[*Local.*—6.]   A   1

EXTENSION TO ST IVES

Valentine made final surveys during May and June 1876 and the following month tenders were invited for the construction of the line. Meanwhile receipts on the Ely to Sutton section for the six months ending 30th June, 1876 showed a 3.1 per cent increase over the receipts for the same period the previous year.

	£	s.	d.
Passengers	476	11	3
Horses	35	9	1
Goods	821	2	7
Total	1,333	2	11

William T. Mousley was awarded the contract for the construction of the new railway tendering at £17,840. The contract specified that Mousley would execute the actual work with all materials, land and ancillary items supplied by the GER. By agreement under the 1876 Act the GER was authorized to take over the Ely & St Ives Railway on a 999 years lease, in return paying any additional expenses required constructing, maintaining and improving the line. The GER also assumed the responsibility for the payment of interest on the debenture and debenture stock of the Ely and St Ives company, 4 per cent on £36,000 initial stock and 5 per cent on the £60,000 extension stock.

When the railway was first mooted it was planned to have only one intermediate station between Sutton and St Ives, at Bluntisham. Application was, however, received from Mr Taylor a landowner at Earith, for a station to serve the local community. In return for the asset Taylor offered to sell his land to the company for £800 instead of £1,050, if the station was built at the locally known, Hermitage Road. The GER agreed to site the station according to Taylor's wishes on condition that if traffic was insufficient to warrant staffing or maintenance they could close it and repay Taylor the outstanding £250.

On 3rd March, 1877 John Valentine the EHSR Company Engineer, reported that the work on the viaduct over the River Ouse was proving troublesome although the foundations for the west end abutments, two large river piers and one small pier were laid in November 1876. The whole valley had since flooded and work had ceased. Messrs Cochrane had, however, completed the order to supply the girder sections and these would be placed in position once the piers were built. The foundations of another bridge at 5 miles 70 chains were laid but again flooding had halted progress of works. The small drain bridges were still to be built but all culverts were completed. The permanent way material for the whole extension had been delivered and 85 occupational crossing gates had been erected. The Engineer concluded his report to the proprietors by advising that tenders had been invited for the building of stations, gate lodges and signal boxes.

Following many complaints from train crews regarding the sighting of signals at Ely Sutton Branch Junction authority was given on 11th July, 1877 to raise the height of certain signals to obviate the problems. The work costing an estimated £110 was completed by October of the same year. Meanwhile on 4th August, 1877 Valentine again reported on the progress of the railway extension to St Ives. Of the 86,000 cubic yards of earthworks required for the line, 74,757 cubic yards had been completed. All bridges and culverts were completed except for two bridges spanning fenland drains, which were being built. Work on the viaduct spanning the River Ouse at Earith was nearing completion. The disastrous wet weather earlier in the year caused the area of flooding to remain until May and all work on the structure had stopped for a period of five months. The Engineer reported that the brick piers were all completed whilst the iron cylinders in the middle of the waterway had been sunk into the blue clay, and the cylinders subsequently filled with concrete. It was hoped to have the whole structure completed at the end of August. Of the stations Valentine was able to report that the new Sutton station was almost completed, while that at Bluntisham would be completed within two weeks. The third station at Hermitage (Earith Bridge) was in the course of erection.

The EHSR Secretary initially advised the Board of Trade on 6th March, 1878 of the notice of intention to open the extension line to traffic and on 20th April the *Cambridge Chronicle* reported that a number of workmen were working on the line between Sutton and St Ives fitting signals and points, and it was hoped the line would open for traffic on 1st May, 1878. The *Cambridge Independent Press* was more specific, for its reporter advised that the line was to be worked on the block system and that points were fitted with Saxby & Farmer patent locking, although it too thought the line would open on Wednesday 1st May. A second application was sent to the BoT on 27th April and a letter from GER headquarters advised that the new line was to be worked by Train Staff and Ticket with block sections.

Major General C.S. Hutchinson duly made the inspection on Friday 3rd May, 1878. The inspector found that the new railway which had been constructed by the EHSR and was to be worked by the GER, was a single line commencing by a junction with the existing line from Ely at Sutton and terminated by a junction with the GER line between St Ives and March at a point two miles north of St Ives. The line offered for inspection was 8 miles 38 chains in length with sidings at the three stations at Sutton, Earith Bridge and Bluntisham. Land had been purchased and the width of some of the formation was wide enough for double track if growth of traffic warranted such improvements in the future. The permanent way was in good order and the lineside fencing was of post and rail formation. The steepest gradient on the line was 1 in 132 and the sharpest curve at Sutton was of 10 chains radius. The four underbridges had cast- and wrought-iron girders on brick abutments, the largest cast-iron span was of 12 feet 9 inches and the wrought-iron 34 ft. A viaduct over the River Ouse had 17 land spans of 30 ft each and two spans over water of 90 ft each and had cast-iron cylinders resting on brick piers with the exception of the water spans in which cast-iron cylinders formed the intermediate supports. There was an overbridge with a 34 ft span constructed entirely of brickwork and four brick culverts, the largest having a diameter of 6 ft 6 in. Hutchinson considered the works to be substantially constructed and to be standing well with sufficient theoretical strength. The girders of the four underbridges, four culverts and the viaduct over the Rive Ouse gave moderate deflections when tested by two heavy locomotives running at speed. The Major General noted the three authorized public level crossings and the signal boxes provided at Needingworth Junction, Bluntisham, Earith Bridge and Sutton. As the traffic was to be worked between Ely and St Ives and the distance between the intermediate stations was over three miles the inspector required the provision of an engine turntable at St Ives in addition to the existing facility at Ely. The GER representative promised to provide a turntable as part of the planned improvements to St Ives station. However, as the station was shortly to become the focus of joint ownership with the Great Northern Railway it was imperative to ensure that the turntable was included in any future arrangements, which were to be to the approval of the BoT. Under these circumstances the engine turntable was to be provided within one year of the inspection. In his report of 4th May, 1878 Hutchinson noted various deficiencies, which required rectification.

1. Sutton Junction and station – the 10 chain radius curve required a check-rail, whilst the down distant signal required clearing of overhanging trees. The signalbox also required widening opposite the chimney breast.

EXTENSION TO ST IVES

2. Earith Bridge station – A box for the crossing keeper was required at the level crossing gates at 4 miles 41 chains, whilst the signal weight on the down signal had been fixed too close to the running line.
3. Bluntisham station – The signalbox required widening opposite the chimney breast whilst the distant signal arm required to be notched.
4. Additional fencing was required at the bridge at 1 mile 54 chains from Needingworth Junction and at the culverts at 5 miles 77 chains and 7 miles 06 chains.
5. Gauge ties to be provided at all facing points.
6. Clocks to be provided in all signalboxes at stations, the latter to be visible from the line.

Hutchinson was provided with two undertakings as to the future method of working the line. The inspector recommended the opening of the line to traffic subject to the speedy completion of the requirements and to a re-inspection taking place at some future convenient time. An undertaking was also required from the GER as to the provision of improvements at St Ives including the installation of an engine turntable

The extension from Sutton to St Ives opened without ceremony on Friday 10th May, 1878. Few passengers travelled on the newly titled Ely & St Ives Railway until the following Monday when full advantage was taken to travel to and from St Ives market. The timing of the afternoon train was considered unsuitable as farmers and corn merchants who attended the market, which ended at 3.00 pm, were forced to wait until 5.30 pm before a branch train departed St Ives for Ely. All other market trains on other routes from St Ives departed soon after 4.00 pm. Some were also concerned that the 9.12 am train did not run on Mondays, when the 7.49 am Mondays-only train ran and was too early for the general public. A number of written complaints requested the GER authorities to alter the timing in the new timetable for June 1878.

The local goods manager had for some years complained of the lack of loading gauges at several goods yards on the branch and on more than one occasion wagons had arrived at Ely or St Ives for forwarding, with loads exceeding the gauge limit. The resultant delay incurred whilst wagons from branch trains were passed under the loading gauges at the junction goods yards meant that perishable goods was not getting the best prices at markets. The correspondence from farmers and growers was increasing and so on 4th June, 1878 the Way & Works Committee finally agreed to the provision of loading gauges at Stretham, Haddenham and Sutton at a cost of £50.

Major General C.S. Hutchinson returned to the branch on 26th October, 1878 and conducted a re-inspection. He found all the outstanding remedial work had been completed. He drew the Engineer's attention to the desirability of moving the facing point gauge ties nearer to the toes of the points and a promise was made to pay special attention to rectify the situation.

The steady increase in traffic at Ely, both on the main line and from the branch, brought additional operating problems and after investigation the GER Board recommended on 20th January, 1879 the rearrangement of facilities at the station costing an estimated £36,230, including £17,700 on new and realigned sidings, £4,800 on lengthening and raising of platforms, £3,300 on resignalling work and £430 on the Newmarket branch junction.

Chapter Three

Great Eastern Takeover

Clause 41 of the Great Eastern Railway Act (42 and 43 Vict. cap. cl), which received the Royal Assent on 21st July, 1879 granted the GER powers to lease the Ely and St Ives Railway for a period of 999 years, on terms agreed by the schedules attached to the Ely, Haddenham and Sutton Railway Extension Act of 1876. The GER in return guaranteed interest of two per cent per annum on the original capital of £38,000 and five per cent on the £60,000 capital for the extension scheme. From 1881 the former was increased to four per cent per annum.

The GER Way & Works Committee authorized the installation of a siding at Haddenham after a Mr Porter made application for the facility. The cost was divided, with Porter paying for work on his property and the GER paying £70 for the siding on railway land. The work was sanctioned on 15th July, 1879 and completed in time for the autumn harvest. However when application was made for a siding and loading dock at Earith Bridge, the matter was deferred on 23rd September, 1879 when the Engineer estimated the cost at an exorbitant £600. The public was constantly advised not to use the line as a public right of way but on 8th October, 1879, a trespasser named Merry Howard was killed by the branch train near Stretham.

The Ely Union at an assessment held on 7th October, 1879 set the parish rating for the Ely to Sutton line at £1,679 against the previous rating of £122 18s. 6d. The GER contested the valuation and appealed against the exorbitant figure. After arguing their case the railway company and the Ely Union finally settled for a rating of £658.

On 16th June, 1880 the GER Directors heard that the Ely & St Ives Railway had spent more on construction than the authorized share capital and under the working agreement the GER was due to pay five per cent of the total outlay. The Solicitor queried whether the GER was due to pay the Directors' fees during construction and it was resolved a payment of £20 was to be paid for establishment expenses. At the GER Board meeting on 18th August, 1880 the takeover of the St Ives company was debated and after investigation, it was recommended on 20th October that the company be taken over by the GER, which would take responsibility for all debentures and debenture stock and issue £125 four per cent preference stock for every £100 extension stock and £100 ordinary stock for every £100 ordinary stock. The GER Solicitor was asked to include the transfer in the Bill for the next session of Parliament but by 2nd November, 1880 it appeared unlikely the terms would be accepted and the transfer was excluded, although provision could be made to add the clause if the Ely & St Ives Directors accepted at a later date.

Further improvements were made to the facilities at Ely station when on 3rd August, 1880 Bennett Brothers were awarded the contract for the provision of additional waiting rooms, staff offices and accommodation at cost of £5,165, a figure which included painting and decorating.

Haddenham goods yard received further attention in 1881 after farmers had complained of the poor state of the cattle pens, which were often slippery and muddy in wet weather, a condition hardly conducive to the safe loading and unloading of livestock into and out of cattle wagons. Authority was duly given on 6th April, 1880 for the paving of the cattle pens at a cost of £6 10s. 0d. Unfortunately nothing was done until the farmers using Sutton goods yard added their voice for improvements. On 5th April, 1881 authority was given for the paving of cattle pens at both stations but by this time the price had increased to £12 10s. 0d. at each location. The increase in cattle traffic from the branch also required the paving of cattle pens at Ely costing £53 and St Ives, costing £460. The work authorized on 4th January and 5th February, 1881 respectively was completed in August of the same year.

Despite the pessimism shown the previous November, the GER authorities managed to include clauses in the Great Eastern Railway Act of 1881 (44 and 45 Vict. cap. cxxxiv) of 18th July, 1881 to raise additional capital. This was a requirement of the lease of the Ely & St Ives Railway to settle outstanding liabilities incurred by overspending on construction between Sutton and St Ives. Almost immediately the Ely & St Ives Directors resolved to ask the GER Directors to lease their company at the earliest opportunity but the matter was not raised at the GER Board meeting until 6th September, 1881. The GER Solicitor confirmed that the GER had powers to lease the local railway, subject to certain conditions, and a full report on the implications of the leasing was requested.

After years of wrangling the GER, who wished access to the northern coalfields, and the GNR who wished to infiltrate into East Anglia, finally reached agreement to form a Great Northern & Great Eastern Railway Joint Committee to administer a combined route from the Eastern Counties to Yorkshire. The authorizing Act, which received the Royal Assent on 1st July, 1879, sanctioned the committee composed of five Directors from each company to oversee the administration, operation and maintenance of the new joint line. The elements of the new route comprised Huntingdon to St Ives opened by the East Anglian Railway in 1847, Needingworth Junction to March, opened by the ECR in 1848, March to Spalding opened by the GNR in 1867 and a new Spalding to Lincoln line, authorized in 1878, opened to Ruskington on 6th March, 1882 and on to Lincoln on 1st August, 1882. From Lincoln the route followed an existing GNR line via Gainsborough to Black Carr Junction on the GNR main line just south of Doncaster. The opening of the new line throughout heralded an expected increase in traffic and the GER General Manager reported on 15th August, 1882, that it was necessary to make temporary signalling arrangements between St Ives and Needingworth Junction, which remained in GER ownership, to enable the block telegraph to be installed between the two signal boxes. The Traffic Committee sanctioned the estimated expenditure of £100 for the temporary work.

In the meantime on the Ely & St Ives Railway, Bluntisham station received attention in 1883 when cattle pens were provided at a cost of £22. The work was sanctioned on 3rd October, 1882 and completed early the following year. The station master at Bluntisham had also complained of the lack of facilities in the station house and on 6th February, 1883 authority was given for the provision of a washhouse and water closet at a combined cost of £35. Installation was completed in that July. In the same period the provision of a trap siding at St Ives costing £40 was authorized on 1st January, 1883 and work was completed in September.

A year later on 1st January, 1884 authority was given for additional sidings at St Ives at a cost of £746. By 5th February an interest payment of £3,085 to ESIR was authorized and a draft lease of the local line to the GER approved. Jewson & Sons Ltd had for some years been forwarding traffic from Haddenham but considered the existing goods yard facilities were inadequate. An approach was made in February 1884 for the provision of a private siding to serve their premises. The siding was sanctioned by the Way & Works Committee on 18th March at a cost of £150 and the GER reached agreement with the firm to charge 5s. 0d. per ton if less than 20,000 tons per annum, whilst offering a five per cent rebate if Jewson forwarded over 20,000 tons. A drawback allowance of 6d. per ton was also available if the tonnage dispatched exceeded 20,000. The siding was completed by mid-October and Major General C.S. Hutchinson inspected the new works at Haddenham on 7th November, 1884. He found that the points of the junction to the goods yard from the main line were secured by a lock, released by a key attached to the Ely to Sutton single line Train Staff. The arrangements were satisfactory save that a bolt was to be provided to hold the facing point close to the stock rail. As well as agreeing to the new siding the GER Way & Works Committee also authorized the provision of a water supply to the cattle pens at Haddenham on 1st April, 1884 at a cost of £22.

On 3rd February, 1885 and 5th January, 1886 the GER Board again sanctioned £3,085 interest payments to the Ely & St Ives Board, whilst on 5th January, 1886 the General Manager recommended the rearrangement of St Ives station and interlocking of the points and signals, at an estimated cost of £11,626. It was also stipulated that the platform should only be 16 ft wide instead of the proposed 20 ft. It was 16th November, 1886, however, before the contract for the interlocking of points and signals at St Ives was awarded to Saxby & Farmer Ltd.

Local inhabitants often used the branch railway as an unofficial public footpath by taking a short cut along the line between villages. As the traffic was sparse few fatalities occurred but on 11th June, 1886, Thomas Dean was knocked down and killed by the branch train as he made his way along the line from Haddenham. The driver sounded the engine whistle but was unable to stop the train before running down the deceased. The public was again warned in the local press not to trespass on the railway.

As freight traffic increased so the layout in the goods yard at Sutton became cramped and farmers and growers complained of the lack of siding space to load and unload wagons. The goods manager investigated and duly requested the provision of additional sidings to ease the situation. Authority was given on 7th September, 1886 for the work to be carried out as a matter of urgency at a cost of £95 and the new sidings were completed in January of the following year. The work was confined to the goods yard and no BoT inspection was required.

On 4th January, 1887 authority was given by the GER Board for the payment of £3,085 interest to the Ely & St Ives Railway. In the same year on 5th April authority was given for the widening of the underline bridge at Ely at an estimated cost of £1,800.

Footplate crews working across the branch were critical of the siting of the starting signals at Bluntisham and after representation, agreement was reached to have both up and down starters renewed and slightly repositioned. The work costing £40 was authorized on 5th April, 1887. On the same day authority was given for alterations to the station master's house at Wilburton at a cost of £100. The small building was primitive and the incumbent and his family regularly complained of the lack of space and toilet and wash facilities. Both the signal work and house improvements were completed by the autumn of the same year.

On 17th May, 1887 the Way & Works Committee sanctioned the resignalling of Ely Sutton Branch Junction at a cost of £390, and a contract was placed with the Railway Signalling Co. of Fazakerley, Liverpool on 15th November, 1887. Work was completed the following year.

The lack of facilities to handle cattle traffic at Stretham had often brought complaints from local livestock farmers and finally on 18th July, 1887 authority was given for the provision of a cattle dock and pens at a cost of £120 and work was completed the following February. On 7th February, 1888 the station master at Stretham was gratified to hear that a sum of £110 had been agreed to make similar improvements to the living accommodation as that authorized at Wilburton the previous year. Wilburton station was further enhanced in 1888 when authority was given on 3rd July for the sinking of a well and improvements to the latrines at a cost of £30. On 3rd January, 1888 the GER authorized the payment of £3,085 as half-yearly interest for the six months ending 31st December, 1887.

Grain traffic continued to increase over the years and an old complaint regarding the storage of the commodity in dry conditions was resurrected. Remedial steps were taken in April 1889 when authority was given for the erection of a grain shed at Bluntisham at an estimated cost of £400.

As a result of the Regulation of Railways Act 1889, railway companies throughout Great Britain were required to standardize on safety. Amongst other things this included the installation of block telegraph for signalling, the interlocking of points and signals and the provision of continuous braking on locomotives and rolling stock required to work passenger trains. Various exemptions were permitted, especially on lightly used lines, for the expense of providing the required infrastructure and equipment was considerable. After deliberating, the GER management decided that the Ely to St Ives line with Train Staff and Ticket working throughout and block signalling already in operation between Sutton and Needingworth Junction only required the eastern end of the line to be brought up to standard. Thus on 21st April, 1891 the contract for signalling improvements and interlocking at Stretham, Wilburton and Haddenham was awarded to the Railway Signal Co. of Fazakerley, Liverpool. In the same year on 2nd June the Way & Works Committee authorized the provision of a cart weighbridge at Sutton at an estimated cost of £120. The structure of the Haddenham Road overbridge spanning the line west of Haddenham station at 11 miles 68 chains from St Ives, was considered too narrow and by 1891 was showing signs of deterioration. Authority was given on 1st September for the brick arches to be replaced by an iron span and the contract for the ironwork was awarded to J. Westwood after the firm tendered at £805 7s. 6d., a price which included five other bridges on the GER.

The continuing increase in freight traffic at Sutton resulted in additional goods accounts work, which was conducted by clerks in the passenger booking office. The small space in the original office became cramped as additional ledgers and documentation filled every available space. On 2nd February, 1892 authority was given for the enlargement of the booking office at a cost of £60 and on completion the problem was alleviated. The early weeks of 1892 also saw the completion of resignalling work and on 16th February, 1892 Major General C.S. Hutchinson inspected the new siding connection at Stretham. He found the new set of points as well as the old were worked by interlocked levers worked from the new signal box containing a 20-lever frame with 15 working and five spare levers. The arrangements were satisfactory. He also examined similar new works at Wilburton and Haddenham and found all to his satisfaction.

On 1st January, 1893 second-class accommodation was abolished on all GER passenger services except in the London suburban area and on Continental boat trains. On 3rd February, 1891 the GER Directors had originally reserved a sum of £20,000 for improvements to Ely station but by 4th April, 1893 the GER Board estimated that it would cost £40,000 to bring facilities up to standard and provision was made in the budget for this expenditure.

After the resignalling of the Stretham to Haddenham section of the branch it was found that certain other modifications were required on the line. At Sutton, it was deemed necessary to provide outer home signals and authority was given on 2nd October, 1894 for their installation at a cost of £120. Two months later on 18th December authority was given for the provision of an up advanced starting signal

Sutton station and crossing loop in the 1890s facing Ely showing the original station buildings on the down platform, which were destroyed by fire in 1921. Note the up platform has a simple covered awning to protect passengers, although this facility was later removed.
Author's Collection

Haddenham station in the 1890s, showing the low station building provided by the EHSR containing the booking office and waiting rooms and the original station master's house, replaced by a new structure in 1900. *Author's Collection*

on the main line at Sutton Branch Junction at a cost of £28. This was required as the section in advance to the next signal box was over four miles distant.

Sutton station at the time of the building of the extension to St Ives was considered adequate for traffic requirements but the gradual increase in traffic by 1895 necessitated the use of the lamp trimming room for alternative use. To obviate the problem of the shortage of space one of the block boxes used by the GER at Cambridge during the Royal Show week was transported to Sutton and became the new lamp room. The work costing £27 was authorized on 19th March and completed within weeks.

In the 1890s Messrs Chivers Ltd opened a jam manufacturing factory at Histon adjacent to the Cambridge to St Ives line. As well as owning over 3,000 acres of land set aside for fruit growing, the firm also bought fruit from farmers in the surrounding area. Compared with the average fenland farmers these fruit growers enjoyed prosperity and at Cottenham, the centre of the fruit growing area, the village maintained facilities more akin to a town with paved streets and gas lighting. To move these supplies of fruit it was proposed to lay a light railway from the junction near Oakington station to Cottenham, with a possible extension to Haddenham under the powers of the 1896 Light Railways Act. On reflection of the costs, estimated between £30,000 and £40,000, it was decided that the horse-drawn waggon service, although slow and cumbersome, was adequate during the short fruit growing season and the idea for the railway was shelved.

After years of leasing and working several small railways in East Anglia, each entailing its own problems the GER Directors resolved to tidy up the excessive costs of administration by purchasing the several leased and worked lines including that from Ely to St Ives. On 6th May, 1896 it was resolved to prepare a suitable Bill to the next session of Parliament. It was initially envisaged that the Ely & St Ives would be offered GER three per cent rent charge stock, to yield a payment equivalent to the current GER payments. On 8th July approval was given for the refurbishment of Ely station including the provision of a longer down side platform and a sloping subway to connect the platforms. Improved goods accommodation was also planned in the scheme, estimated at £18,158. By 7th October the Engineer had advised that the sloping subway would cost an additional £1,460 and the authority for the work was increased to £19,618.

The GER Board initially approved of the terms of the takeover of the Ely to St Ives Railway on 2nd December, 1896. The local Directors, subject to the approval of the shareholders, agreed to sell their line outright for £128,000, receiving in exchange GER four per cent debentures. This arrangement was entirely acceptable to the debenture holders and shareholders of the Ely company, for as well as receiving an income equal to their existing arrangements, an additional £1,750 was available to meet outstanding expenses incurred in the winding-up of the company.

At about 7 am on Thursday 16th January, 1897 the 45-year-old wife of Thomas Barnard, signalman at Ely Sutton Branch Junction signal box, walked from their cottage alongside the line to deliver his breakfast. After exchanging pleasantries with her husband she returned from the signal box to the cottage in the darkness of the winter morning but was unfortunately struck and killed by the engine of the 6.55 am Cambridge to Norwich train. Barnard was unaware of the accident until platelayer Fen discovered the body during his inspection of the line. At a later inquiry the driver of the train explained he was unaware of the tragedy and a verdict of accidental death was recorded.

The Ely & St Ives company and the GER entered into an agreement on 19th July, 1897 authorizing the main line company to acquire the Ely and St Ives line on and

[61 & 62 VICT.] *Great Eastern Railway (General Powers)* [**Ch. lxvi.**]
Act, 1898.

CHAPTER lxvi.

A.D. 1898.

An Act to confer further powers upon and to amend certain Acts relating to the Great Eastern Railway Company to authorise the Company to subscribe towards the undertakings of the Elsenham Thaxted and Bardfield and the Kelvedon Tiptree and Tollesbury Light Railway Companies and to acquire the undertakings of the Ely and Saint Ives the Ely and Newmarket the Colchester Stour Valley Sudbury and Halstead and the Mellis and Eye Railway Companies and part of the Great Northern and Great Eastern Joint Railway to make further provision as to certain funds of the Company and for other purposes.

[1st July 1898.]

WHEREAS it is expedient that the Great Eastern Railway Company (in this Act called "the Company") be authorised to construct the works and to purchase the additional lands hereinafter described and to exercise the other powers in this Act specified:

And whereas the Company have acquired by agreement for the purposes of their undertaking certain other lands herein-after described and it is expedient that the purchase of such lands and the expenditure of money by the Company in respect thereof be confirmed:

And whereas the works authorised by this Act include the conversion into a fixed bridge of the existing swing bridge by which the Company's branch railway leading to the "Pepper Warehouses" is carried over the River Lee or the River Lee Navigation at Bow Creek and it is expedient that certain provisions of the Great Eastern Railway Act 1862 relating to the existing swing bridge be repealed:

[*Price* 4s.]

from 1st July, 1898. By clause 2 of the agreement the GER would settle any terminable debentures of the Ely & St Ives, which required settlement after 1st July, 1898. The GER was permitted to raise £127,706 4 per cent debenture stock as from 1st July, 1898 and issue £125 4 per cent debentures for every £100 Ely & St Ives 5 per cent debentures and £100 Ely & St Ives 5 per cent ordinary stock and issue the balance as £100 debentures to the registered holders of Ely & St Ives 4 per cent stock. On completion of the purchase, the GER would pay to the Ely & St Ives the sum of £1,750 as full compensation to the Directors for loss of office and would release the local company of its £5,129 obligations. James B. Bond, Secretary to the Ely & St Ives and W.H. Peppercorne, Secretary to the GER, signed the document, which was subject to ratification by future Act of Parliament.

Considerable improvements were made at St Ives during the autumn of 1897, which eased the operation of trains through the station complex. Lt-Col G.W. Addison conducted the BoT inspection of the new works on 12th January, 1898. He found that a new crossover had been laid between the main lines to March and Ely, north of the station. The position of some of the signals had been altered and the former through road from the up line to the sidings on the down side of the railway had been removed. The points and signals in that portion of the goods yard were worked from St Ives Yard signal box containing a 36-lever Saxby & Farmer frame with 30 working and six spare levers. The only alterations required by Addison was that levers Nos. 4 and 34 were to be interlocked and that arrangements were to be made for rotating the locking between levers Nos. 4 and 5, so that after No. 5 signal had been lowered it was not possible to pull No. 5 lever a second time until No. 4 lever had been pulled and put back to danger. Addison returned on 6th April, 1898 and found the requirements made in his report of 13th January had been attended to.

At a special General Meeting of the Ely & St Ives Directors and proprietors held at Hamilton House, Bishopsgate, London on 21st February, 1898, the gathering discussed the Bill being presented to Parliament by the GER to enable the main line company to subscribe towards the Elsenham, Thaxted & Bardfield Light Railway and the Kelvedon, Tiptree & Tollesbury Light Railway, and for the acquisition of the Ely & St Ives, Ely & Newmarket, Colchester, Stour Valley, Sudbury & Haverhill, and Mellis & Eye railway companies. After resolving a few minor problems the gathering approved of the takeover and the Bill proceeded.

The Great Eastern Railway General Powers Act 1898 (61 and 62 Vict. cap. lxvi), which received the Royal Assent on 1st July, 1898, authorized the main line company to acquire the Ely & St Ives Railway by raising £127,706 four per cent debentures and exchanging them for the Ely & St Ives company shares at the rates mentioned above. At a special Board meeting held on 26th July, 1898, the GER Directors approved of the creation of £517,844 four per cent debenture stock to purchase the Ely & St Ives, Ely & Newmarket and Colchester, Stour Valley, Sudbury and Halstead railway companies.

The last Board meeting of the Ely & St Ives Railway held on Friday 3rd August, 1898 was a somewhat sombre affair, for the death of John Sutherland Valentine, the original Engineer of the EHSR and later Chairman was announced. Frederick Camps was elected Chairman in his place but ultimately never chaired a meeting. The final expenditure incurred by the Ely & St Ives company amounted to £134,835 13s. 10d. and this included £13,000 in payment of matured debentures and £5,129 13s. 10d. which was not repayable until the end of the 999 years lease.

The GER on takeover of the erstwhile Ely & St Ives Railway carried out a complete survey of the assets and quickly found that the original station house at Haddenham

Ely station *c*.1910 facing south from the up platform showing the down side platform undergoing repairs to the canopy. A St Ives branch train is approaching to terminate at the down platform. In the extreme distance is Ely Station South signal box located at the end of the up platform. This signal box, together with Ely Dock Junction signal box, controlled the signalling and points at the south end of the station. *Author's Collection*

Ely station *c*.1910 viewed from the up side island platform looking north, and showing the down main platform at which the St Ives branch passenger trains terminated. The station buildings are fronted by ornate canopies added at different periods hence the difference in height. The platform wall is littered with numerous posters and advertising hoardings and to the extreme left is a 17 gallons milk churn, possibly offloaded from a St Ives branch train. Ely Station North signal box, seen at the extreme end of the platform, controlled the signals, points and level crossing at the north end of the station. *Author's Collection*

was dilapidated and in need of replacement. On 21st March, 1899 authority was given for the construction of a new station master's house at an estimated cost of £550 and a new booking office, estimated at £150. The contract was duly awarded to A. Saint on 18th July after he tendered for the complete work at a cost of £412. Difficulties with the subsoil and finding a solid base for the foundations added to the costs and delayed completion until December 1900 at a cost of £751. Along the line at Earith Bridge several complaints had been made regarding the lack of loading facilities for livestock, notably horses and on 1st October, 1901 authority was given for the provision of a horse dock at an estimated cost of £138. The dock was finally completed in August 1902 at a reduced cost of £122. The new decade brought further improvements at Wilburton where four cottages were authorized on 17th December, 1901 at an estimated cost of £875. The contract was awarded to R. Shanks but, as at Haddenham, difficulty was experienced finding a substantial base for the footings of buildings in the marshy fenland. The lack of ladies' accommodation at Wilburton was also cause for concern as was the fact the booking office measured only 10 ft x 6 ft and was extremely cramped. To obviate the deficiencies the Way & Works Committee sanctioned the provision of new ladies facilities and an extension to the booking office on 15th July, 1902 at an estimated cost of £120. Both cottages and station work was completed in May 1904, at above the estimated prices, the cottages costing £966 and the station work £155.

In the meantime at Sutton, Messrs Drake & Sons of New Mill requested the provision of a siding to serve their works near the old station. The work was authorized on 7th October, 1902 at a cost of £390 and was completed in April 1903 at a reduced cost of £282 but not before a Mr Sheard of Sutton House had complained regarding the unpleasant smells emanating from the works, a factor totally outside of the control of the GER.

On 16th November, 1903 the crossing hut at Needingworth Junction level crossing was destroyed by fire and on 1st December the Way & Works Committee sanctioned a replacement hut to obviate the crossing keeper having to stand in the open in all weathers with nothing but a temporary tarpaulin sheet as protection. By 1904 Brown & Goodman were sending considerable tonnages of grain and flour traffic from Earith Bridge to Godmanchester and requested the provision of a stage and crane to assist with the loading of the commodities into wagons. After investigation it was found the loading could be achieved without the necessity for an additional siding and authority was given on 18th October for the loading dock and crane at a cost of £150. The GER were somewhat lethargic in providing the equipment and it was November 1905 before work was completed at the reduced cost of £122.

On 19th December, 1905 the GER management approved of the installation of advanced starting signals at various stations to improve the smooth operation of trains. The signals would allow a second train to pull into the station platform, whilst the previous train drew ahead to the advanced starting signal. St Ives was included in the list of proposed stations and St Ives Junction signal box was to be provided with an advanced starter on the up line and St Ives Yard signal box an advanced starter on the down road. Then on 2nd January, 1907 it was proposed to install additional signals at Ely. As there was much goods shunting between Ely Dock Junction and Ely South signal boxes, when the platform line was occupied, it was often necessary to pass goods traffic down the up Newmarket branch line. It was recommended that the Ely Dock Junction signalman should slot all five signals applicable to the up branch line at the South signal box. It was also recommended that a disc signal be provided, applicable to trains passing from the up branch line

Looking south from Ely Station South signal box towards Cambridge in 1911. The engine shed is to the left, whilst the locomotive beyond the building is on the 55 ft diameter turntable. The down yard and goods shed are on the right with an 0-6-0T shunting wagons. Ely Dock Junction signalbox is in the central distance.
National Railway Museum

The north end of Ely station looking south in 1911 with the up main and down main lines crossing underbridge No. 1569 spanning the River Ouse. The engine nearest the camera stands just short of Ely North signal box on a short siding used to hold locomotives relieving northbound services. The line diverging in front of the siding served a small coal yard.
GERS/Windwood 1426

View taken from the front of Ely Dock Junction signal box in 1911 showing the single line branch to Fordham and Newmarket diverging to the left and the up and down main lines to Cambridge on the right. The loop line from Ely station leading to the Fordham line is to the left. St Ives branch trains followed the up main line to Ely Sutton Branch Junction where they diverged to the west whilst down branch trains followed the down main line between the junction and Ely. Ely Sutton Branch Junction distant signal for the branch can be seen in the caution position on the up side of the up main line at a slightly lower level than the distant for the up main line, which is in the clear position. Ely Dock Junction signal box was subsequently repositioned in the 'V' of the Fordham and Cambridge lines on the up side of the main line in 1928.   *National Railway Museum*

Ely station from the south in 1911. Ely engine shed, which supplied some engines to work the St Ives branch is on the right, whilst Ely Station South signal box is in the centre of the view at the up end of the island platform. In the foreground is the up independent line to Fordham running from the up back platform, whilst carriage storage sidings are alongside. The down side goods reception sidings are to the left and to the lower left cattle wagons stand on the low level sidings on the approach to the goods shed. St Ives branch services departed from either the up main or up back platform.   *National Railway Museum*

Looking north from St Ives yard signal box in 1911 showing the down and up main lines to and from March and followed by Ely trains to and from Needingworth Junction. Beyond the rake of wagons on the goods yard reception siding can be seen the extensive cattle pens in the cattle market which adjoined the goods yard and was served by its own siding. Much cattle traffic came by way of the Sutton branch. *GERS/Windwood 1502*

The south end of St Ives station with up and down main line platforms to the left and the Huntingdon branch in the foreground. This was the junction of the GN&GE Joint line from Huntingdon with the GER route from Chesterton Junction (Cambridge) to Needingworth Junction and on to Ely via Sutton. The GN&GE Joint double line continued north from Needingworth Junction. *GERS/Windwood 1499*

to the down main line, and that a draw-ahead signal be provided on the Newmarket branch down home signal at Ely Dock Junction to enable a train to be drawn from the branch line as far as the signal box, when the main line ahead was blocked and there to await the signalman's instructions. The estimated cost of the alterations was £152. The work was completed in December 1908 at a cost of £139.

After several years of neglect the branch stations were included in a repair and painting programme and on 15th June, 1911 work at Bluntisham was awarded to Clarke at a cost of £54 18s. 0d. The following year on 6th June, 1912 three further contracts were awarded at Haddenham to Clarke who tendered at £57 8s. 0d., Wilburton to Vigor who tendered at £40 and Stretham to A. Coe priced at £33.

The outbreak of World War I on 4th August, 1914 found the GER with other British railway companies coming under Government control (the Railway Executive Committee). Train services initially ran to pre-war timetables as passengers travelled on business or pleasure. Goods traffic quietly flourished as increased produce was dispatched from the fenland farms of Cambridgeshire and Huntingdonshire to towns and cities to make up for the loss of imported food. A few local railwaymen quickly answered the call to arms and joined the colours in the first months of hostilities. As the months progressed British farmers were again urged to increase production of fruit and vegetables. Growers and cattle breeders of the fens answered the call and additional freight trains ran across the Ely to St Ives line in addition to the booked workings. Hay and straw traffic also increased providing fodder and bedding for horses at the many military establishments in East Anglia and London. The branch was not so strategically placed as many other GER routes but the line carried a few additional trains for troops on training manoeuvres.

The strain of the war years severely taxed the resources of the railways and in December 1916 the Railway Executive Committee issued an ultimatum to the effect that they could only continue if drastic reductions were made to ordinary services. Locomotive availability was especially short through lack of coal supplies. The Lloyd George Coalition thus agreed to the reduction of passenger train services from 1st January, 1917, but despite this edict the Ely to St Ives branch services remained virtually intact.

In 1914, soon after the commencement of hostilities, the GER set up a War Relief Fund with collections being made at main line and branch stations. In the three months ending 31st March, 1917 £1 19s. 11d. was collected at St Ives, with £1 16s. 9d. for the three months ending 30th September and £1 5s. 7d. for the final three months of the year. The first three months of 1918 resulted in collections of £1 19s. 1d. at St Ives and 3s. 6d. at Wilburton. No collections were made at the other branch stations in the same period.

On Armistice Day in November 1918 flags were exhibited at some of the branch stations. The renewed peacetime operation was rudely interrupted from 26th September to 8th October, 1919 when a railway strike halted services on the line. The advent of the internal combustion engine on the roads from Ely to Sutton, Mepal and Somersham and Ely to Haddenham, Earith and St Ives brought the first regular bus services from the same year. Soon Ortona Motor Services of Cambridge were operating competitive bus services in the district served by the branch railway. This brought a rapid decline in passenger traffic, which had always been of a secondary nature to the goods traffic. The stations were unfortunately remote from the villages they were supposed to serve and in most cases the walk between village and station or return involved a climb as most stations were in the valley bottom and the settlements on the higher fenland ridge. Stretham and Wilburton suffered more than

The north end of St Ives with the down platform to the left and the up platform on the right in 1911. The goods yard with large goods shed is in the background. The water column at the end of the down platform and a similar column at the Cambridge end of the up platform were fed from a water tank with the supply coming from a well. *GERS/Windwood 1495*

St Ives goods yard in 1911 with the extensive goods shed to the left and St Ives Yard signal box on the up side of the up main line from March. The signal box contained a 36-lever Saxby & Farmer frame but as a result of rationalization the box was abolished on 21st June, 1931 when control of points and signals transferred to St Ives Junction signal box. *GERS/Windwood 1503*

St Ives station from the north showing the up and down main lines to March with the short up reception road to the left. The extensive goods yard overshadowed by the large goods shed was evidence of the importance of this Huntingdonshire junction and trade created by the town. Sutton branch goods trains were outsorted and re-formed within the sidings before continuing their journey. *GERS/Windwood 1501*

Looking west from St Ives GN&GE Joint line platform towards Huntingdon on 19th October, 1911. The line was single with the points set for the main line, whilst the right-hand rails formed a siding serving successively Potto Brown's and then Brown & Goodman's mill. By 1904 the premises had been taken over by Chivers Jam Manufacturing Printing Works. The other line is the run-round loop. Through trains from Ely to Huntingdon via St Ives used this platform. *GERS/Windwood 1494*

St Ives station looking north-west in 1911 with the Huntingdon branch to the left and the double track March line curving to the right. St Ives Junction signal box is located in the 'V' of the junction between the two lines. Ely branch passenger services terminated in the up platform and departed from the down platform, whilst goods services ran direct to the goods yard. Through services between Ely and Huntingdon had to reverse at the station. Note the River Ouse in full flood. *National Railway Museum*

Looking towards the junction of the Huntingdon branch and the Cambridge to March double track line with St Ives Junction signal box to the left and the up branch starting signal to the right. The continuation of the down reception line and the run-round loop for Huntingdon branch trains is to the right. *GERS/Windwood 1500*

most being 1½ miles and one mile away from their villages respectively. Haddenham and Sutton were slightly nearer whilst Earith Bridge served a scattered community and Bluntisham was also a half mile from the village. In comparison the buses offered an almost door-to-door service.

In 1921 a miners' strike affected coal supplies and although the branch services were not curtailed the number of passenger trains was reduced. A downturn was also experienced with freight receipts, for with the ending of the war many surplus military vehicles were made available to farmers and industrial concerns. Short haul produce was conveyed locally on the gradually improving roads instead of by rail, thus saving the double handling into and out of railway wagons. The railway company, however, still retained long haul freight traffic as the primitive road vehicles were incapable of continuous long journeys. As if things could not get any worse Sutton station was then destroyed by fire.

After the passing of the 7.30 pm goods train on Saturday 24th September, 1921 signalman Howard at Sutton signalled 'Train Out of Section' to Earith Bridge and then waited for the train to clear the branch at Ely Sutton Branch Junction before closing and locking the signal box. Just after 8.00 pm he left the station, knowing that the platform staff had already vacated the premises and the next train was not due until the following Monday morning. He noted nothing amiss as on his way home he passed a terrace of eight houses known as Bow Cottages. No. 3 was occupied by John Stimpson, whose daughter Mrs Keeler was staying for the night. At about 2.40 am on Sunday 25th September Keeler was woken by the cries of her baby and getting out of bed found the bedroom was bathed in light and thought it was the approaching dawn. On glancing through the curtains the young mother was aghast to see that the buildings of Sutton station were ablaze and roused her father from his slumbers. Stimpson immediately called three of his neighbours, one of whom called the Sutton Fire Brigade and another roused station master H.W. Doughty from his bed. By the time Stimpson was at the station, the north end of the building was well and truly gutted but as the station master's office was not so seriously damaged he entered through the broken door and rescued some papers just before the roof collapsed. Within minutes Captain G. Few of the Sutton Fire Brigade and his men arrived but with lack of a plentiful supply of water were powerless to stop the flames from spreading. A hand pump was borrowed from Drake's Forage Factory and attempts were made to keep the walls doused with water. By 4.00 am the entire station roof had collapsed and the whole site was a burning cauldron, although for a time the roof tiles quenched the flames. As the railway telegraph was destroyed in the conflagration, station master Doughty roused the local postmaster and used the Post Office telegraph to summon help. A message was sent to Ely and relayed on to Cambridge where the GER Fire Brigade was alerted at 4.30 am. A special train was arranged and set off an hour later en route for Ely. In the meantime arrangements were made to open the branch and the train subsequently arrived at Sutton at 6.50 am having picked up the Ely Auxiliary Fire Brigade en route. The newcomers were, however, too late and by the time they arrived they could only douse the remaining flames. Of the 50 ft x 30 ft station building little remained save that the walls were standing. All interior fixtures and fittings were destroyed and coins were welded together by the heat. The remains of the booking hall clock stopped at 3.58 am, whilst the frame of an automatic chocolate machine stood gaunt in the morning light, its contents well and truly melted. The cause of the outbreak was unknown but it was optimistically noted that the walls of the station showed no signs of cracking and it was thought a new station building could be built using the original framework. By Monday 26th September a booking office had been set up in a temporary hut in the station approach road, whilst other transactions were transferred to the goods shed office.

Government control of the railways continued until 15th August, 1921 when it was evident the railway companies could not be returned to pre-war days. The railways had been overstretched by the war effort and the variety of large, medium and small companies had little chance of recovering when maintaining Victorian systems and business values. In 1918 the Coalition Government hinted at nationalization, a matter that had been simmering after the formation of the Railway Nationalization League in 1895. The Labour Party, with railway union backing, declared such a move as policy and this was followed by the creation of the Railway Nationalization Society in 1908. However, it was also the view of many industrialists and traders that the railway should act as a public corporation rather than a profit making business and in 1919 the *Railway Gazette* had published a number of serious proposals for nationalization, which was openly debated by ministers, although rejected by public opinion. In the event the Government decided against nationalization by reforming the companies into four groups.

With a view to counteracting the increasing bus competition and working its many branch lines with the utmost economy, the GER operating and commercial superintendents jointly proposed the introduction of the conductor-guard method of working on a number of lines including the Ely to St Ives branch. The Traffic Committee was advised that the Ministry of Transport had given their approval to the modification required for working the existing branch lines. The Downham and Stoke Ferry branch had operated under such conditions since 1895 and the annual estimated savings for all lines involved in the proposals was £7,000. At a meeting on 16th June, 1922 it was reported that at several places served by road transport the railway company had no station or halt. It was well known and all too obvious that a further reduction in passenger receipts could be expected as the motorbus routes expanded. The cost of providing large stations was prohibitive but with the Ministry of Transport's relaxation it was possible to provide cheaply built line side halts. On various branches these were ultimately provided but no such locations were to be found on the Ely to St Ives line. The total expenditure to provide enough modified coaching stock for the introduction of conductor-guard working was estimated at no more than £400 for the whole scheme. The modified working incurred expenditure of £300 on the Ely to St Ives line, with expected annual savings of £2,700.

In the meantime after months of indecision the Traffic Committee on 13th July agreed to the provision of a new station at Sutton to replaced the fire-gutted building after the Engineer had estimated the cost at £572. However on 9th November, 1922 the contract for the rebuilding of Sutton station was awarded to S.S. Ambrose after the firm tendered at the reduced price of £398 15s. 0d.

In December 1922, the GER just prior to amalgamation introduced the conductor-guard method of working. On introduction of the revised working the booking offices at Stretham, Wilburton, Earith Bridge and Bluntisham stations were closed for passenger work as tickets were issued on the train by the guard. To enable the guard to collect fares whilst the train was travelling between stations, suitably modified six-wheel coaches were introduced with internal centre gangways and a centre door at the end of each coach to enable the guard to walk between each vehicle. The normal formation of the branch train was a three-coach set, formed of composite, a full third and a brake third. There was cautious optimism that the new method of working would bring an upturn in passenger revenue.

Chapter Four

Grouping and Nationalization

In accordance with the 1921 Railways Act, from 1st January, 1923 the GER was amalgamated with the Great Northern, Great Central, North Eastern, North British and several smaller companies to form the London & North Eastern Railway. The new ownership brought few changes to the Ely and St Ives branch save that Haddenham station was renamed Haddenham (Cambs) on and from 1st July, 1923 to differentiate it from Haddenham station on the former Great Western and Great Central Joint line located north of Princes Risborough. Industrial action soon affected affairs when a seven-day railway strike from 20th January, 1924 brought a further decline in traffic. The few passengers who had regularly patronized the railway service for short journeys turned to the competitive bus services, some never returning to the branch line. The conductor-guard method of working certainly reduced operating costs but also failed to bring about an increase in passenger traffic at the branch stations. However, the programme of repairing and painting stations continued under the new regime and on 4th June, 1925 Arundel Painters Limited was awarded the contract for refurbishing Stretham, Wilburton and Haddenham stations after tendering at £307 12s. 0d.

The branch was once again affected by an industrial dispute when during the General Strike of May 1926 union members withdrew their labour in support of the miners. Train services could not be guaranteed and the Ely to St Ives branch service was suspended for several days. Fortunately within a week or so regular railwaymen returned to work but the impact of the continuing miners' strike meant coal stocks were low. The LNER authorities decided on the only course of action available and reduced train services for a short period to conserve coal supplies. From 31st May, 1926, when the revised timetable was introduced, only two passenger trains made return trips across the branch.

On 26th January, 1928 the Divisional General Manager, Southern Area, reported that Needingworth level crossing was extensively used by road traffic but the crossing was not protected by fixed signals. The crossing keeper was only advised of an approaching train by the ringing of a bell on the block telegraph circuit. A sufficiently good view of the level crossing was not obtained by enginemen of approaching trains because of the curvature of the line whilst the crossing keeper's view of trains approaching from St Ives or Bluntisham was similarly impeded. In the interests of safety it was proposed to provide gate distant signals for both directions of travel, worked by the crossing keeper from a ground frame and interlocked with the gates. The Traffic Committee readily agreed the £225 expenditure and work was completed by June of the same year.

The Divisional General Manager, Southern Area, reported on 6th June, 1928 that it was proposed to close St Ives Yard signal box and concentrate the control of all signals and points at the station on St Ives Junction signal box, located 270 yards to the south. The scheme was to include the provision of track circuits and the electrical operation of certain points on the main line. A two-lever ground frame, electrically released from the Junction signal box was to replace the existing five-lever ground frame, whilst the public level crossing gates were also to be electrically released from the Junction signal box. The cost of the scheme was estimated at £3,096 but after taking into consideration the £600 value of ultimate renewals and credit for the recovered materials, estimated at £42, the net cost equated to £2,454. The saving of two signalmen's positions realized another £337 but this had to be offset by the estimated annual maintenance costs of £57 bringing the net saving to £280 per annum. The Traffic Committee duly approved of the scheme on 28th June, 1928.

Despite the introduction of the conductor-guard working, the loss of traffic caused by the various strikes and the attractions of the almost door-to-door service by the competitive bus company was always of concern to the railway authorities. The decline on the Ely to St Ives line was serious as passenger numbers and passenger receipts reduced considerably. As the undermentioned statistics show, only three passengers were booking weekly at Stretham in 1923 reducing to two in 1926, before rising to five in 1927. In 1927 only 12 passengers joined trains at the station in the first six months of the year. If that was dire the following year only four passengers used the station in the same period. The next station on the branch, Wilburton fared even worse, from four weekly passengers in 1924 reducing to three in 1925, two in 1926 and 1927 before increasing to five in 1928. In truth the station went months without a passenger joining or alighting from a train. Takings at Bluntisham were equally poor for in 1925 passenger bookings were five per week rising to six in 1928. Only 427 passengers utilized Earith Bridge station in 1923 with receipts of £24. Four years later only 649 passenger journeys were made during the whole year raising receipts to £52. Sutton with 5,161 passengers and Haddenham with 7,953 passengers in 1927 returned the best statistics but with the overall figure of less than 15,000 passenger journeys per year or 288 passengers per week on average, the LNER commenced investigations into the future of the passenger services.

	Passengers	Passenger receipts	Parcels receipts	Season ticket receipts	Total
1923		£	£	£	£
Stretham	168	31	456	2	489
Wilburton	463	61	412	10	483
Haddenham	6,795	730	1,128	184	2,042
Sutton	11,255	949	1,486	154	2,589
Earith Bridge	427	24	462	24	510
Bluntisham	338	25	711	7	743
Total	*19,446*	*1,820*	*4,655*	*381*	*6,856*
1924					
Stretham	277	48	377	1	426
Wilburton	191	23	638	12	673
Haddenham	6,729	649	1,193	211	2,053
Sutton	11,193	944	1,380	128	2,452
Earith Bridge	440	24	522	27	573
Bluntisham	340	24	635	7	666
Total	*19,170*	*1,712*	*4,745*	*386*	*6,843*
1925					
Stretham	273	44	407	1	452
Wilburton	152	25	751	16	792
Haddenham	7,458	696	1,359	46	2,101
Sutton	9,798	887	1,374	101	2,362
Earith Bridge	477	21	640	35	696
Bluntisham	254	18	576	7	601
Total	*18,412*	*1,691*	*5,107*	*206*	*7,004*

GROUPING AND NATIONALIZATION 47

	Passengers	Passenger receipts £	Parcels receipts £	Season ticket receipts £	Total £
1926					
Stretham	122	22	358	1	381
Wilburton	90	12	1,206	12	1,230
Haddenham	7,185	582	1,113	64	1,759
Sutton	5,398	575	1,225	92	1,892
Earith Bridge	508	29	650	22	701
Bluntisham	243	24	773	8	805
Total	13,546	1,244	5,325	199	6,768
1927					
Stretham	281	43	322	–	365
Wilburton	117	20	647	7	674
Haddenham	7,953	610	737	90	1,437
Sutton	5,161	547	680	35	1,262
Earith Bridge	649	52	511	19	582
Bluntisham	503	47	1,064	3	1,114
Total	14,664	1,319	3,961	154	5,434
1928					
Stretham	292	43	262	–	305
Wilburton	251	32	613	25	670
Haddenham	8,391	691	637	100	1,428
Sutton	5,392	624	630	28	1,282
Earith Bridge	630	47	422	6	475
Bluntisham	319	30	641	6	677
Total	15,275	1,467	3,205	165	4,837

The LNER Directors had for long been concerned with the poor returns earned from passenger traffic where competitive bus services running on roads paralleling the railway had seen further improvements. At a special Board meeting it was resolved to stem the loss of receipts by introducing 20 railway company operated bus services with the purchase of 60 motor buses. One of the centres for the new services was St Ives, where it was envisaged routes would operate to Holme via Ramsey and Huntingdon via Godmanchester, using two 20-seater vehicles, and to Ely via Sutton, using four 32-seater vehicles, in competition with other services. Allocations would, however, be varied in the event of the LNER coming to terms with local bus proprietors. The Engineer estimated the cost of providing garage accommodation at St Ives at £5,000 exclusive of lighting and petrol pumps. On 29th November, 1928 authority was given for the outlay on the garage at St Ives but no further developments were made for the company was negotiating financial and operating interests in the existing local bus companies.

The refurbishing of Ely station was long outstanding and on 25th April, 1929 Wellerman Brothers Ltd gained the contract for repairing and repainting after tendering at £13,652 16s. 0d. against a provisional estimate of £14,960. The contract was subject to the firm accepting and completing the work within nine months. A scheme was also presented for a new goods yard at Ely. This included the rearrangement and extension of siding accommodation for the marshalling of trains and for locomotive servicing, costing an estimated £35,243. Additional land was required and the full scheme included additional siding accommodation for 308 wagons.

'F3' class 2-4-2T No. 8061 pulling into Ely with a train from St Ives in 1927. *J.E. Kite*

Earith Bridge station, located 5 m. 60 ch. from St Ives, had a 200 ft-long platform, constructed of timber on the down side of the single line. The station buildings are typical of the structures provided on the extension beyond Sutton to Needingworth Junction and included accommodation for the station master, alongside the single-storey station offices. Earith Bridge signal box built to Saxby & Farmer style which had the smallest frame on the branch with 12 levers, 10 working and 2 spares, is to the left of the picture whilst the loop goods siding is in the foreground. After the withdrawal of passenger services the signal box, along with that at Bluntisham, was abolished on 17th August, 1932, after which the points to the goods yard were operated from a 2-lever ground frame released by Annett's key attached to the Needingworth Junction to Sutton single line Train Staff. *Author's Collection*

GROUPING AND NATIONALIZATION

1. Abolition of the present goods yard and warehouse, the site of which was required for marshalling sidings.
2. Conversion of two existing recently purchased buildings into a warehouse and goods office.
3. Provision of additional marshalling accommodation with up and down independent lines.
4. Provision of additional siding accommodation in the new goods yard including cart roads.
5. Provision of additional accommodation at the locomotive depot to facilitate the coaling of engines from a truck, a new engine inspection pit road, extension of the turntable road and an improvement in the locomotive watering facilities.
6. Provision of electric lighting.
7. Consequential alterations to the carriage sidings and cattle pens.

The scheme was initially deferred but after further estimates from the engineer a revised and reduced costing of £34,566 was accepted and the work authorized on 6th June, 1929.

The following year the opportunity was taken to enlarge the goods yard at St Ives. The existing yard had capacity for 168 wagons, with seven in the goods shed, 45 on sidings with cart access and 116 in sidings without cart access. The yard layout was considered completely unsatisfactory for the growth in traffic and a complete reconstruction of the yard was planned to provide additional accommodation for 94 wagons, including cart access for 72 wagons. A new goods shed was required as a replacement for the existing structure as 'renewal was long overdue'. Other alterations included the provision of new cattle pens, a new 5-ton capacity crane outside the goods shed to replace the existing 1-ton capacity crane and a 12-ton capacity weighbridge to replace the existing 7-ton capacity weighbridge. It was also the intention to replace the existing gas lighting with electric lighting. The scheme costing £17,058 was placed before the Traffic Committee at their meeting on 20th February, 1930 and after discussion authority was given for the work to proceed. New up and down reception lines were also included in the scheme and the BoT inspection was made on 4th January, 1932 when it was noted that the points and signals at the station were controlled from St Ives Junction signal box containing a new Westinghouse A2 75-lever frame, with 66 working and nine spare levers. As a result of the resignalling St Ives Yard signal box and Fenstanton signal box had both been abolished on 21st June, 1931.

On the branch the traffic receipts of the early 1920s had shown little improvement over the receipts of the late 1890s, and the economic depression at the end of the decade and the early 1930s meant there was little hope of an upturn in trade on the branch. With improvements in local roads came the increase in the use and reliance on motor vehicles and rural passenger rail services suffered. The LNER experienced overall traffic losses, which deemed it necessary for the management at Marylebone and Liverpool Street to seek further economies. Various branch lines in East Anglia were investigated as to their viability in the future passenger railway network, and as a result passenger train services were withdrawn on the Downham to Stoke Ferry branch in Norfolk and the neighbouring Somersham to Ramsey East branch in Huntingdonshire, on and from 22nd September, 1930. Unfortunately within months the Ely to St Ives branch was to follow a similar fate.

The Divisional General Manager, Southern Area duly reported to the Traffic Committee on 22nd December, 1930 that passenger traffic receipts on the Ely to St Ives branch had gradually declined and the gross value of traffic, local to, originating from, or terminating on the branch amounted to only £7,562 in 1928. To offset this the line carried an appreciable amount of freight and indications were that the tonnage would

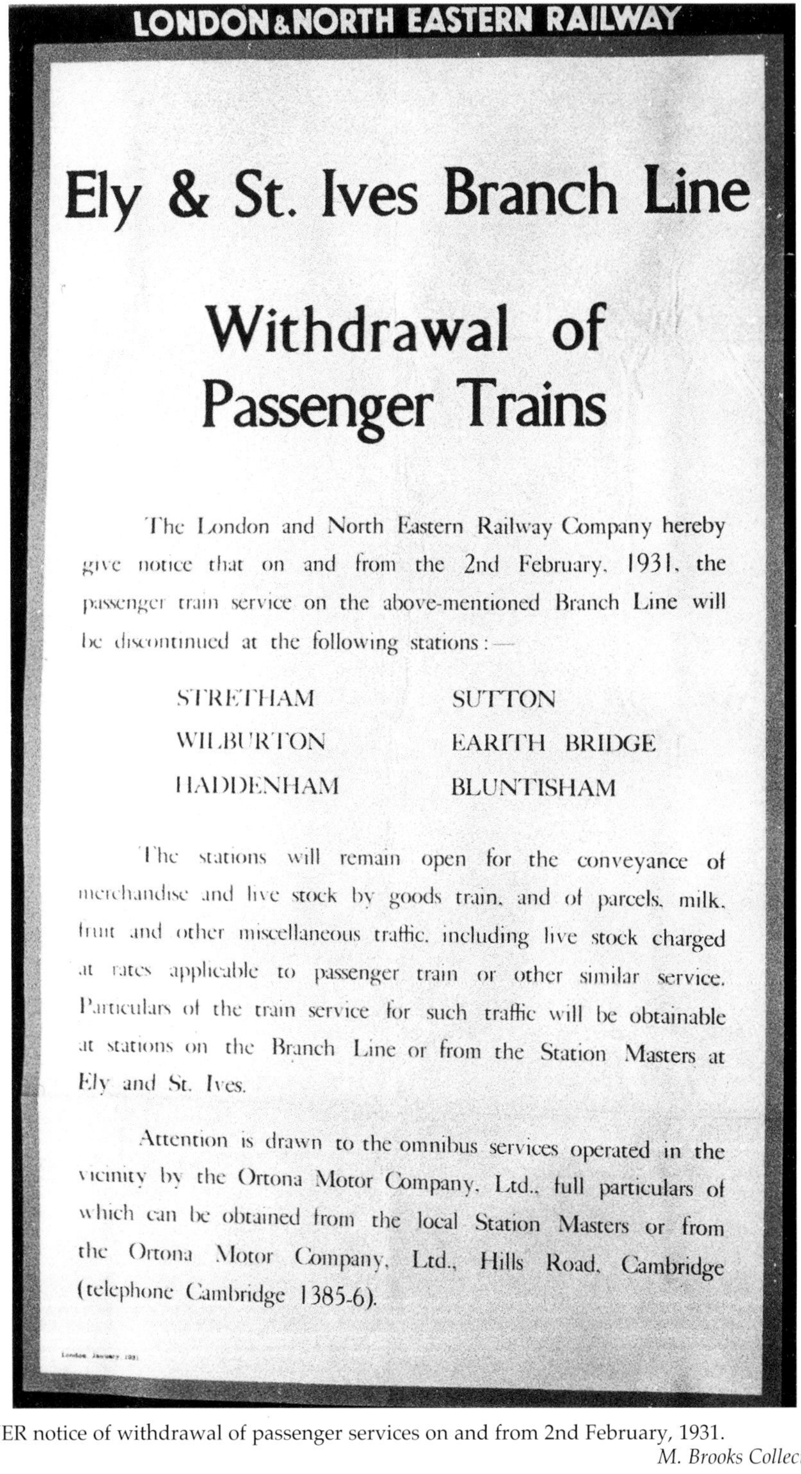

LONDON & NORTH EASTERN RAILWAY

Ely & St. Ives Branch Line

Withdrawal of Passenger Trains

The London and North Eastern Railway Company hereby give notice that on and from the 2nd February, 1931, the passenger train service on the above-mentioned Branch Line will be discontinued at the following stations:—

STRETHAM	SUTTON
WILBURTON	EARITH BRIDGE
HADDENHAM	BLUNTISHAM

The stations will remain open for the conveyance of merchandise and live stock by goods train, and of parcels, milk, fruit and other miscellaneous traffic, including live stock charged at rates applicable to passenger train or other similar service. Particulars of the train service for such traffic will be obtainable at stations on the Branch Line or from the Station Masters at Ely and St. Ives.

Attention is drawn to the omnibus services operated in the vicinity by the Ortona Motor Company, Ltd., full particulars of which can be obtained from the local Station Masters or from the Ortona Motor Company, Ltd., Hills Road, Cambridge (telephone Cambridge 1385-6).

LNER notice of withdrawal of passenger services on and from 2nd February, 1931.
M. Brooks Collection

increase. In the interests of economy it was proposed to withdraw the passenger service from the line on and from 2nd February, 1931, with the exception of one morning train from St Ives to Ely which was necessary to convey milk and perishable produce. It was also intended to adjust the timing of goods trains in order to cater for parcels and miscellaneous traffic. To equip the line for freight train working only, would involve signalling alterations and the provision of a petrol driven trolley for the permanent way department. The total cost of the work and provision of the trolley was estimated at £933. The withdrawal of the passenger service after allowing for the loss of receipts, estimated at £1,881, was expected to produce a net saving of £1,780. The Traffic Committee duly accepted the proposals and authorized the expenditure of £933. The decision was noted and endorsed by the Works Committee on 8th January, 1931.

Arrangements were subsequently made with Ortona Motor Services Ltd, later absorbed by the Eastern Counties Omnibus Co. Ltd, to provide an alternative public service. Ortona was already working a bus service between Ely and St Ives, two days a week and with the closure of the line, agreed to provide a service each weekday augmented to two or three services each way. The buses were timed to connect with trains at both Ely and St Ives. In addition Ortona arranged for its Sutton to Ely service to be extended from Ely city centre to the railway station to afford a connection with main line train services.

In comparison with railway closures in the 1950s and 1960s little opposition was made by local inhabitants served by the railway and the local bus services, already used by the local populace without cars, were readily accepted. The withdrawal of the passenger train service from the branch received scant mention in the local press, little inconvenience was experienced as so few people used the trains.

The Divisional General Manager, Southern Area, reported on 15th October, 1931 that following the completion of the new goods yard and marshalling accommodation at Ely, new up and down independent lines had been installed but the down side independent line had not been brought in to use pending consideration of a proposal for effecting economies by simplifying the layout of the junction between the Sutton branch and the main lines. After the withdrawal of the branch passenger services it was considered uneconomical to retain Ely Sutton Branch Junction signal box for the passage of two goods services in each direction. It was therefore proposed to execute further modifications to enable the signal box to be abolished:

1. Remove the existing branch junctions with the up and down main lines and connect the St Ives branch with the down independent line over which both up and down goods trains passing over the branch and the down main line would travel.
2. Displace the workings from Sutton Branch Junction signal box, which necessitates the employment of two signalmen and concentrate the work on Ely Dock Junction signal box.
3. Alter the position of the connection between the down main line and the down independent line, the points of which would be operated electrically from Ely Dock Junction signal box.
4. Consequential signalling alterations and provision of track circuits.

The gross cost of the works was estimated to cost £2,132, with engineering priced at £2,082. This could be reduced by recovering material to the value of £233, whilst the net cost of renewals due within five years but now rendered unnecessary, amounted to £947, which reduced the net engineering cost to £902. The surveyor, however, reported that 15 poles of land required to enable the branch junction to be altered would cost £50 bringing the net cost to £952. It was estimated that the original capital

Bluntisham station in 1931 facing towards Ely with the station buildings on the 250 ft-long platform on the down or north side of the main single line. Empty pigeon baskets loaded on the barrow on the platform await return to their home station. Partially obscured by trees are the goods shed, alongside the 400 ft-long shed loop siding, and the signalbox which controlled points and signals at the station. Of similar construction to those at Sutton and Earith Bridge it contained a 16-lever Saxby & Farmer frame with 10 working and 6 spare levers. *Author's Collection*

A 1930s view of the rather spartan Sutton 'new' station opened for the extension to St Ives with the 250 ft down platform and the 1922-built station buildings on the left and the 230 ft up side platform on the right, with the up starting signal in the right foreground. To the far left a wagon can be seen in the goods yard, showing the alignment of the original EHSR line.
Author's Collection

cost of the displaced works was £501. The Traffic Committee considered and approved of the scheme on 22nd October, 1931 and learned that by dispensing with the services of two signalmen and allowing for additional cost of maintenance, estimated at £6, would result in a net annual saving of £298. Tenders were duly invited for the resignalling work and the signal box was abolished on 17th July, 1932. The BoT inspection was conducted on 22nd December, 1932, when it was noted that the signals and points previously worked from Sutton Branch Junction signal box were now operated from a replacement Ely Dock Junction signal box dating from 1928 containing a Westinghouse A2 82-lever frame, with 77 working and five spare levers. A new Ely Station South signal box was also provided in 1933 containing a 75-lever frame, with 55 working and 20 spare levers. Ely North signal box now contained a 41-lever frame with no spare levers.

Soon after the withdrawal of the passenger services the LNER authorities abolished the branch signal boxes; Stretham, Earith Bridge and Bluntisham, were closed on 17th August, 1932 and Wilburton and Haddenham on 7th September, 1932, leaving Sutton as the only intermediate signal box. To save costs Needingworth Junction signal box was only manned for 12 hours to handle the branch traffic and was equipped with a switching-out key for the main line.

After closure of the intermediate signal boxes the structure at Haddenham was purchased late in 1932 and rebuilt as a house and greenhouse at Wilburton Road, Haddenham by Frank Steel. Subsequently his son Richard Steel was born in the former signal box on 20th March, 1940 (surely a unique experience for mother, baby and signal box!). At about the same time in 1932 Wilburton signal box was purchased, placed on wheels and towed by road to Stretham by Fred Peacock of Haddenham.

In the late 1920s and early 1930s the branch was at its busiest between June and November when train loads of fruit pickers, often Londoners taking working holidays, were conveyed by special trains to the branch stations, where they were picked up by local farmers and growers and conveyed by carts and horse-drawn covered vans and primitive motor lorries to their temporary camps in orchards and fields. The efforts of the pickers was evident by the continual loading of fruit produce in vans and wagons at Sutton, Haddenham and other stations ready for the booked freight service or special goods trains to convey the produce away to Ely or St Ives and on to distant provincial markets. The station yards were a constant hive of activity with the unloading of fen tumbrels and tipping carts.

During the 1930s until the outbreak of World War II goods traffic continued to be conveyed by two freight trains which ran weekdays only in each direction. Milk and parcels traffic previously conveyed by passenger train was carried in a van attached to all freight trains. In the late 1920s sugar beet was introduced into the area and during the autumn and winter months from October to January considerable tonnages were conveyed to the beet factory at Ely, Wissington and Peterborough. Other items conveyed included cattle and livestock, building materials, manure, agricultural components and above all fruit traffic, which flourished in the summer months. Passenger trains continued to use the line on infrequent occasions, in connection with specials or excursions and a few times trains were diverted across the branch after a mishap or because of engineering work on the main lines. A passenger coach continued to be attached to the first up train on Mondays and the return afternoon freight train for the convenience of drovers attending St Ives market.

To enable the widening of the A10 London to Kings Lynn main road 85 square yards of railway land adjacent to level crossing No. 84 was ceded to the Isle of Ely County Council on 16th April, 1934. In the same year flooding occurred across roads near the railway on Grunty Fen. The clerk to Grunty Fen Drainage and Improvement Commissioners duly requested the LNER to clear the dyke adjacent to the branch line to obviate the blockage but was informed the company had no responsibility for the waterway. Along the line at Haddenham, similar problems were experienced and once again the Civil Engineer reported the company had no responsibility for clearing or maintaining the defective dyke. Then in 1937 a small pocket of railway land at Earith Bridge was sold to the River Ouse Catchment Board for the princely sum of £5.

Prior to the outbreak of World War II, the LNER with other major railway companies came under the control of the Railway Executive Committee. To safeguard against air raids, especially during the hours of darkness, the station and yard lamps were dimmed and staff utilized shielded handlamps to attend to train and shunting duties. Again the agricultural nature of freight handled at the branch stations was of utmost importance as the vital provisions of home-grown food, grain, vegetables, fruit and sugar beet were dispatched and conveyed to home markets. In addition to these exports, the war years brought an influx of tinned foods and dried milk for distribution to the Ministry of Food storage depots in the area. Rationing of petrol also brought the withdrawal of many road vehicles from the highways and byways and the urgency of foodstuffs forced more traffic on to the railway. The close proximity of military airfields brought a steady flow of armaments and stores for the personnel and materials were conveyed to Sutton for onward transit to the Royal Air Force airfield at Mepal. During hostilities occasional passenger trains ventured across the branch conveying military personnel. Bluntisham and Earith Bridge goods yards were also used for traffic destined for Somersham airfield when that station was overstretched. It was during this period that ammunition trains served the yard at Sutton, mostly travelling at night and the bombs and shells were unloaded and removed by road to ammunition sites in the locality. The ammunition was usually conveyed in open wagons, sheeted over to conceal their deadly cargo, although the prominent red flashed labels advised 'Shunt With Great Care' and 'Place As Far As Possible From The Engine, Brake Van and Wagons Labelled Inflammable'. The Luftwaffe had knowledge of the movement of armaments but the closeness of the airfields proved a deterrent although one German bomber attempted to blow up the River Ouse viaduct. Fortunately the bomb fell well clear and the branch survived. On another occasion in 1940 a parachute mine dropped near Wilburton station failed to explode. The station and adjoining cottages were evacuated until the mine was detonated. The subsequent explosion caused superficial damage to the buildings.

During hostilities a further five perches of land was sold to the River Ouse Catchment Board in April 1941, whilst occupational crossing No. 67 at 12 miles 36 chains between Haddenham and Wilburton was closed and the gates removed, the line of fencing being restored on 12th November, 1943. In the same year a new ferro-concrete 5 ft diameter culvert was laid under the line by the Great Ouse Catchment Board to assist with drainage.

At the height of the London blitz and occasionally thereafter until 1945 when Cambridge goods yards were choked with essential provisions for the capital, traffic was held back waiting clearance at Northumberland Park, Spitalfields and Temple Mills. Vital supplies for London and some East Anglian destinations were then diverted from the former Midland Railway main line at Kettering via Huntingdon to St Ives and then over the branch to Ely. The small ex-Midland Railway '2F' class 0-6-0 tender locomotives delegated to work these trains throughout, reversed and ran-round the formation at St Ives before continuing tender first to Ely; Cambridge depot provided pilotmen for the London Midland & Scottish Railway (LMS) Kettering crews working the trains.

The nationalization of the railways from 1st January, 1948 brought little change to the Ely to St Ives line, which essentially retained its GER/LNER atmosphere until the withdrawal of steam traction from the branch. Locomotives working the line soon lost the NE or LNER on the tender sides, whilst the wagon stock including former private owner vehicles, appeared in the new British Railways (BR) livery. After the war fruit, parcels and milk traffic quickly transferred to road and gradually other items were lost from the railway. Fruit traffic had travelled by road to markets from the early 1950s. The remaining imports of coal and coke and exports of sugar beet were easily handled by one freight train, which ran across the branch each weekday and latterly Saturdays excepted. Road transport with its door-to-door service went from strength to strength in East Anglia and soon coal merchants were receiving an increasing tonnage of fuel by road. Two further land sales were made to local landowners; on 28th May, 1953 with 26 perches of property disposed of at Bluntisham for £25 and 1 rod and 18 perches of land at Earith Bridge for £40 on 28th April, 1955.

Two annual booked passenger excursion trains ran from St Ives to Ely en route to Yarmouth for the races and/or Hunstanton but by 1955 their future was in the balance as the track and permanent way between Sutton and Earith Bridge had deteriorated. After consultation with the Civil Engineer the excursions were allowed to continue across this section subject to a 10 mph speed limit. The excursions continued for another two years until the section from Bluntisham to Sutton was at first abandoned in 1957 and later closed to all traffic on and from 6th October, 1958. The track east of Bluntisham through Earith Bridge was subsequently lifted and the section thence to Sutton used as a siding for the storage of condemned wagons. The excursions for 1958 started from Sutton and ran only to Hunstanton.

Just before closure of the line through Earith Bridge station, wagons were stored on the Sutton to Earith section, having been being taken in from the Earith Bridge end before track removal. Initially they were stored close up to the Haddenham Road level crossing but as the number of wagons increased from the east, the line of empty vehicles reached the occupational crossing just west of Sutton. Being close to public access thieves subsequently removed valuable whitemetal bearings from about 50 wagons so that when BR required to transport the wagons away for scrap the carriage and wagon department were forced to use a float of bearings before they could be moved.

The two sections of the former through route, now divided into two sections Needingworth Junction to Bluntisham and Sutton to Ely, received the benefit of British Railways' modernization programme in 1959 when diesel-electric locomotives gradually replaced the 'J15' and 'J17' class steam locomotives on the freight work. March-based Brush type '2', later class '31', were sometimes assisted by Ipswich- and March-based BR/Sulzer type '2s' later class '24', but the latter were soon ousted and the Brush type '2' locomotives maintained the workings.

The eastern end of the line remained open for a further six years handling the dwindling sugar beet and vegetable traffic, but by 1962 sugar beet was also conveyed direct from the farms to the sugar beet factory. Consequently the Ely to Sutton and St Ives to Bluntisham freight trains conveyed few wagons from the branch station goods yards and often days went by without the goods train making the trip. In 1963 the infamous Beeching Report was published and whilst referring specifically to passenger traffic, the map included with the report also quoted freight receipts. All the branch stations showed loadings of 0 to 5,000 tons per annum and the poor receipts only confirmed to railway management that the two stubs of the Ely to St Ives branch were expensive assets to maintain with little chance of improvement in trade. Indeed as the year progressed traffic continued to dwindle and thus in April 1964 the inevitable announcement was made that goods facilities at Stretham, Wilburton, Haddenham and Sutton were to be withdrawn

'J15' class 0-6-0s were often used on goods workings between Ely and St Ives. No. 65477 and brake van stand on the main single line at Earith Bridge before collecting the covered van standing on the adjacent yard loop siding and continuing the journey to Sutton.   *D. Lawrence*

'J17' class 0-6-0 No. 65532 pauses at Bluntisham with a down freight train from St Ives to Ely in the summer of 1957. The station is typical of the imposing structures provided on the Sutton to Needingworth section of the line, in stark contrast to the small buildings on the eastern section of the branch. The 2-lever ground frame in the foreground, released by Annett's key on the Needingworth Junction to Sutton section single line Train Staff, operated the points to the goods yard located on the down side of the line east of the station. Bluntisham Road overbridge No. 2289 at 3 m. 60 ch. from St Ives spans the line behind the train.   *Dr I.C. Allen*

GROUPING AND NATIONALIZATION

Steam brake-only 'J17' class 0-6-0 No. 65583 standing at Haddenham, as her crew pose for the cameraman, before continuing with the branch goods service to Sutton and St Ives. The station building is typical of the small structures erected on the Ely, Haddenham & Sutton Railway section of the line. The Haddenham (Cambs) nameboard was provided by the LNER on 1st July, 1923 to differentiate the station from Haddenham on the former Great Central & Great Western railways joint line north of Princes Risborough. *Dr I.C. Allen*

'J17' class 0-6-0 No. 65548 standing at Haddenham with the Ely to St Ives freight in 1957. A rake of vans occupies the down reception siding. From 1891 until 1932 Haddenham signal box was sited on the up side of the line at a point where the two parallel sidings from the goods yard converged on the loop siding. *Author's Collection*

'J17' class 0-6-0 No. 65577 makes for Ely with the branch freight train consisting of a covered van and a 'Toad E' goods brake van. It is passing the tall Stretham down fixed distant signal, complete with decorative finial and signal arm raised at a higher level than the lamp spectacles. Staff delegated to trim the lamps and replenish the reservoirs with oil on these tall signals had extreme difficulty in relighting the lamps on windy days, for the fens are rarely becalmed. *Dr I.C. Allen*

'J17' class 0-6-0 No. 65587 eases over the main A10 London to Kings Lynn road level crossing near Thetford Corner with a Sutton to Ely goods working after the guard has opened the gates for the passage of the train. *R.C. Riley*

GROUPING AND NATIONALIZATION

The village of Haddenham was built above the flat lands on one of the Fen Islands and consequently the railway meandering south from Sutton entered a relatively deep cutting on the approach to the station. London Midland Region class '2MT' 2-6-0 No. 46467 approaches Haddenham with the St Ives to Hunstanton excursion train formed of eight former LMS corridor coaches in 1957. Sutton was located on the ridge in the far distance. The class '2MTs' were favoured for working these excursion trains as they were equipped with tender cabs, which afforded the crew protection when running tender first. *Dr I.C. Allen*

on and from Monday 13th July, 1964, a date synonymous with many freight station closures in East Anglia. Bluntisham yard and mill provided a considerable amount of traffic via St Ives but it was considered uneconomical to retain this short section and when the contract between BR and the traders expired the traffic was subsequently withdrawn and the line closed on and from 5th October, 1964. Needingworth Junction signal box was finally abolished on 16th June, 1965, the same day as Sutton signal box, which had been retained in use to enable demolition trains to use the line. The track of the Ely to St Ives branch remained *in situ* for some months before contractors cut up the rails, removed sleepers and other fixed assets. Vandals set fire to Sutton station, which was fully engulfed in flames for the second time in its history, but this time there was no rebuilding and the remaining debris was duly demolished.

The former GER line north of St Ives to the site of Needingworth Junction and the GN & GE line thence to March South Junction was closed to passenger traffic on and from 6th March, 1967, freight facilities having been withdrawn in stages between 1964 and 1966 from the intermediate stations. St Ives lost its passenger service from Cambridge on and from 5th October, 1970, although freight continued to run from Chesterton Junction over the former double line, later converted to single, until 16th July, 1977. The route is now part of the Cambridge to St Ives busway.

Three years after closure of the Ely to St Ives branch the sale of redundant land began in earnest, with the following examples of disposals. The BR Estate & Rating Department initially found ready buyers for the trackbed but after 1970 prospective purchasers were difficult to find:

With the up starting signal clear 'J17' class 0-6-0 No. 65567 propels her train of two vans and a brake van out of the up platform at Sutton as far as the down home signal shown in the background. This enabled the engine to haul her train forward to Ely. Allotment's footpath crossing No. 60 at 10 m. 10 ch. from St Ives is located at the end of the platform. Because of the flat terrain crossed by the branch there were 74 level crossings between Needingworth Junction and Ely Sutton Branch Junction.   *Dr I.C. Allen*

19.06.68	Sutton	906 sq. yds	H. Stimpson	£14
22.06.68	Bluntisham	Nos. 1 & 2 Station Cottages	F. Banyard	£250
04.07.68	Sutton	2,860 sq. yds	D.V.J. Peacock	£18
09.07.68	Sutton	527 sq. yds	E.W. Burton	£10
25.07.68	Sutton	2 acres 461 sq. yds	M.J. Stimpson	£100
26.07.68	Sutton	2,419 sq. yds	E.B. Haddock	£15
26.07.68	Sutton	1 acre 288 sq. yds	R.F. Peacock	£50
29.05.69	Haddenham	2 acres 1,403 sq. yds	A. Giddings	£100
13.08.69	Haddenham	1 acre 629 sq. yds	Gonville & Caius College	£60
16.08.69	Stretham	3,175 sq. yds	E.A. Veal	£40
03.11.69	Sutton	933 sq.yds	Sutton Poor Charities	£14
25.06.70	Stretham	3,533 sq. yds	D.A. Chapman	£50
28.07.70	Stretham	2,420 sq. yds	B.R. Howard	£60
03.09.70	Wilburton	3 acres 435 sq. yds	J. Langley	£185
04.09.70	Wilburton	5 acres 3,000 sq yds	Wilburton Farmers Ltd	£340
25.11.70	Stretham	1,452 sq. yds	F.J. Russell	£20
02.04.71	Stretham	2,299 sq. yds	W.P. Yarrow	£30
18.01.73	Stretham	2 acres 3,109 sq. yds	A. Traube	£202
21.12.76	Haddenham	1 acre 2,187 sq. yds	Cambridgeshire CC	£675

The disused station buildings at Hahdenham were used after closure as a Girl Guide centre known locally as 'Haddenham Hall' but after the building was vacated in February 1995 it was demolished and the platforms levelled. Elsewhere Earith Bridge station area was levelled to become part of a marina.

Today most of the trackbed has reverted to farmland fields or, because of its raised position above the fenland, as access roads. Little evidence is available to distinguish the former branch at the site of Ely Sutton Branch Junction but the stations at Stretham, Wilburton, and Bluntisham remain in use as private residences as reminders of the erstwhile Ely, Haddenham & Sutton and later Ely & St Ives Railway.

Chapter Five

The Route Described

The GER always considered the direction of travel to be down from St Ives and up from Ely despite the railway being constructed from Ely towards St Ives. The mileage quoted was initially from Liverpool Street to Ely via St Ives but later the Engineer established the mileage from St Ives Junction and these are quoted in the description of the line. The gradient chart included, however, shows the through mileage from Liverpool Street via Clapton.

The original buildings at St Ives station, 70 miles 31 chains from Liverpool Street via Clapton, were constructed by the ECR in 1847 in Cambridge white brick. The Cambridge to March line platform buildings, awnings and footbridge No. 2273 were added later by the GER, the buildings also being of white brick but with red brick trimmings fronted by standard 'Ashbee' style awnings.

Ely branch passenger trains usually arrived at the curving up platform at St Ives station. After shunting and the locomotive running round the stock, the down train departed from the down side platform. Passenger trains continuing on to Huntingdon terminated at the up platform, whilst the engine ran round the train via the down main line. Having re-coupled to the stock, the engine then propelled the train clear of the junction before setting off over the crossover on to the Huntingdon single line. On the return journey from Huntingdon the train stopped in the single branch platform at St Ives whilst the engine ran round the stock. Having re-coupled, the train was propelled clear of the junction before setting off via the down main line to Needingworth Junction and Ely. Goods trains terminating at St Ives were crossed from the up line to the goods yard, located north of the station on the down side of the line, where the outsorting of stock took place. Down goods services departed directly from the goods yard en route to Ely. Goods facilities at St Ives included the down and up loop lines, each capable of holding 92 wagons plus engine and brake van, four sidings in the down goods yard with capacity for 82 wagons and one siding on the up side with capacity for 17 wagons. .

The section of line from St Ives to Needingworth Junction was GER but from 1882 north of the junction was part of the Great Northern and Great Eastern Joint Line with zero mileage measured from Huntingdon. The reason for this was that the former GER route from Huntingdon to St Ives via Godmanchester also became part of the GN and GE Joint Line from the same date. Leaving St Ives the Ely branch trains climbed at 1 in 566/792/1120 on the double track line before falling at 1 in 314 followed by a climb at 1 in 214 to Needingworth Junction, 1 mile 71 chains, with the signal box controlling the junction on the down side of the main line. The single line branch to Ely swung away to the east falling initially at 1 in 203 over Lowndes Drove level crossing No. 14, also known as Junction Crossing at 2 miles 03 chains, with the attendant crossing keeper's cottage on the down side of the line west of the crossing. Beyond the crossing the line climbed at 1 in 220 across arable land on a straight course where there were several occupational crossings before passing Heath Barn south of the line. The railway then ran across a shallow embankment and fell at 1 in 203 through Low Wood before entered a cutting on a 1 in 203 rising gradient to pass underbridge No. 2289 at 3 miles 60 chains, carrying the A1123 Huntingdon to Ely road over the railway, and into Bluntisham station 3 miles 62 chains from St Ives, on a 1 in 203 falling gradient.

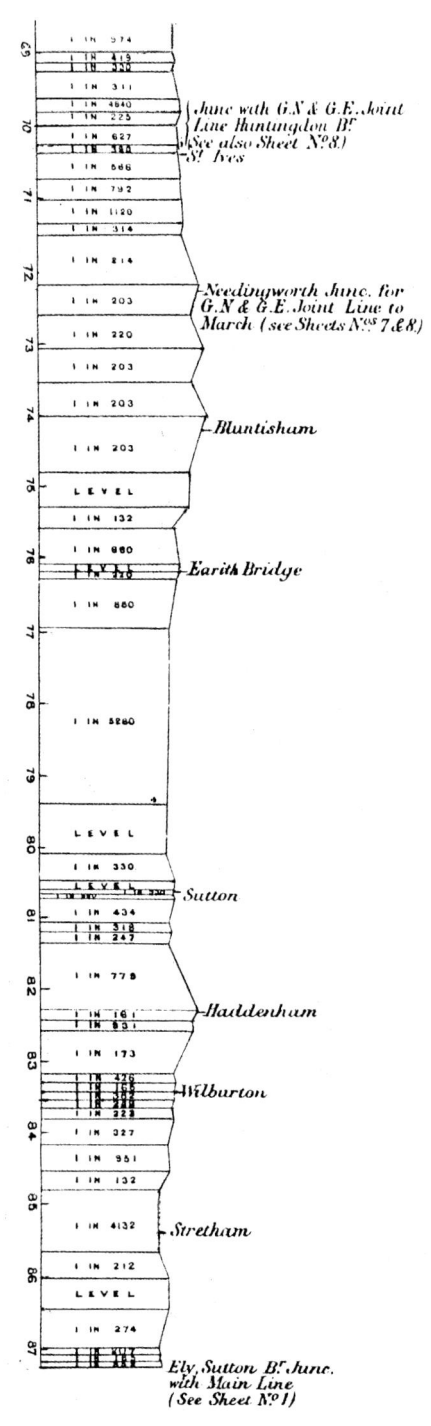

Gradient Profile

The station served the villages of Bluntisham and Colne, ½ and 1½ miles to the north of the railway respectively. The platform 250 feet in length was situated on the down side of the line between the goods loop to the east and the overbridge to the west. The platform was host to the station master's house, booking office, station master's office and waiting rooms. Bluntisham was the first Train Staff and Ticket station on the branch and the 400 ft-long goods loop/shed road on the down or north side of the main single line east of the station was used to pass trains. At the west end of the loop a short 150 ft siding served a cattle dock and pens, whilst the 220 ft siding to the east served a coal ground and was used as a headshunt. Alongside the loop the railway company erected a goods shed. Because of the restricted clearance of this shed and the absence of a second platform, it was only permissible to pass two goods trains or a goods and passenger train at Bluntisham and not two passenger trains, the goods train being shunted in the loop siding to allow the passenger train to pass on the single line. The points and signals were controlled from the station signal box located on the up side of the line opposite the loop.

Leaving Bluntisham the railway curved slightly to the right past the 4 mile post and continued on a falling 1 in 203 gradient for half a mile passing the hamlet of Little London, with a view of St Mary's church on the down side of the line and then followed a level course over Wadsby Folly underbridge No. 2290 at 4 miles 28 chains and Bury Fen underbridge No. 2291 at 4 miles 32 chains in quick succession. The railway then crossed bridge No. 2292 at 4 miles 55 chains, the viaduct over the River Ouse on the level. This viaduct was the most substantial civil engineering structure on the branch, with 19 spans and was used as a landmark by RAF crews approaching Mepal or Somersham airfields during and after World War II. The railway then fell at 1 in 132 past the 5 mile post to follow a straight course with the village of Earith to the north before negotiating a 40 chains left-hand curve rising at 1 in 660 to level track to cross Earith Mill underbridge No. 2293 at 5 miles 36 chains where the railway crossed No. 18 Drove. Beyond the bridge the line negotiated a 20 chains left-hand curve passing Shelford's Farm and over the Long Stanton to Earith road, later B1050, and the Old West River by West River underbridge No. 2294 at 5 miles 52 chains, then immediately into Earith Bridge station, 5 miles 60 chains from St Ives.

Earith Bridge was located in a cramped position between the bridge over the Old West River and a level crossing. The 200 ft platform located on the down side of the single branch line was host to the usual station buildings. The track layout at this station, which was originally to be called the Hermitage after a local sluice and farm, was completed by a 310 ft goods loop on the up side of the line with 150 ft and 200 ft shunting traps at each end, the former serving a loading dock. Entry to the loop was by facing points from each direction and signals and points were controlled from the Earith Bridge signal box, located on the down side of the line west of the station. The yard, for a short time had a 10 cwt capacity fixed crane.

Away from Earith Bridge the line fell at 1 in 220 over the Hill Row Causeway level crossing at 5 miles 63 chains from St Ives, initially on a straight course passing the 6 mile post, before falling at 1 in 880 for three-quarters of a mile. The railway then negotiated a short 45 chains radius right-hand curve before following a straight course across South Fen with the high embankments guarding the New Bedford Level or One Hundred Foot Drain on the down side of the line. The line then fell at 1 in 5,280 for the next 2½ miles passing the 7 mile post as the railway continued on the straight crossing and re-crossing many culverts spanning the fenland drainage dykes.

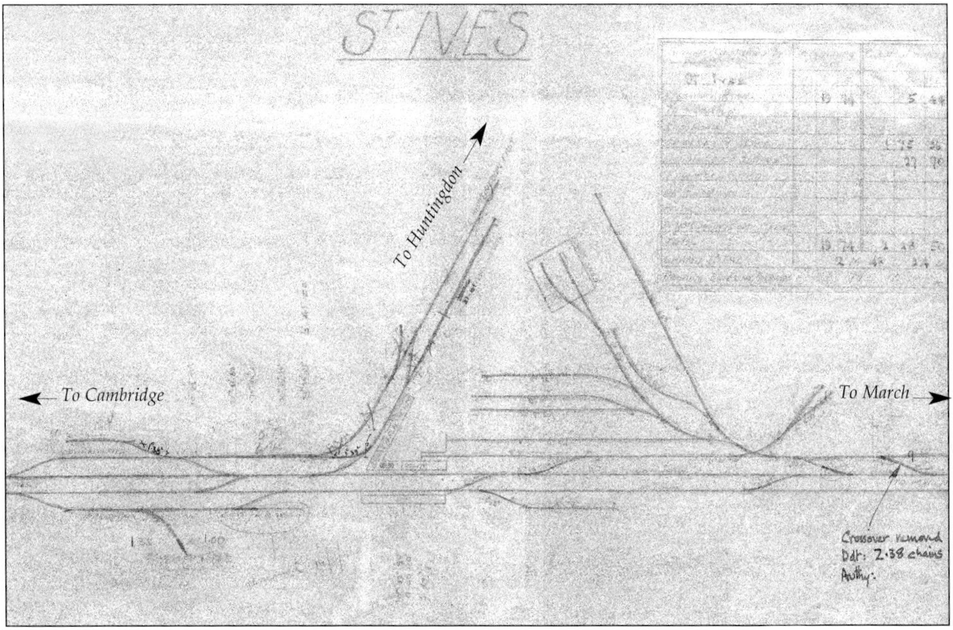

Civil Engineer's diagrammatic plan of the track layout at St Ives, *circa* 1950.

The curved approach to St Ives station from the north with the down advanced starting signal on the left and the goods yard to the right. *R. Powell*

THE ROUTE DESCRIBED

'D16/3' class 4-4-0 No. 62521 departs from St Ives with a Cambridge train on 28th August, 1954. Ely branch trains terminated at the up platform and departed from the down side platform at St Ives. To the left is the Great Northern & Great Eastern Joint line to Huntingdon served by a single platform. St Ives Junction signal box shown in the 'V' of the junction at the end of the platform controlled all points and signals at the station in the latter years after the abolition of St Ives Yard signal box in 1931. *Eric Sawford*

Looking south-east from St Ives down main platform with the Junction signal box to the right. After rationalization of signalling at the station and the abolition of St Ives Yard signal box, St Ives Junction Station signal box was provided with a 75-lever Westinghouse A2 frame to control all points and signals. The up starter and up loop inlet signals are to the left and in the distance are the splitting home signals for the down March line and the single line to Huntingdon. *R. Powell*

The single platform at St Ives serving the line to Huntingdon, view facing towards Cambridge with the junction with the March line just beyond the signal box. *Stations UK*

St Ives station from the footbridge showing the down and up main lines to March and the ornate canopies over the platforms. The goods yard is beyond the down platform. *R. Powell*

St Ives goods yard, the terminal for the Ely branch freight trains, with the loading dock to the right. *R. Powell*

Looking north from St Ives with the trailing connection from the goods yard immediately to the left and the crossover forming the sidings to the coal drops and St Ives cattle market. The points from the goods yard lead to the down main line to March and the up main line parallel. The Ely branch trains used the down and up main lines between St Ives and Needingworth Junction.

R. Powell

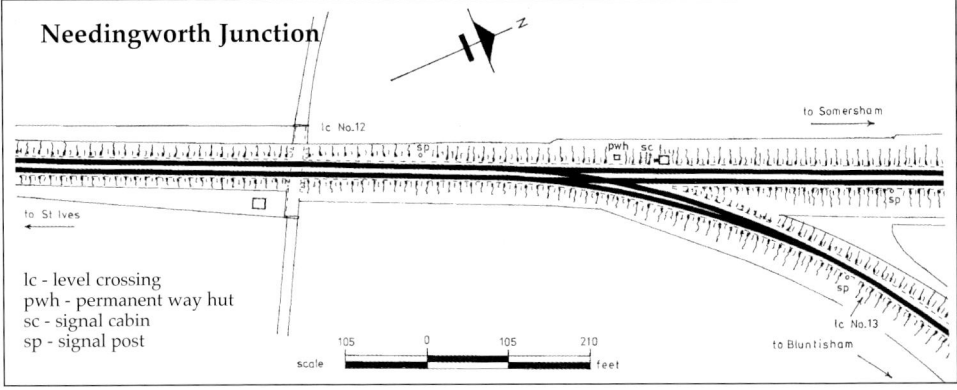

Needingworth Junction

lc - level crossing
pwh - permanent way hut
sc - signal cabin
sp - signal post

The approach to Needingworth Junction from the Ely branch with the timber- and brick-built signal box in the centre background. The branch up home signal and the gate distant share the same post, whilst the sleeper timbers of occupational crossing No. 13 at 1 m. 75 ch. from St Ives are near the signal post. *R. Powell*

Needingworth Junction, facing north with the GN and GE Joint line straight ahead and the branch to Sutton and Ely to the right. The signal box of brick and timber construction was opened on 10th May, 1878 and was equipped with a 16-lever Saxby & Farmer frame, initially with 12 working and four spare levers and later with 11 working and five spares. The box was abolished on 16th June, 1965. *Author's Collection*

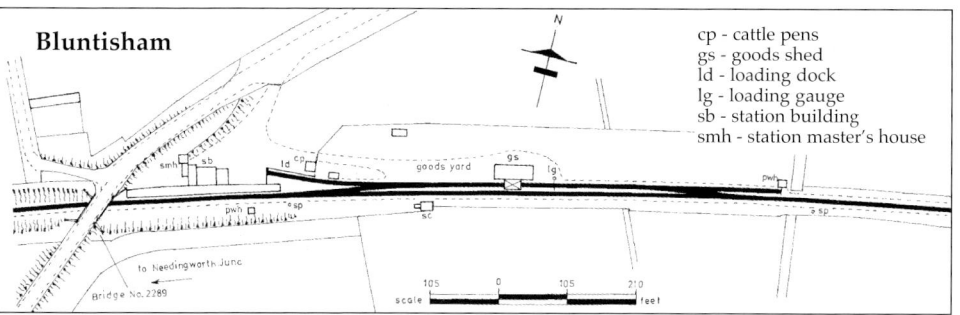

Bluntisham

cp - cattle pens
gs - goods shed
ld - loading dock
lg - loading gauge
sb - station building
smh - station master's house

Bluntisham station with the 250 ft-long platform on the down or north side of the single line. Bluntisham was a Train Staff station, splitting the single line section from Needingworth Junction to the west and Sutton to the east. It was not permissible to cross two passenger trains at the station and conflicting movements required the goods train to stand in the 400 ft-long shed road for the passenger train to pass. After the signal box was abolished on 17th August, 1932 Bluntisham ceased to be a Train Staff station and the single line section became Needingworth Junction to Sutton. In this view facing towards Ely the yard is almost full to capacity with covered vans. The cattle dock road is behind the platform and the 220 ft coal road/headshunt is a continuation of the loop road. *Stations UK*

Close up view of Bluntisham station house, booking office and store, showing the station architecture used on the extension of the line from Sutton to St Ives. *John Watling*

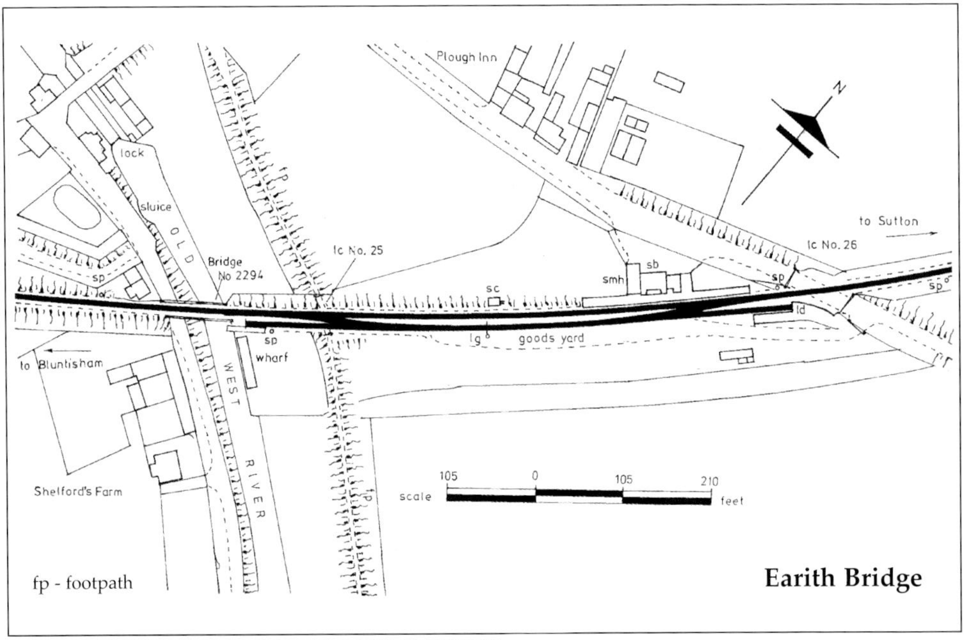

Earith Bridge

Earith Bridge station, 5 m. 60 ch. from St Ives, showing an example of the larger buildings provided on the St Ives extension. View towards facing Ely showing the gates of Hill Row Causeway public level crossing No. 26 at 5 m. 63 ch. It was originally intended to call the station 'The Hermitage' after a local sluice and farm but wiser counsels prevailed. *John Watling*

Earith Bridge station viewed from the east in July 1961 showing the main single line in the foreground and the 200 ft headshunt siding to the left and the loop siding. The trackbed is weed covered and the wagons at the platform are being used for the removal of the permanent way.
R. Powell

Earith Bridge station after the removal of track and demolition of the platform facing, view facing west.
John Watling

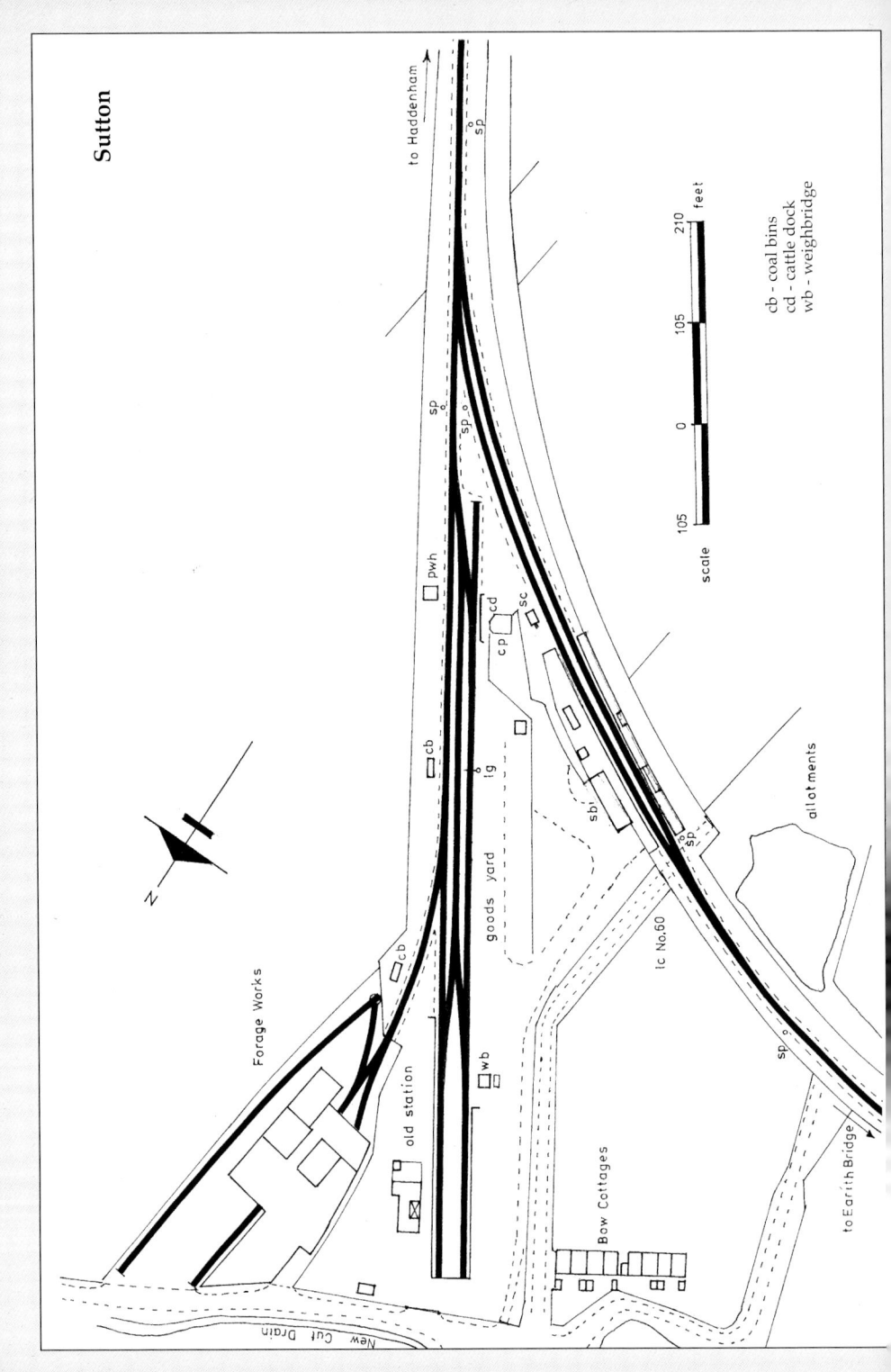

Just past the 8 mile post it swung to the right on a 45 chains radius curve to pass over South Fen underbridge No. 2295 at 8 miles 49 chains and bisect Rymanmoor Drove level crossing at 8 miles 63 chains with its attendant gatehouse on the up side of the line west of the crossing. Beyond the crossing the line straightened out on level track before climbing at 1 in 330 parallel to the south of the town of Sutton for almost a mile, with views of the parish church of St Andrew prominent on the skyline with its excellent tower displaying quatrefoil freezes and battlements and two octagonal stages. This section of line possessed numerous occupational crossings, which were always considered a source of danger by footplatemen working the branch trains. On the up side of the railway were views of North Fen and beyond the 120 ft high North Hill, west of Haddenham. At the end of the straight section the branch ran on level track and followed a sharp 10 chains radius right-hand curve to enter Sutton station, 10 miles 16 chains from St Ives, on a 1 in 330 falling gradient.

The station was situated half a mile south-east of the town, known locally as Sutton-in-the-Isle, and was the second Train Staff and Ticket station after Needingworth Junction signal box and boasted a 780 ft crossing loop. The up platform, 230 ft in length was host to a waiting shelter only, whilst the 250 ft down platform boasted the station master's house, booking and parcels office, waiting room and staff room. The signal box, situated a few yards east of the down platform, controlled all points and signals including the points leading to the goods yard. From the junction points the former EHSR single line led to the old Sutton station, which from 1878 served as a goods station. The track layout in the extensive goods yard was completed by two sidings, the 680 ft-long up yard road, serving Coote and Warren's coal ground and the 850 ft-long down yard road, connected by points from the 370 ft yard loop siding, one of which terminated at the second old station platform. The cattle pens were served by the 140 ft cattle dock siding. From the old single line, facing points on the down side 450 ft from the buffer stops led to Drake's Forage Works, with its four sidings, which provided considerable traffic and revenue for the railway.

Departing from Sutton 'new' station the railway climbed at 1 in 330 and 1 in 238 on the 10 chains radius right-hand curve to follow a south-easterly course. After negotiating the points at the junction of the extension line and the original EHSR line the railway fell at 1 in 434 before rising at 1 in 318 and again falling at 1 in 247 as the single line branch crossed a fen drain. A straight course was then followed across North Fen as the line climbed at 1 in 779 past the 11 mile post as the railway bisected Milkinghill occupational crossing No. 65 at 11 miles 07 chains and then Milkinghill underbridge No. 2296 at 11 miles 08 chains, both near the adjacent Salmon's Farm and Haddenham End. The straight section gave way to a 30 chains radius left-hand curve where facing points in the up direction off the main single line led to extensive clay pits and the Isle of Ely Brickworks siding. The private siding agreement with Frederick Jewson dated from 17th May, 1884 but the siding closed in 1904. The points were released and locked by the Annett's key attached to the single line Train Staff. After the points the line entered a relatively deep cutting still climbing at 1 in 779 as the curve eased to 40 chains radius to pass under the Haddenham Road bridge No. 2297, at 11 miles 68 chains, carrying the Chatteris to Haddenham road over the railway, to enter Haddenham station 11 miles 71 chains from St Ives.

Haddenham station, some three-quarters of a mile north of the village had a 230 ft-long platform, located on the south or up side of the single branch line adjacent to the overbridge. The track layout was one of the largest on the branch, with a 480 ft-long reception siding serving a cattle pen on the down side of the line, opposite the platform with access via facing points in the up direction. A 50 ft headshunt was also

Sutton station, 10 m. 16 ch. from St Ives facing towards St Ives with the Saxby & Farmer signal box to the right. The loops 780 ft in length served up and down platforms, the former devoid of any shelter, whilst the latter housed the station buildings. Sutton station was the busiest on the branch and possessed the only crossing loop where passenger trains could pass, the Train Staff and Ticket sections being Ely Sutton Branch Junction to Sutton, Sutton to Bluntisham and Bluntisham to Needingworth Junction. *R. Powell*

'J17' class 0-6-0 No. 65548 runs round her train at Sutton station in readiness to shunt the stock into the goods yard. By the mid-1950s little traffic was generated, other than domestic coal and in season, sugar beet loadings. This is reflected in the short train consisting of a covered van, a 16 ton all-steel open wagon and a former LMS goods brake van. *Dr I.C. Allen*

This view of the second Sutton station from the 230 ft-long up platform facing towards Ely, shows the main station buildings on the 250 ft-long down platform and the Saxby & Farmer brick-built signal box. The original terminus of the Ely, Haddenham & Sutton Railway was on the site of the goods yard, behind the signal box but when the extension was constructed to St Ives the second station was built on the curve to the west of the goods yard. The original station buildings burnt to the ground in 1921 and were not replaced until 1922 when S.S. Ambrose was awarded the contract at a cost of £398 15s. 0d. *Stations UK*

'J17' class 0-6-0 No. 65578 running tender first through the down loop platform at Sutton on 28th July, 1961. As the line beyond Sutton was lifted by this time, the engine is running round the train prior to shunting the wagons into the goods yard. The tower of St Andrew's church can be seen to the right. *R. Powell*

Drake's Forage Works at Sutton showing the track layout within the premises. Private owner wagon No. 163 owned by Joseph Bylam Ltd of Leicester and Kings Lynn stands loaded with coal in the foreground.   *Author's Collection*

The entrance gate to Drake's Forage Works at Sutton, which was served by a siding connection from the goods yard.   *Author's Collection*

THE ROUTE DESCRIBED

The fire-ravaged buildings of Sutton station on 31st January, 1966 as a result of arson by vandals.
John Watling

The weathered GER station nameboard at Sutton on 20th March, 1961.   *John Watling*

The junction between the main single line and the goods yard to the south of Sutton station. The up and down loop lines leading to the platforms are to the left, and the single connection leading to the goods yard and former terminus until the line was extended, straight ahead. The signals are the down starter and the goods yard starter. *R. Powell*

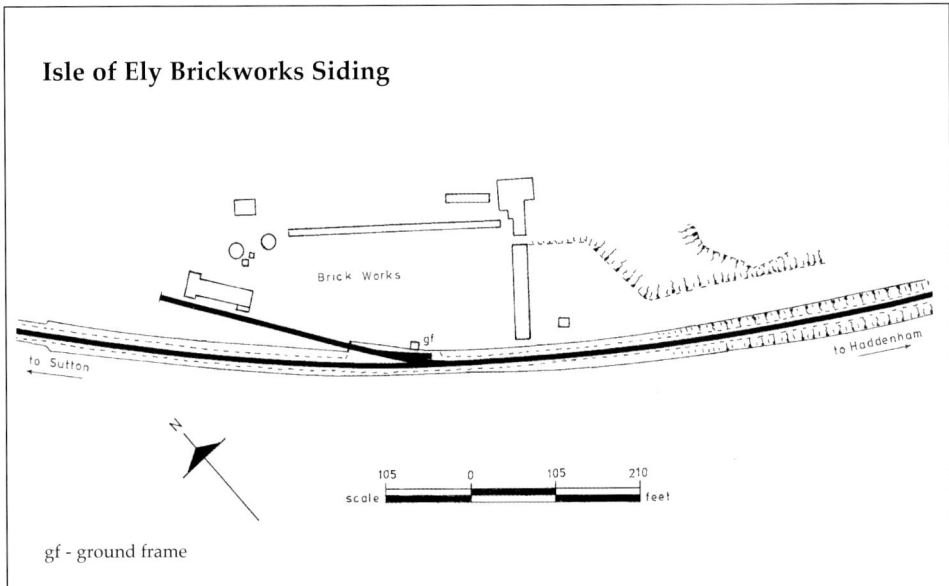

Isle of Ely Brickworks Siding

gf - ground frame

THE ROUTE DESCRIBED 79

Haddenham station buildings showing the LNER nameboard and GER oil lamps, view facing Ely on 31st July, 1961.
John Watling

Haddenham

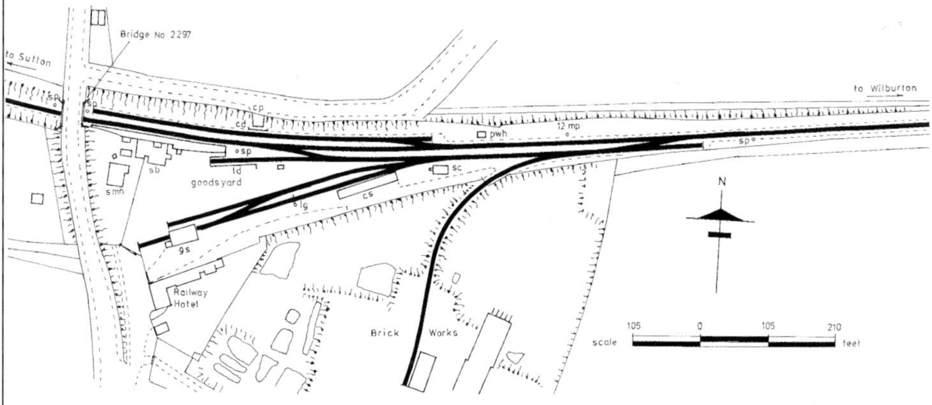

cs - coal stage

Haddenham station and goods yard facing St Ives, showing the second station master's house built in 1900 as a replacement for the original accommodation adjacent to the station building. Open wagons occupy the 170 ft dock road at the back of the platform whilst on the right is the 480 ft-long down reception road serving the cattle dock and cattle pens. From 1891 until 1932 all points and signals at the station were controlled by Haddenham signal box but after abolition, the points from the main single line to the yard were operated by 2-two lever ground frame released by Annett's key on the Ely to Sutton single line Train Staff. One of the ground frames can be see at the end of the platform. Haddenham Road overbridge No. 2297 forms a backdrop at the far end of the 230 ft-long platform. *John Watling*

Haddenham station, 11 m. 71 ch. from St Ives looking towards St Ives with Haddenham Road overbridge No. 2297 at the end of the platform. In this 1964 view the down reception siding has already been removed. Note the rails of the cattle pens to the right. *R. Powell*

Haddenham station with its single platform on the up side of the main single line. The goods yard behind the station building had an extensive layout including the 470 ft-long shed road serving the goods shed, the 380 ft yard loop and the 400 ft yard road. The brickworks, denoted by the chimney in the background, was served by a 280 ft-long private siding. *Stations UK*

Haddenham goods shed, which had capacity for storing 50 quarters, later increased to 100 quarters of grain. *John Watling*

THE ELY & ST IVES RAILWAY

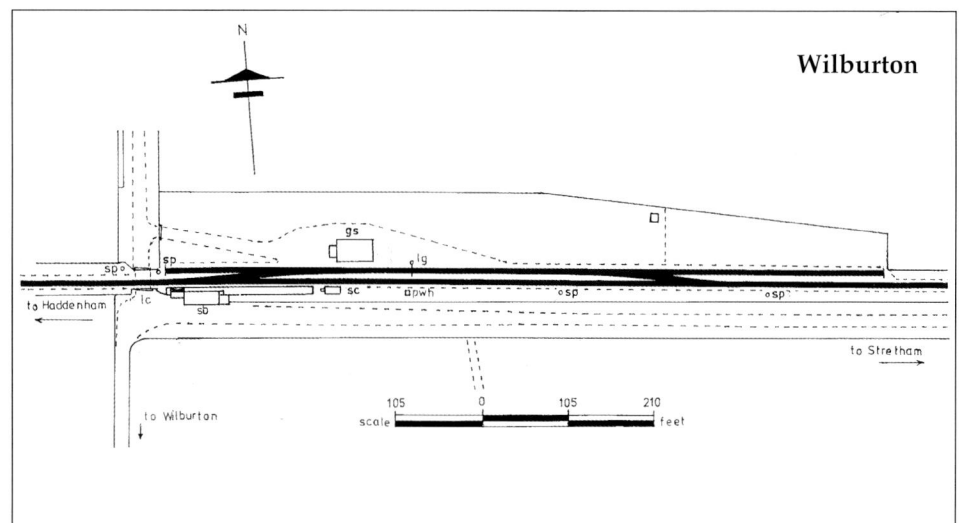

Wilburton station facing towards St Ives on 22nd July, 1964. Located 12 m. 79 ch. from St Ives the 180 ft-long platform was on the up or south side of the line with the gates guarding the Wilburton to Wentworth road level crossing No. 69 at 12 m. 77 ch. at the west end of the platform. The 160 ft-long headshunt is to the right and points leading to the 340 ft-long goods loop siding in the foreground.   *R. Powell*

located on the down side. To the east of the station was the 380 ft goods loop siding on the south side of the main single line with the 130 ft-long up headshunt at the east end and the 170 ft dock siding at the western end. Access from the main single line to the goods loop was by facing points in each direction. From the goods loop, two sidings, yard road 400 ft, and shed road 470 ft, connected by a crossover road served the goods yard, the southernmost siding also served the coal ground as well as the goods shed. A further private siding, 280 ft in length, installed in the 1880s ran from the goods loop to serve a clay pit and brickyard opened in 1921, crossing in its path marshy land by an embankment. Points and signals at the station were controlled from the Haddenham signal box located on the up side of the goods loop line.

From Haddenham the branch initially fell at 1 in 161 past the 12 mile post before following a straight course climbing at 1 in 831 and then falling at 1 in 173 as the line crossed the edge of fenland. After following a straight course past Tiger Farm and then Hawk's Nest Farm on the up side of the line and over the adjacent occupational crossing at 12 miles 52 chains on a 1 in 426 rising gradient, the branch negotiated a slight right-hand curve and fell at 1 in 165 to bisect the Wilburton to Wentworth road by level crossing No. 69 at 12 miles 77 chains and enter Wilburton station 12 miles 79 chains from St Ives.

Wilburton station platform was the shortest on the branch and was only 180 ft in length. It was host to spartan station buildings, which included station master's accommodation, booking office, booking hall, at one time only measuring 10 ft x 6 ft, and waiting room as well as a porter's room and lamp room combined. A small canopy on the front of the station buildings provided meagre protection for passengers. The track layout consisted of a 340 ft goods loop on the down or north side of the line with access from the main single line by facing points in each direction. At the east end of the goods loop was the 310 ft refuge siding and at the western end the 160 ft headshunt. The goods loop served a goods shed, originally built by the EHSR as a grain store, but after World War II the building was allowed to deteriorate. The points and signals were controlled from Wilburton signal box located on the up side of the line at the east end of the station platform. Wilburton station was also situated in an isolated position, a mile north of Wilburton village which was located on the high fenland ridge to the south of the railway.

From Wilburton the single track branch ran on a straight course parallel to a side road to the south of the line, on a rising 1 in 382 gradient before falling at 1 in 239 past Crow's Farm on the down side of the line and rising again at 1 in 223 before bisecting Grainger's/Grunty Fen occupational level crossing No. 79 at 14 miles 40 chains. The line then fell at 1 in 327 as a fen island ridge closed in to the south of the line before climbing at 1 in 951 over three occupational crossings. The railway then fell at 1 in 132 around a slight left-hand curve on a 1 in 4132 falling gradient to enter Stretham station, 14 miles 74 chains from St Ives.

The platform, 200 ft in length, was located on the up or south side of the branch, immediately west of the level crossing. Station buildings included station master's house, booking office, waiting room, lamp room and toilets, whilst over the platform was a small canopy offering protection to passengers. The station and platforms were illuminated by oil. The track layout consisted of a 300 ft goods loop on the up side of the main single line, west of the station. This served a cattle pen and coal ground and access was offered by facing points in both directions from the main single line. At the western end of the loop was the 340 ft refuge siding, whilst at the eastern end was the 180 ft dock siding, in later years used extensively for the loading of sugar beet. Points and signals were controlled from the Stretham signal box, situated on the

Wilburton station facing St Ives; the canopy is raised at a rakish angle over the narrow platform to clear the carriage roofs. Note the sparseness of the location and the entrance gate to the goods yard on the extreme right. *Author*

The small station at Wilburton 12 m. 79 ch. from St Ives, had the shortest platform of any station on the branch, a mere 180 feet in length on the up or south side of the single main line. This view taken on 21st May, 1962 shows the spartan station buildings, which included the single-storey station master's accommodation on the left and a booking office, booking hall, at one time only measuring 10 ft by 6 ft, and waiting room as well as a porter's room and lamp room combined. This was fronted by the small canopy, which provided meagre protection for waiting passengers in this windswept part of the fens. Wilburton station was located a mile north of the village, which was on the high fenland ridge south of the railway, and consequently saw little passenger traffic. The buffer stops in the foreground are at the end of the 160 ft headshunt siding. *John Watling*

The exterior of the small station at Wilburton on 7th September, 1964. The station offices are nearest the entrance and the station master's accommodation beyond. *John Watling*

Looking east towards Ely from the platform at Wilburton on 22nd July, 1961. The flat fenland terrain is much in evidence and the main single line recedes into the distance. Running parallel to the main single line is the loop goods siding serving the corn shed provided in 1868 and the loading gauge beyond. To the left is the 160 ft-long headshunt siding. Wilburton signal box, controlling the points and signals at the station between 1891 and 1932, was located on the up side of the line at the east end of the platform. *R. Powell*

Two views of the large ornate corn shed at Wilburton, built in 1868 at a cost of £197 for storing farmers' grain awaiting transit. The loop goods siding runs alongside the shed with the main single line to the left. *(Both) John Watling*

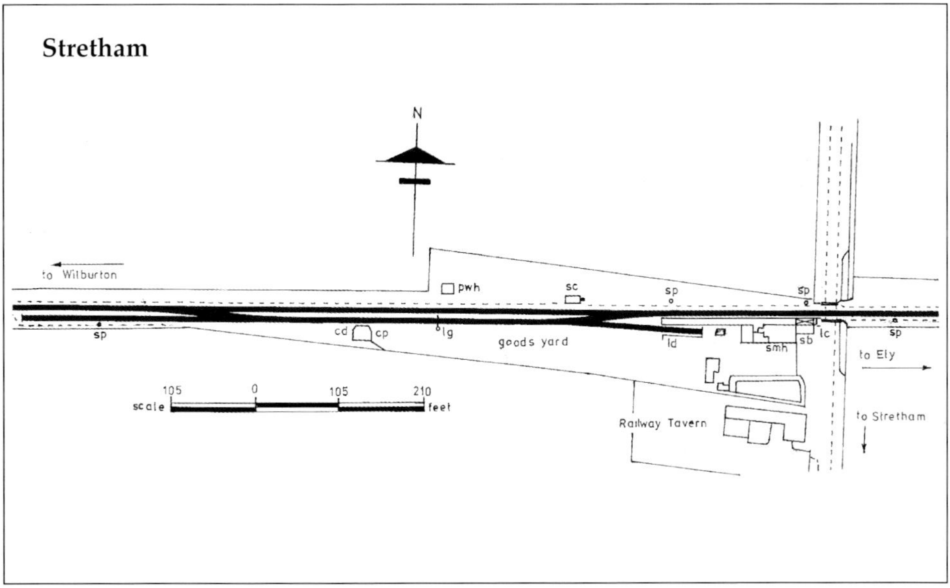

Stretham

The remote Stretham station viewed from the east looking towards St Ives with level crossing No. 80 at 14 m. 75 ch. from St Ives in the foreground. The station foreman is closing the gates across the railway after the passage of the branch goods train on 28th July, 1961. *R. Powell*

Stretham station, 14 m. 74 ch. from St Ives with the 200 ft-long platform on the up or south side of the line. This view looking east towards Ely shows the points leading to the loop goods siding operated by a 2-lever ground frame released by Annett's key attached to the Ely to Sutton single line Train Staff. Stretham signal box, which operated the points and signals at the station from 1891 until 1932, was located to the left of the picture. *R. Powell*

Stretham station and station house facing Ely. This remote station at one time had an adjacent hostelry known as the 'Railway Tavern', whose owner acted as the local coal merchant. The inn was probably necessary for intending passengers as Stretham village was over 1½ miles away to the south! *John Watling*

THE ROUTE DESCRIBED 89

down side of the line opposite the goods loop. The station was rather isolated and exposed to the elements especially if a north or east wind blew across the fens and during these periods it often required two or three attempts to light the platform oil lamps. Stretham village was over 1½ miles away to the south of the railway and passenger traffic was never heavy. The only building in the vicinity of the station was the Railway Tavern whose owner also acted as the local coal merchant.

Immediately on leaving Stretham the line crossed the Stretham to Witchford road by level crossing No. 80 at 14 miles 75 chains, on a 1 in 4132 falling gradient before climbing at 1 in 212 past the 15 mile post to cross fenland fields. The railway then negotiated a 30 chains radius curve left-hand curve on level track to follow a north-easterly course bisecting a minor road at Thetford Corner level crossing No. 83 at 15 miles 58 chains. The curve continued on 40 chains radius as the railway then crossed the main London to Lynn, later A10, road by Cambridge road level crossing No. 84 at 15 miles 60 chains on a 1 in 274 falling gradient. Undulating gradients of 1 in 207 rising past the 16 mile post, and then 1 in 185 falling/352 rising followed as the line negotiated a straight course passing Braham Farm on the down or north side of the line. A 22 chains radius left-hand curve brought the branch to Ely Sutton Branch Junction, 16 miles 54 chains from St Ives, where facing points led to the down main line which branch trains followed on level track to terminate at Ely station 17 miles 55 chains from St Ives and 70 miles 33 chains from Liverpool Street via Clapton Junction and Cambridge. After the withdrawal of the branch passenger services and the abolition of Sutton Branch Junction signal box in July 1932, all trains for Sutton and St Ives used the down reception line from Ely Dock Junction to gain access to and from the branch.

The layout at Ely consisted of a down platform served by a loop line and an up side island platform. The down or western platform was host to the main station offices, including station master's office, booking office, general and ladies waiting rooms, toilets, parcels office, telegraph office and refreshment room. The up side platform buildings consisted of staff rooms, waiting room, toilets and small refreshment room. In GER and LNER days the St Ives branch train usually departed from the island platform using the up main or up loop lines. Leaving the platform St Ives trains followed the up main line as far as Ely Sutton Branch Junction, 1 mile 1 chain south of Ely station where facing points led to the branch. From Ely station to Ely Sutton Branch Junction trains were controlled by Ely South and Ely Dock Junction signal boxes, the latter 56 chains from Ely station at the junction for the line to Bury St Edmunds.

Ely had considerable siding capacity for handling the interchange of freight, which was generated from the various converging lines and branches. These included two down reception sidings with capacity for 80 and 50 wagons, three up reception sidings holding 90, 35 and 35 wagons respectively, eight sorting sidings with capacity for 257 wagons and nine yard sidings on the down side holding 30, 40, 30, 20, 22, 12, 12, 25 and 30 wagons respectively. Six refuge sidings on the down side held 28, 26, 55, 40, 28 and 30 wagons, whilst the four refuge sidings on the up side held 54, 54, 51 and 50 wagons respectively. At one time the cattle pens sidings had capacity for 34 wagons.

The mileposts on the Ely to St Ives branch were generally on the down side of the single line branch whilst the gradient boards were on the up side. The speed limit on the branch was for many years 30 mph although in 1885 no train worked by an engine weighing over 32 tons was to exceed a speed of 15 mph between Ely Sutton Bridge Junction and Sutton. This was later restored to 30 mph but after 1957 a restriction of 10 mph was in force between Bluntisham and Sutton because of the

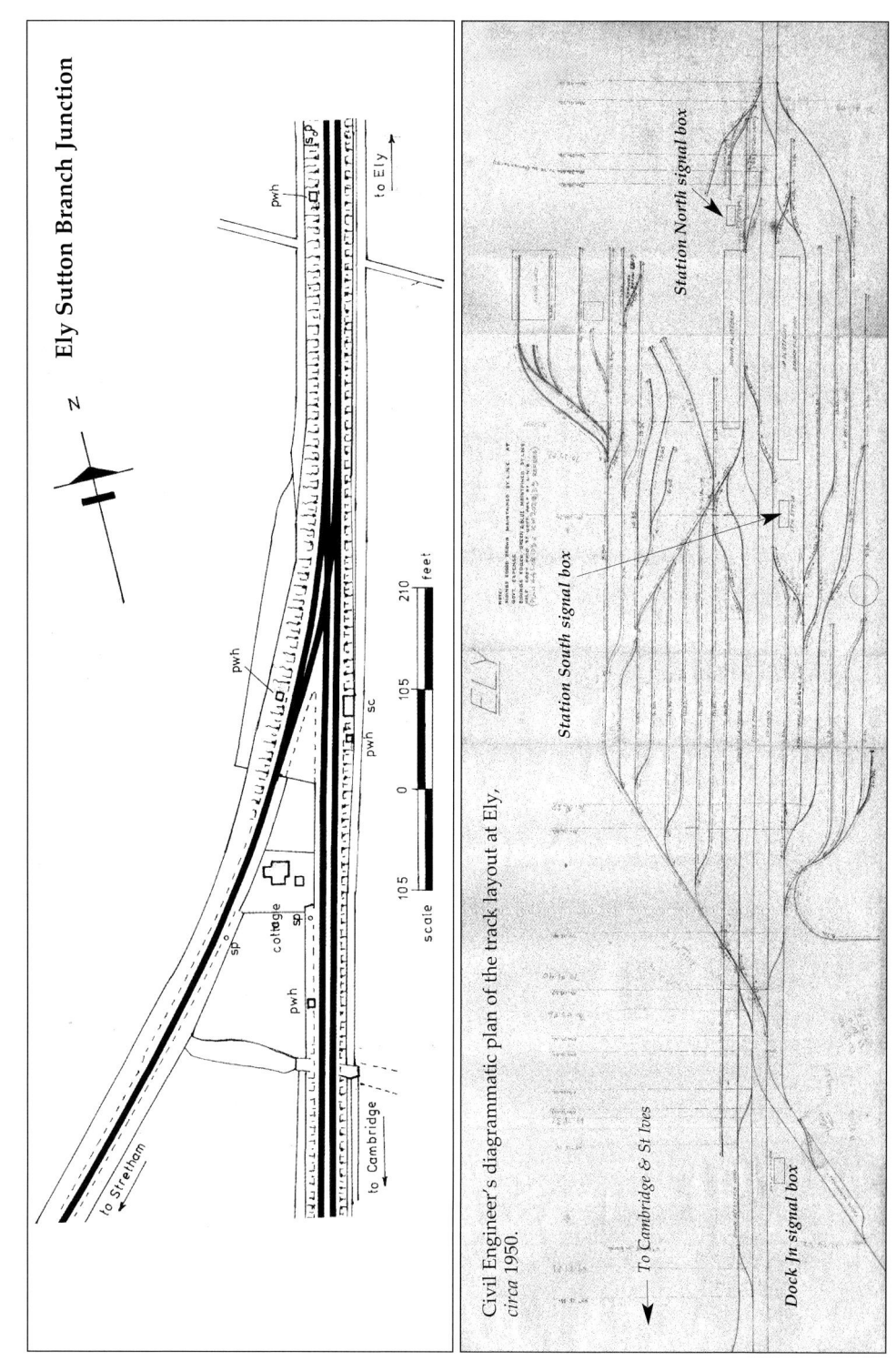

Civil Engineer's diagrammatic plan of the track layout at Ely, circa 1950.

THE ROUTE DESCRIBED

A 'J17' class 0-6-0 running into the down goods yard at Ely with the branch freight train from Sutton on 28th July, 1961.
R. Powell

In the 1961 summer timetable the branch freight train to Sutton was a through working from Brandon. 'J17' class 0-6-0 No. 65578 pulls into the up main platform at Ely before continuing with the train to Sutton on 28th July, 1961.
R. Powell

With the magnificent Ely Cathedral visible on the skyline, 'J17' class 0-6-0 No. 65578 prepares to depart from Ely down yard with the branch freight train to Sutton on 28th July, 1961. By this time the line beyond Sutton to Bluntisham had been closed and lifted. *R. Powell*

'J17' class 0-6-0 No. 65589 passing through the down platform road at Ely after working the branch freight train from Sutton in August 1960. *R. Powell*

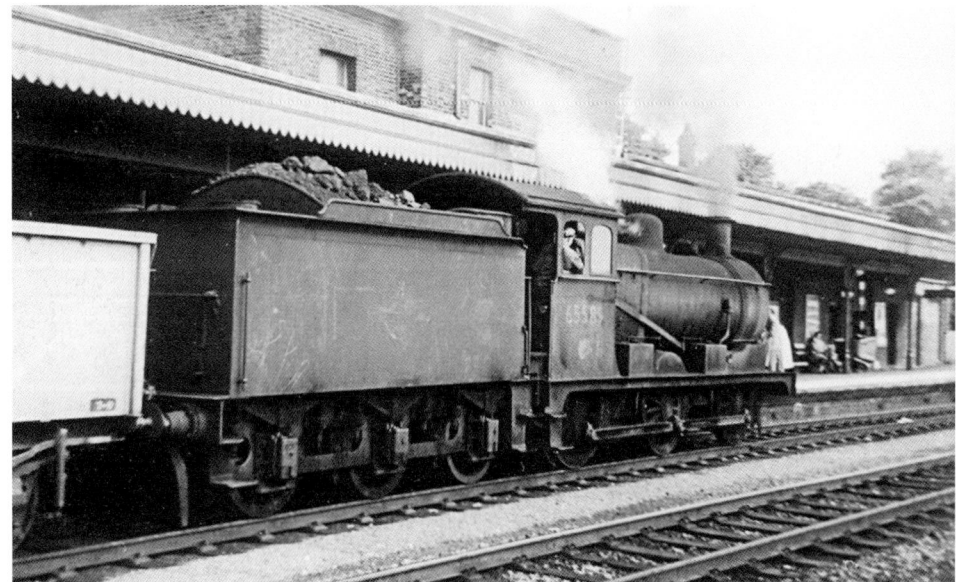

THE ROUTE DESCRIBED   93

Ely Dock Junction and signal box on 16th October, 1979. The line to Soham, Newmarket and Bury St Edmunds curves away to the left, whilst the double track main line to Cambridge passes in front of the box. The down goods line, which used by Sutton branch trains after 1932, runs parallel to the down main line (*centre*). *R. Powell*

The north end of Ely station facing north with the down platform and Ely Station North signal box to the left, equipped with a 37-lever Stevens frame to control points and signals. The down and up main lines are to the centre and the back platform road to the right. Stuntney Road (Ely Station), later A142, level crossing No. 130 at 70 m. 38 ch. from Liverpool Street via Clapton, bisects the line between the platform end and the signal box. *GERS/Windwood 1457*

Looking towards Ely station from near Ely Dock Junction with the down goods line used by St Ives branch services second from the left and the down and up Cambridge main lines to the right. The connection from Soham, Newmarket and Bury St Edmunds is to the extreme right.   *R. Powell*

poor condition of the permanent way. At Ely station trains were not permitted to exceed the following speed limits.

Down platform line	15 mph
Down centre line	20 mph
Down side line	5 mph
Up line	20 mph
Up back platform line	5 mph

In GER days a platform bell was sounded at both Ely and St Ives five minutes before the departure time of the train to warn passengers, and again at departure time as starting advice to the guard for the train to depart. At other branch stations the platform bell was sounded on the approach of the train. This procedure was later abandoned.

The south approach to Ely station with Ely Station South signal box to the right. The signals from the right are the down main home in the 'on' position, the down platform loop home in the 'off' position and down goods loop starter. In the background the up main inner starter and up main advance starter signals are in the 'off' position whilst the up loop signal is at danger.   *R. Powell*

Chapter Six

Permanent Way, Signalling and Staff

Permanent Way

The initial permanent way of the EHSR was of double-headed rails, weighing 65 lb. per yard in 21 ft lengths, fishplated at the joints by 16 in., four-hole plates. The sleepers were of Baltic timber half-round in shape and measuring 8 ft by 9 in. by 4½ in., laid 2 ft apart at the rail joints and 3 ft 2 in. apart at the intermediate places. The rails were affixed to the sleepers by fang bolts at the joints and a mixture of wood screws and dog spikes elsewhere. The permanent way was laid on a mixture of sand and gravel ballast, nine inches in depth. Captain Tyler on his inspection remarked of the similarity of the permanent way of the EHSR and the West Norfolk Junction Railway, both the work of W. Simpson.

The permanent way provided for the extension between Sutton and Needingworth was originally to be of 75 lb. per yard flat-bottom track but because of the requirements for stronger rails, 80 lb. per yard double-headed rails in 24 ft lengths were laid. The rails were fishplated at the joints and laid on cast-iron chairs weighing 26 lb. each. The chairs were fixed by spiked trenails to sleepers of red fir measuring 8 ft 11 in. x 10 in. x 5 in., eight sleepers bearing each length of track. The ballast was again formed of sand and gravel, nine inches in depth below sleeper level on ordinary track and on embankments but 15 inches deep in cuttings.

The original gravel ballast was soon replaced by clinker and ash formation. Second-hand track of GER 80 to 85 lb. per yard in 30 ft and later 45 ft length, replaced the original rails and, after amalgamation, the LNER laid 87 to 92 lb. per yard bullhead rails in 45 ft and 60 ft lengths. The GER found ashes and clinker were ideal for the ballasting of many of their branch lines and supplies were readily available from the motive power depots on the system. When supplies of ashes were not available from locomotive sheds, wagon loads were obtainable from Tate and Lyle's sugar refinery at Sivertown and after 1925 from the British Sugar Corporation factories at Wissington, Ely and Peterborough. Ashes and clinker were also found suitable for infilling on the sections of line which crossed fenland where the track formation was susceptible to slight subsidence during exceptionally dry weather when the peat and silt tended to dry out. Once wet weather returned the formation usually returned to its normal state.

The maintenance of the permanent way was covered by gangs based at St Ives and Ely with a ganger and sub-ganger at each of the branch stations for the day-to-day inspections and minor remedial repairs. After the withdrawal of the passenger train services from 1931 the maintenance was rationalized and a petrol driven permanent way trolley was allocated to enable the sub-gangs to be merged.

In 1915 the Bluntisham gang, consisting of J. Rayner, foreman platelayer, J. Bentley, second man and C. Papworth and A. O'Dell platelayers, earned the platelayer's award for the St Ives to Bluntisham section of permanent way. Of the permanent way staff who worked on the line, in 1924 George Brooks ganger occupied the gate cottage at Rymanmoor Drove crossing, which was rent free as he and his wife were responsible for opening and closing the level crossing gates at all times of the day and night. Similar rent-free accommodation was available to underman Samuel Chapman who resided in the gate cottage at Willingham Road

ELY, SUTTON AND ST. IVES BRANCH.
Jewson's Siding between Haddenham and Sutton, about 500 yards from the Haddenham Station.

Facing Points leading to the above Siding are laid into the Main Single Line, about 500 yards on the Sutton side of Haddenham Station.

The Lever working these Points and the Catch Points in the Siding is secured by "Annett's Patent Lock." This lock can only be opened and the Lever released by a key attached to the "Ely and Sutton" Train Staff, and the key cannot be withdrawn until both Points have been replaced in their proper positions, and the Lever relocked.

Trucks can only be worked in and out of this Siding by Down Trains, and as the Engine-driver of the 6.10 p.m. Goods Train from St. Ives to Ely (which is appointed to work the Siding), is now in possession of a **Ticket** on leaving Sutton for Ely, the Station Master at Sutton, must, when the Train is required to call at the Siding, after handing the Ticket to the Engine-driver, deliver the "Ely and Sutton" Train Staff to a competent man of his Station Staff, who must accompany the Train to the Siding, where he must hand over the Train Staff to a competent man sent by the Haddenham Station Master to work the Siding. After the work is done the man from Haddenham will be responsible for seeing that the Trucks are placed inside the Catch Points, and that the Points are replaced and locked in their proper position before handing the Train Staff back to the Sutton man, who must at once return on foot to the Sutton Station and deliver up the Staff to the Station Master.

Instructions for working Jewson's siding between Haddenham and Sutton, 1891.

ST. IVES TO ELY.

St. Ives	Junction		...	...	See Cambridge and St. Ives Branch.
,,	Yard Box		12	...	...
,,	Needingworth Junc.	1	61	...	Closed and switched out each Week-night after last Sutton Branch train is out of section until 20 minutes before first Branch train is due in the morning; and after last Sutton Branch train is out of section on Saturdays until 20 minutes before first Branch train is due on Mondays.
Bluntisham	Station	1	77	...	Closed at Night, and on Sundays.
Earith Bridge	,,	1	70	...	,, ,, ,,
Sutton	,,	4	43	...	,, ,, ,,
Haddenham	,,	1	60	...	,, ,, ,,
Wilburton	,,	1	3	...	,, ,, ,,
Stretham	,,	1	70	...	,, ,, ,,
Ely	Sutton Branch Junc.	1	65	...	See Cambridge Main Line.
,,	Dock Junction		54	...	,,
,,	Station South Box		24	...	,,

Opening and closing of signal boxes 1910.

NEEDINGWORTH JUNCTION TO ELY DOCK JUNCTION

	St. Ives Needingworth Junction				7.0 a.m. to 5.30 p.m. (M to S)		
	Bluntisham		1747				No Signal Box.
	Earith Bridge		1734				No Signal Box.
Telephone Block, Train Staff and Ticket	Sutton Station	4	905		For running of Sutton Branch trains shown in W.T.T. and for Branch trains specially advised (M to S)		
	Haddenham (Cambs)		1102				No Signal Box.
	Wilburton		173				No Signal Box.
	Stretham		1676				No Signal Box.
	Ely Dock Junction	2	620		Continuously...		The Branch Line joins the Down Reception Line 950 yards south of Ely Dock Junction. The Goods Loop is worked under "No Block" and is used for all trains to and from the Sutton Branch.

Opening and closing of signal boxes 1947.

PERMANENT WAY, SIGNALLING AND STAFF

crossing and to Ganger Harry Wallis who resided at Holywell crossing cottage. Other staff included J.G. Few sub-ganger at Sutton who died in January 1929, aged 71 years, after many years service on the branch; T. Wright, ganger at Stretham, who retired on 30th May, 1930; C.E. Maile, ganger at Earith Bridge, who retired on 29th October, 1935; R. Hawes, ganger at Sutton, who retired on 7th July, 1937, William Hinkins, sub-ganger at Bluntisham, who died on 1st March, 1940 and H. Gillett platelayer at Wilburton.

In addition to attending to day-to-day maintenance, the permanent way gangs were responsible for cleaning toilets where no mains drainage existed, as well as the maintenance of fencing and gates. On hot and dry sunny days they also patrolled the line acting as beaters to extinguish small fires caused by stray sparks from passing locomotives damaging crops in lineside fields.

The maintenance and upkeep of the infrastructure and permanent way on the Ely to St Ives branch was the responsibility of the Cambridge district engineer under the permanent way inspector in charge of District No. 3.

Signalling

The Ely to Sutton section of line was initially worked on the Train Staff and Ticket principle in accordance with special order No. 1191 dated 1st April, 1866. With the opening of the extension, Train Staff and Ticket working continued and the line was split into three sections, Ely Sutton Branch Junction to Sutton, Sutton to Bluntisham and Bluntisham to Needingworth Junction. The single line Train Staffs utilized on the branch were: Ely Sutton Branch Junction to Sutton, triangular in shape and coloured red and inscribed Ely and Sutton, Sutton to Bluntisham hexagonal in shape and blue in colour, and Bluntisham to Needingworth Junction square in shape and coloured yellow and incorrectly stamped Bluntisham to St Ives. The Tickets used in conjunction with the Train Staff were similar in colour to their respective staffs. On the withdrawal of the passenger service in 1931 and the subsequent abolition of signal boxes at all branch stations except Sutton, the line was divided into two sections, Ely Dock Junction to Sutton and Sutton to Needingworth Junction.

Signalling on the EHSR originally consisted of a station signal at each of the stations, and auxiliary or distant signals at Ely Sutton Branch Junction and Sutton, supplied and installed by Messrs Stevens. Special instructions were issued regarding auxiliary signals. In the event of an auxiliary signal being at danger, the driver of an approaching train had after coming to a stand immediately move his train forward with great care so far as the line was clear, so as to bring his train well within the protection of the signal. Drivers were especially cautioned that failure to carry out the regulation could cause an accident, which would otherwise have been avoided. If it was not practicable to draw the train far enough within the signal to afford sufficient protection from a following train, the guard was required to immediately go back with hand and 'percussion' [*sic*] signals to protect his train. Distant signals were later installed at Haddenham. When the extension was opened, block signalling supplemented the Train Staff and Ticket working and Tyer's single line block instruments were installed in the new signal boxes. Signalling equipment, signal boxes, frames and signals on the section from Sutton to Needingworth Junction were supplied by Saxby & Farmer Ltd. These signal boxes were built of brick to the standard Saxby & Farmer design except Needingworth Junction, which was of brick and timber construction. Sutton measuring 16 ft long by 10 ft wide with the operating floor 7 ft 6

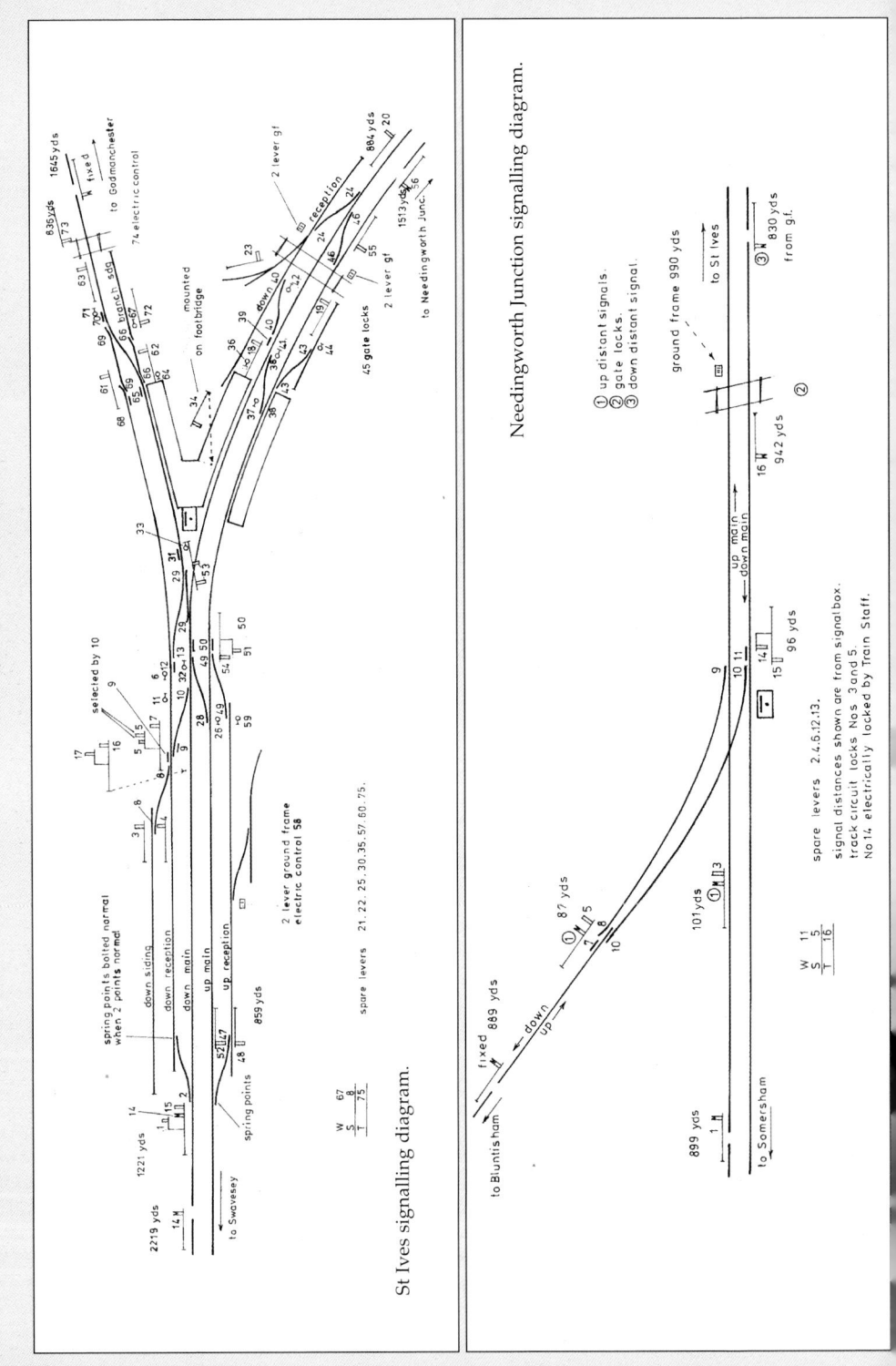

PERMANENT WAY, SIGNALLING AND STAFF

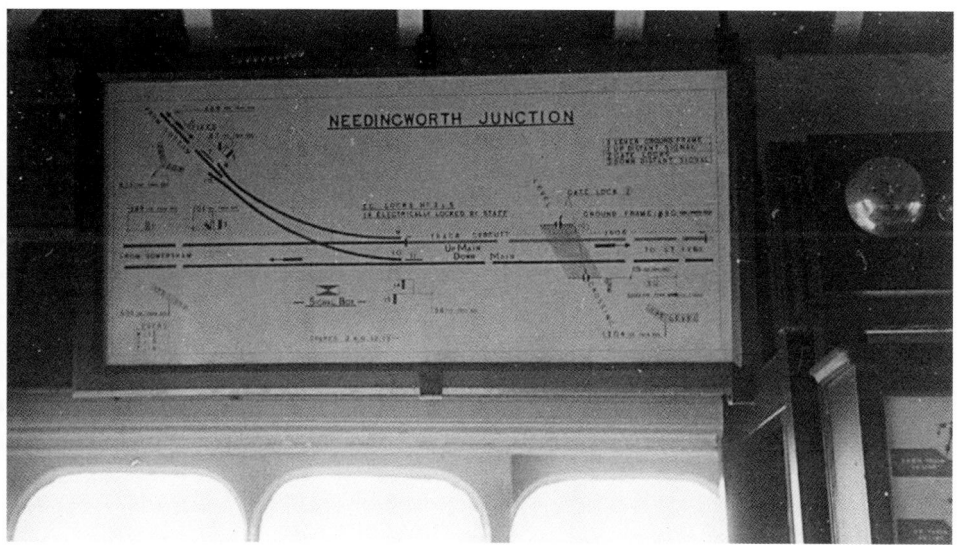

The signal box diagram at Needingworth Junction on 6th September, 1963. Note the ornate curve to the tops of the windows of this Saxby & Farmer designed signal box. *R. Powell*

The 16-lever Saxby & Farmer frame at Needingworth Junction signal box on 6th September, 1963 when the Ely branch was still open as far as Bluntisham. The box originally had 12 working and four spare levers but by this time alterations had resulted in 11 working and five spares. *R. Powell*

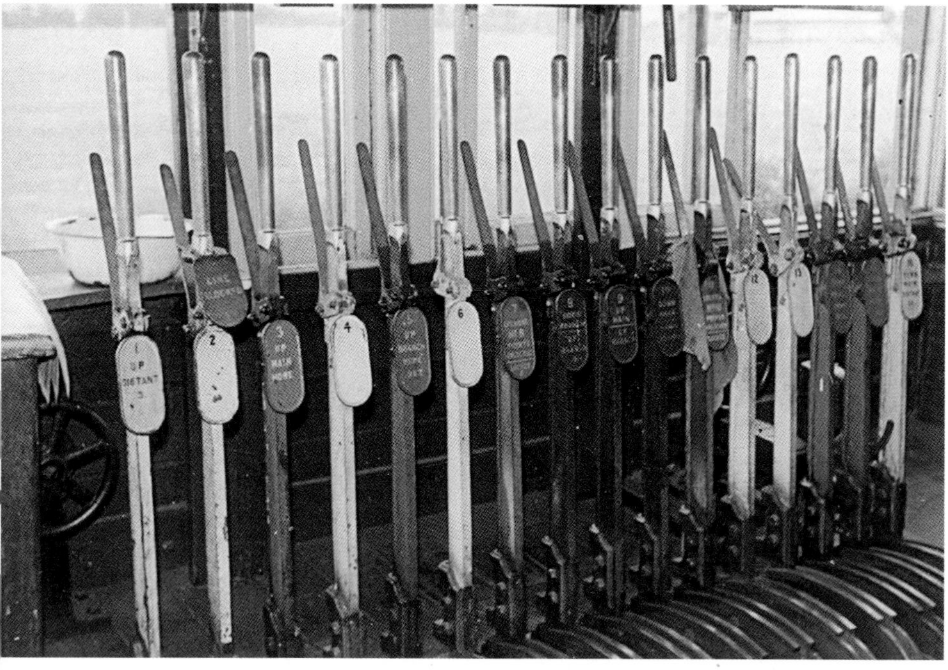

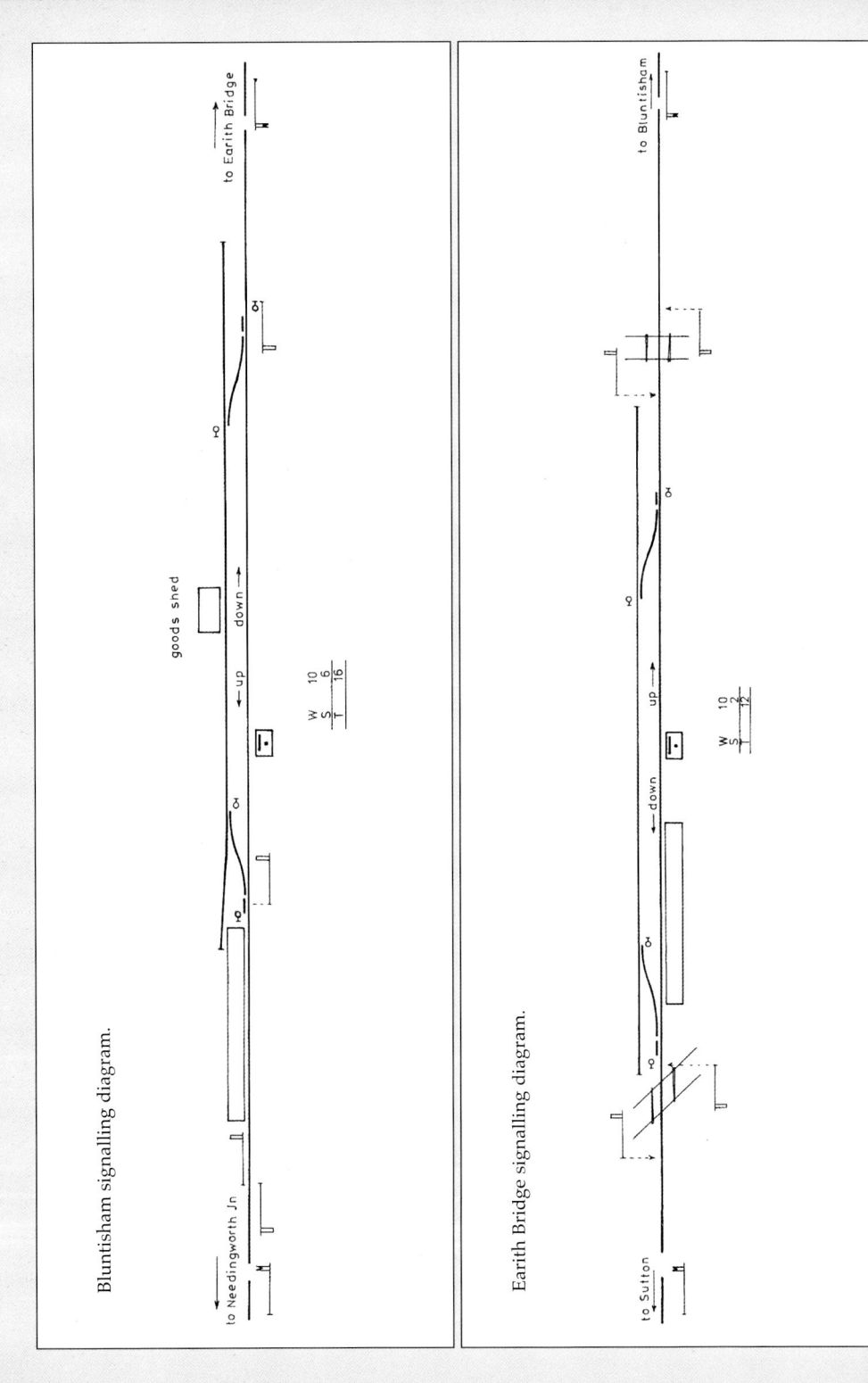

PERMANENT WAY, SIGNALLING AND STAFF 101

in. above rail level had an 18-lever frame with 15 working and three spare levers, later 11 working and seven spares, whilst Earith Bridge measuring 14 ft x 10 ft with operating floor at 7 ft above rail level boasted the smallest frame on the line with 12 levers, 10 working and two spares. Bluntisham signal box measuring 16 ft long by 10 ft wide with operating floor 8 ft above rail level had a 16-lever frame with 10 working and six spares whilst Needingworth Junction measuring 14 ft long by 12 ft wide with operating floor at 7 ft 6 in. had the same size frame but with 12 working and four spare levers, later 11 working and five spares. Soon after the opening of the extension, level crossing gatehouses were supplied with block repeater bells. The single needle telegraph was installed at each station to assist communication whilst the junction and station signal boxes were supplied with a circuit phone at a cost of £500.

The Regulation of Railways Act 1889 amongst other things required the interlocking of points and signals. Ely Sutton Branch Junction and Sutton signal boxes received interlocking when the line first opened to traffic, as did the signal boxes on the extension in 1878. The remaining three stations were without such refinements until 21st April, 1891 when a contract was placed with the Railway Signal Co. of Fazakerley, Liverpool for interlocking and other signalling improvements at Stretham, Wilburton and Haddenham. The new signal boxes at the eastern end of the line were of timber construction. Sutton Branch Junction, measuring 20 ft in length by 11 ft 4 in. in width with the operating floor 7 ft 6 in. above rail level, boasted a 20-lever frame with no spare levers, whilst both Stretham and Wilburton each measuring 20 ft long by 11 ft 6 in. wide with operating floors at 5 ft 6 in. and 5 ft 9 in. above rail level respectively, had 20-lever frames with 15 working and five spare levers. Haddenham signal box serving a larger track layout and measuring 22 ft long by 11 ft 6 in. wide with operating floor 9 ft above rail level, had a 24-lever frame with 18 working and six spare levers. Further signalling improvements were made in October 1894 when authority was given for the installation of outer home signals at Sutton costing £30.

The branch stations were provided with distant, home and starting signals for each direction of travel, with Sutton having the added benefit of outer home signals, although after the withdrawal of passenger services these were abolished. Ely Sutton Branch Junction signal box had distant, home and starting signals on the main line and a down distant and home signal and up starting signal on the branch. Needingworth Junction signal box also had distant, home and starting signals for each direction of travel on the St Ives to March line and up distant and home signals and a down starting signal on the branch. Whilst the gates of Lowndes Drove level crossing were protected by the signals of Needingworth Junction, those at Rymanmoor Drove, level crossing No. 35, were guarded by gate distant signals for each direction of travel with the crossing keeper working the signals from a small ground frame. With the rationalization of branch operation these signals were subsequently removed.

Around the turn of the century modifications were made to the distant signals on the branch. At that time the GER distant signal arms were painted the same red as stop signals and showed the same red and green aspects to drivers at night. To avoid confusion with the home and starting signals the distant signals were fitted with a Coligny Welch lamp which showed an additional white > at night. In common with GER practice each wooden signal arm was stamped on the reverse with the name of the controlling signal box. With the coming of the LNER, the distant signals were gradually repainted the familiar yellow with black > and the Coligny Welch lamps removed or modified to serve as ordinary lamps.

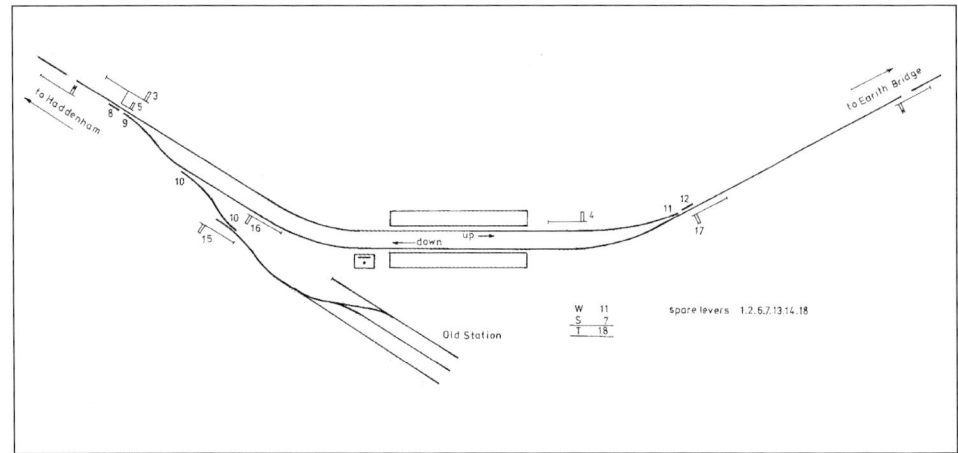

Sutton signalling diagram.

Sutton signal box built by Saxby & Farmer Ltd was typical of the signal boxes on the Sutton to Needingworth branch extension. It boasted an 18-lever frame with 15 working and three spare levers in 1921, later 11 working and seven spares. *John Watling*

PERMANENT WAY, SIGNALLING AND STAFF 103

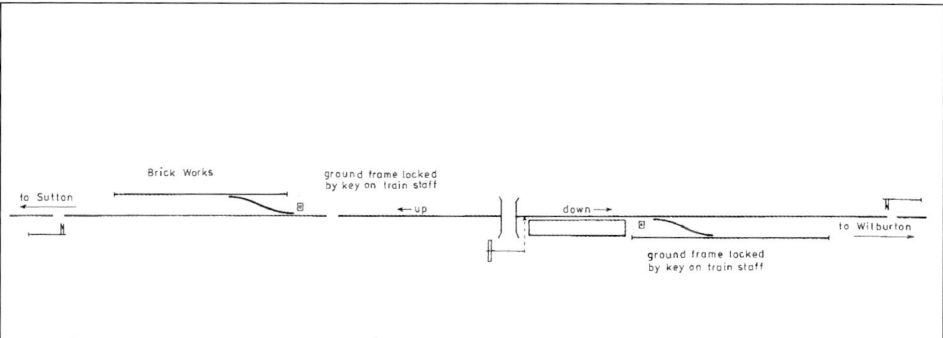

Early signalling diagram for Haddenham.

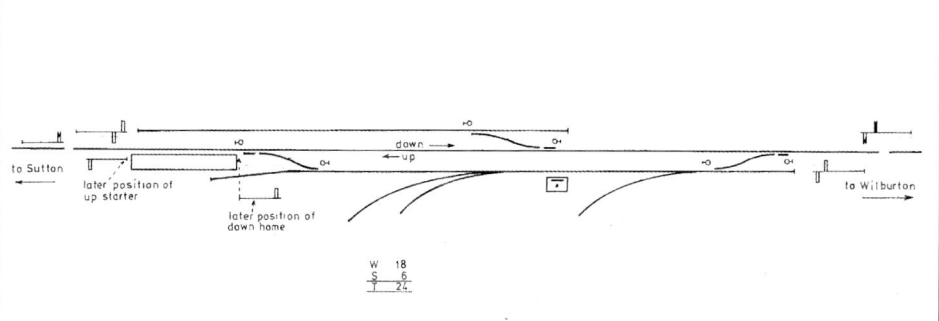

Haddenham signalling diagram.

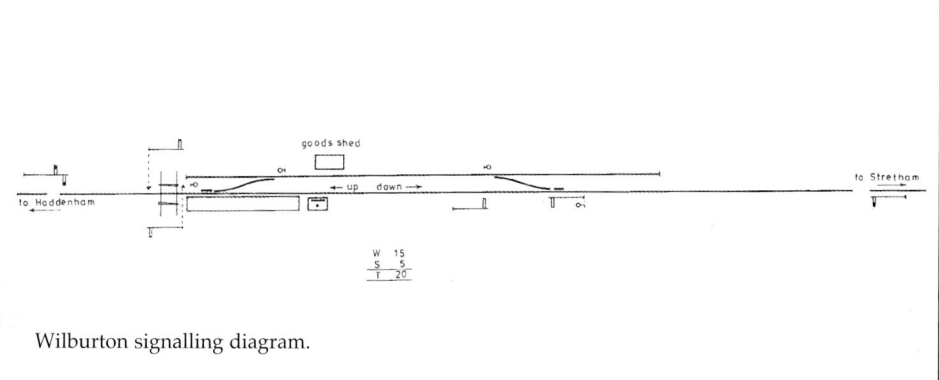

Wilburton signalling diagram.

104   THE ELY & ST IVES RAILWAY

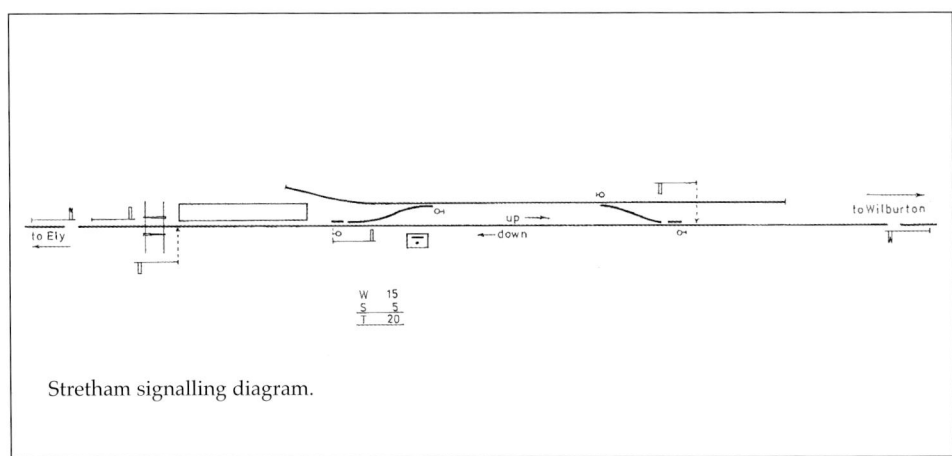

Stretham signalling diagram.

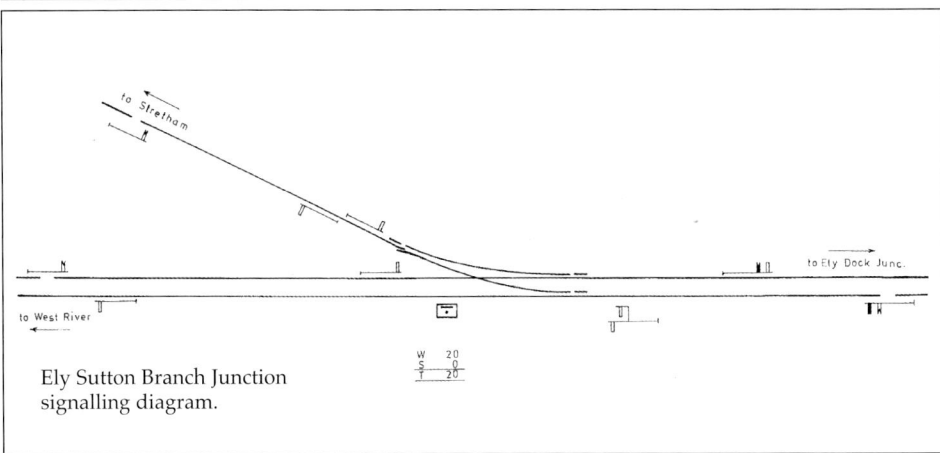

Ely Sutton Branch Junction signalling diagram.

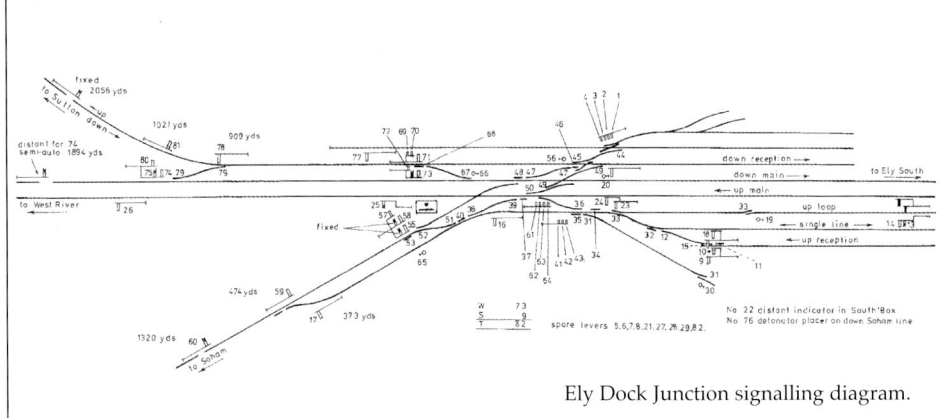

Ely Dock Junction signalling diagram.

In GER days the signal boxes at Needingworth Junction, Bluntisham, Earith Bridge, Sutton, Haddenham, Wilburton and Stretham were open for Sutton branch trains shown in the working timetable and for branch trains specially advised, whilst Sutton Branch Junction signal box was open from 5.30 am Mondays-only, 6.00 am Mondays-excepted to 9.00 pm weekdays only. In 1891 Needingworth Junction signal box was closed and switched out each weeknight after the last Sutton branch train was out of section until 20 minutes before the first branch train was due in the morning and after the last Sutton branch train was out of section on Saturdays until 20 minutes before the first branch train was due on Monday. In 1928 after the LNER had taken over, Sutton Branch Junction signal box was open from 6.00 am until 10.00 pm weekdays only whilst Needingworth Junction signal box opened from 7.00 am to 10.00 pm weekdays only. The other signal boxes were only open for the passage of branch trains or trains specially advised. By this date porter/signalmen were operating the signal boxes at Stretham, Wilburton, Haddenham and Earith Bridge and to save delays the signal box circuit phones at these stations were transferred to the station buildings.

Jewson's, later Isle of Ely Brick Co. siding was located 500 yards on the Sutton side of Haddenham station with points facing up trains and these were released and bolted by Annett's key attached to the Ely to Sutton Train Staff. The operation of the siding points was straightforward if the driver of a train calling at the siding was in possession of the Train Staff but special instruction were issued when the driver of a down train appointed to work the siding was only in possession of a Train Staff Ticket. On leaving Sutton for Ely, the station master at Sutton was required, when the train was to call at the siding, after handing the Ticket to the driver, deliver the Ely to Sutton Train Staff to a competent member of his station staff, who accompanied the train to the siding. On arrival at the siding the Train Staff was handed over to the competent man sent by the Haddenham station master to work the siding. On completion of shunting the Haddenham member of staff was responsible for ensuring the trucks were placed inside the catch points and that the points in the main line were locked in the proper position. The Train Staff was then handed back to the Sutton man who, after the departure of the train towards Haddenham and Ely, returned on foot to Sutton to deliver the Train Staff to the station master.

After the withdrawal of passenger train services in 1931, the signal boxes remained in use for only a short period. Sutton Branch Junction signal box was abolished on 17th July, 1932 when arrangements were made to pass the branch traffic over the down reception line between Ely Dock Junction signal box and the site of the junction. Stretham, Earith Bridge and Bluntisham signal boxes were abolished from 17th August, 1932 when the points to the goods yard sidings were worked by ground frame released by Annett's key attached to the Train Staff. At the same time all signals except the gate distant signals were removed. Less than a month later on 7th September, 1932 the signal boxes at Wilburton and Haddenham were abolished and replaced by ground frames. The line was then worked by telephone block and divided into two single line sections using the Train Staff and Ticket from Ely Dock Junction to Sutton and Sutton to Needingworth Junction. With the closure of the section of line between Sutton and Bluntisham on and from 6th October, 1958 the branch was divided into two separate sections of single line. Whilst operation of the section from Ely Dock Junction to Sutton remained unchanged, the section of line from Needingworth Junction to Bluntisham was operated by 'One Engine in Steam' principle using the Train Staff. Sutton signal box

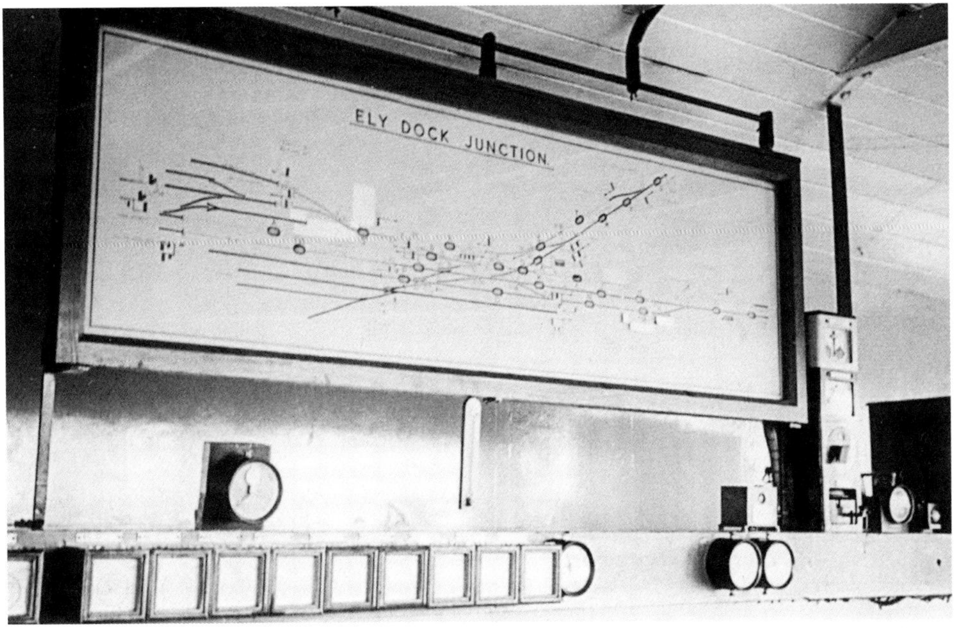

The signalman's diagram in Ely Dock Junction signal box in October 1979. *R. Powell*

The interior of Ely Dock Junction signal box showing the block shelf and part of the 82-lever Westinghouse A2 frame. *R. Powell*

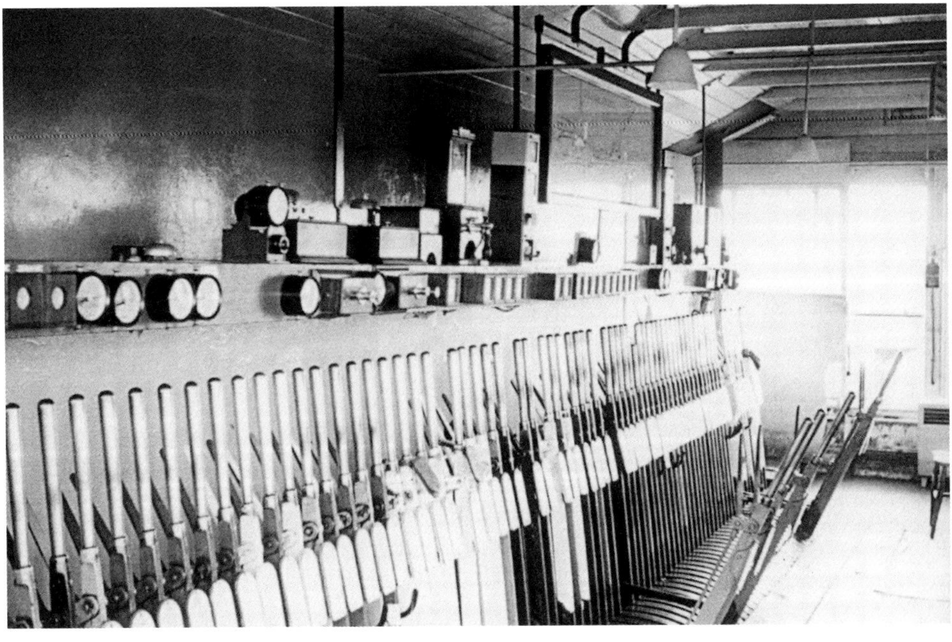

Ely Dock Junction signal box located on the up side of the Cambridge main in the 'V' of the junction with the line to Soham and Newmarket. This signal box, provided in 1928 as a replacement for a smaller GER signal box, was equipped with a 82-lever Westinghouse A2 frame, with 75 working and seven spare levers.
R. Powell

In 1928 Ely Dock Junction signal box was relocated to the up side of the Cambridge main line just south of the 'V' junction with the single line to Fordham, replacing the former GER signal box dating from 1881. This new signal box controlled access to and from the St Ives branch via the reception loop line after the abolition of Ely Sutton Branch Junction signal box from 17th July, 1932.
Author

Ely Station South signal box located on the up side of the main line immediately south of Ely station was provided by the LNER in 1933 as a replacement for smaller GER structure and contained a 75-lever Railway Signal Co. frame, with 55 working and 20 spare levers. *R. Powell*

Ely Station South signal box signalled St Ives branch trains to and from Ely Dock Junction.
Author

The interior of Ely Station South signal box showing the signalman's diagram, the block shelf and part of the 75-lever Railway Signal Co. frame. Signalman Ted Saggs is signalling a train forward to Ely Dock Junction box.
R. Powell

The signalman's diagram in Ely Station South signal box.
R. Powell

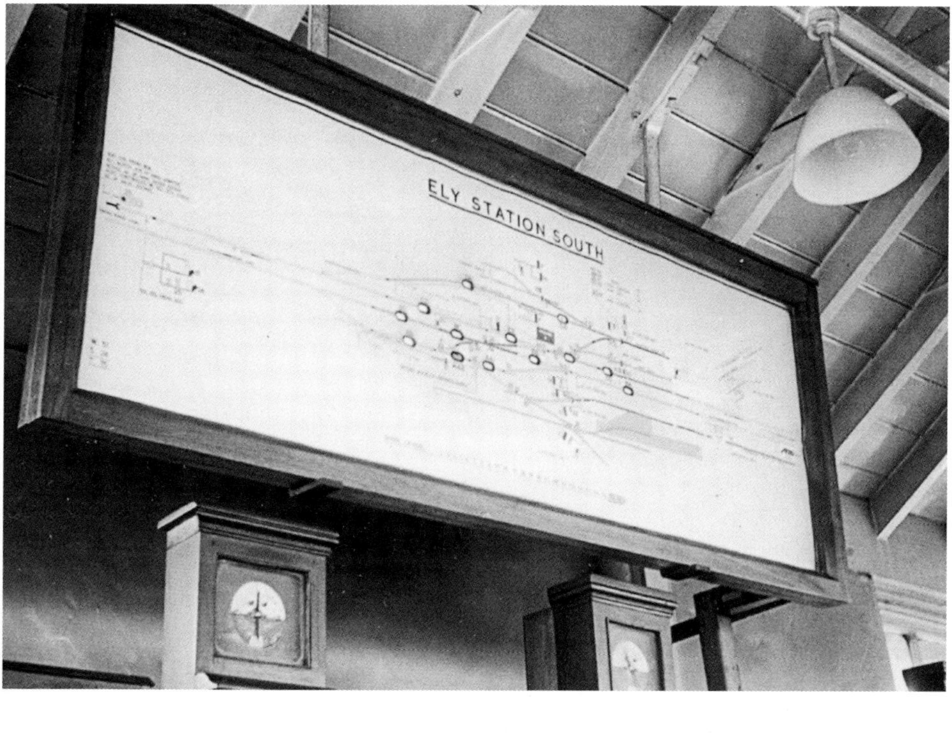

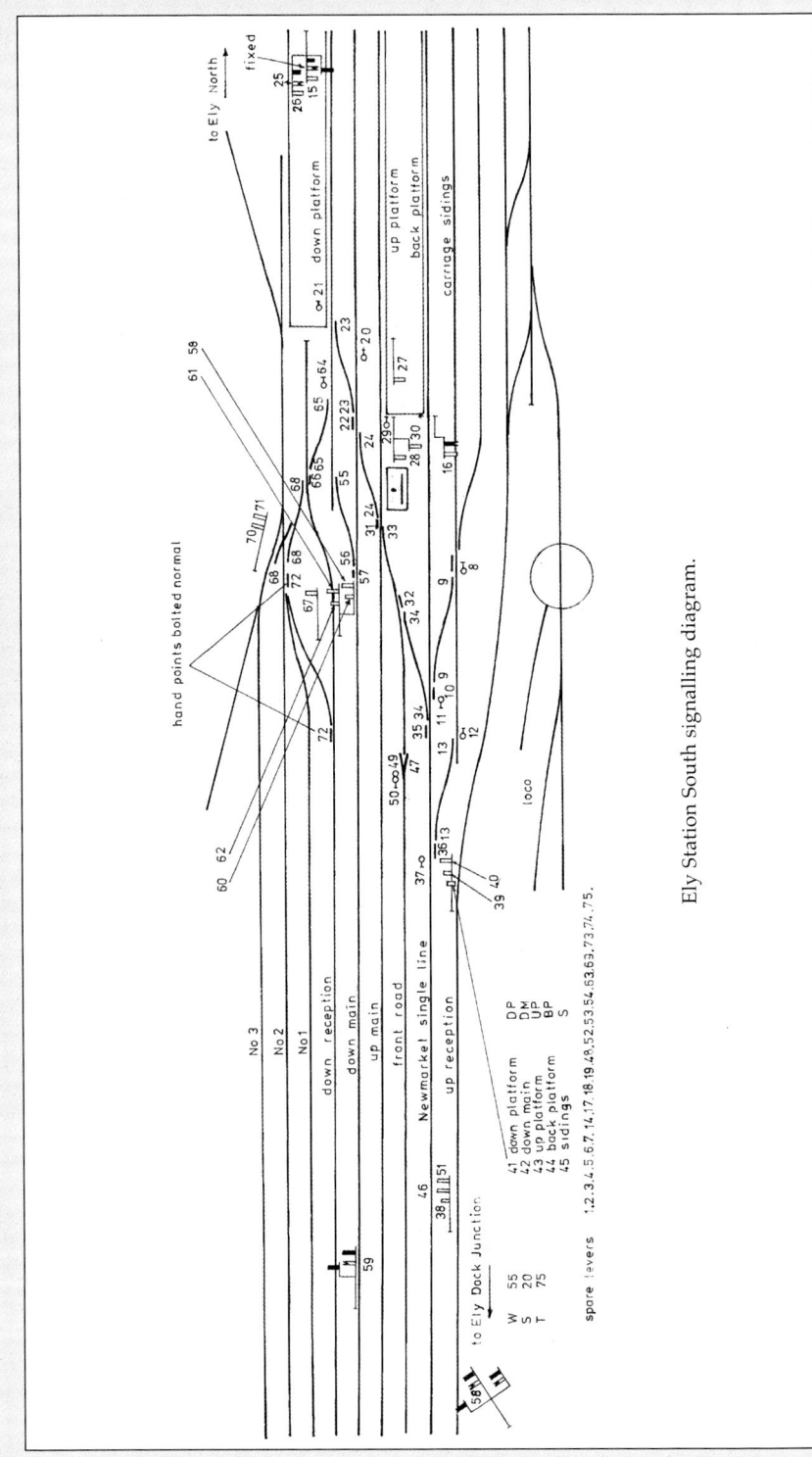

Ely Station South signalling diagram.

PERMANENT WAY, SIGNALLING AND STAFF 111

remained in use as a Train Staff station until the withdrawal of the freight services and was finally abolished on 16th June, 1965, the same day that Needingworth Junction signal box was abolished.

At the extremities of the branch Ely Dock Junction signal box, which with Ely South signal box, controlled the movement of the St Ives branch trains between Ely station and Sutton Branch Junction until 1932, was of timber construction 29 ft in length by 11 ft 5 in. wide with the operating floor 12 ft above rail level and contained a 50-lever Stevens frame with 48 working and two spare levers, later 46 working and four spare levers. In the general scheme of improvements at Ely made in 1928 by the LNER this box was replaced by a new structure on the up side of the Cambridge main line in the V of the junction with the line to Fordham and contained an 82-lever Westinghouse 'A2' frame, with 75 working levers and seven spares, later 77 working and five spare levers. Ely Station South GER signal box had a 60-lever Stevens frame with 59 working and one spare lever replaced in 1926 by a 65-lever LNER relock frame; but as with Ely Dock Junction the signal box was rebuilt in 1933 when it boasted a 75-lever Railway Signal Co. frame with 55 working and 20 spare levers. Movements at the north of Ely station were controlled by Ely Station North signal box containing a Stevens 37-lever tappett frame, with 36 working and one spare lever but during the station improvements the frame was increased to 41 working levers with no spares.

At St Ives train movements were controlled from two signal boxes. St Ives Yard to the north of the station of timber construction measured 26 ft in length by 11 ft 4 in. wide with the operating floor 12 ft 6 in. above rail level and contained a 36-lever Saxby & Farmer frame with 31 working and 5 spare levers, whilst St Ives Junction signal box, located at the junction of the Huntingdon and March lines was 33 ft 3 in. in length by 11 ft 6 in. wide with the operating floor 6 ft 9 in. above track level. This contained a 52-lever Saxby & Farmer frame with 44 working and eight spare levers. As part of the rationalization programme at St Ives, the yard box was abolished on 21st June, 1931 when the control of the signals and points was transferred to St Ives Junction signal box, which received a 75-lever Westinghouse 'A2' frame, with 67 working and eight spare levers, latterly much reduced. The Junction signal box was abolished on 30th April, 1972. Ely Station South signal box was abolished on 30th June, 1985 and Ely Station North and Ely Dock Junction signal boxes closed on 11th April, 1992, these as a result of Cambridge power signal box taking over the control of the Ely station area.

It is not always remembered that the railways first brought standard time throughout the country. Before the coming of the railway each town or village varied in time from minutes to hours. The standard scheme finally adopted by the GER before the advent of the telegraph and wireless, was like other companies, of giving a 10 am time signal via the single needle telegraph to each signal box and station on the system. By the time the headquarters at Liverpool Street had telegraphed down the line and the message had been manually passed on, some three minutes had elapsed before the stations and signal boxes on the Ely to St Ives branch had received their time check. The gap in time was generally accepted and adjustments made, as this was a far better system of ensuring a standard time throughout the land than was possible by any other system. Once standard time was set, clocks and watches in the villages served by the line were invariably aligned to station time.

Station Masters

The first station master at Stretham was James Welham Rowe who transferred to the new line from the Norwich district. He remained at the branch station until he was promoted to Hilgay in August 1872 from where he moved to Snettisham on the Hunstanton branch in February 1874, until retirement in 1905. Mr A. Whiteman was station master at Sutton from 1870 to 1875 when he was transferred on promotion to Shelford on the Cambridge main line. Whiteman later saw service at Somersham from 1881 to 1899, when he moved on promotion to Whittlesea from where he retired on 28th February, 1913 aged 65 years. Mr F. Hillier station master at Magdalen Road was appointed to Sutton in 1891 but stayed for only a short period before moving on to take charge at Littleport. In May 1911 station master Pollintine was promoted from St Ives to March and G.W. Newell was transferred from Histon to St Ives to take up the vacancy. He retired from the station on 4th August, 1928. Mr S.N. Wright replaced Newell and he served at St Ives until January 1930 when he was promoted to assistant yard master at Whitemoor. In April 1912 station master Thompson at Stretham was transferred on promotion to Linton on the Shelford to Sudbury line, and was replaced by William George Wybrew who remained at Stretham until January 1920, paying annual rent of £15 0s. 0d. per annum for the station accommodation, increased to £16 0s. 0d. from 1st July, 1915. He was promoted to Burwell and later Mildenhall. He finally retired because of ill health as station master Audley End including Saffron Walden. Along the line at Wilburton, Frederick C. Fosdike was station master paying annual rental of £16 0s. 0d. for the station accommodation in 1914, increased to £17 0s. 0d. from 1st July, 1915. Mr F.A. Jordan replaced Fosdike on 1st January, 1916. Frederick Thomas Pool was station master at Earith Bridge from January 1908 until December 1917 when he was promoted to Long Stanton. In appreciation of his services at the station, local traders presented him with a case of treasury notes.

Early in 1922 Harry William Doughty, station master at Sutton, took over the extra responsibility for Earith Bridge and Bluntisham stations. He lived in the station master's house at Sutton paying an annual rental of £21 in 1924. Doughty retired on 21st February, 1930 after 50 years' service and 30 years as station master at Sutton. At a staff gathering he was presented with an Aladdin lamp. In 1924 Charles Howard was station master at Haddenham paying an annual rental for the station house of £20, reduced to £13 8s. 4d. in 1925 and surrendered on 29th August, 1925. Further rationalization took place in August 1922 in connection with the introduction of conductor-guard working and the closure of the booking offices when F.A. Jordan, station master at Wilburton, was transferred to Coldham on the March to Wisbech line, whilst his colleague R.J. Hoare station master at Stretham was transferred to Gosberton on the GN&GE Joint line, Mr Howard then assumed control of the two stations; he retired in 1925 and died on 2nd December, 1932.

G.B. Tassell a clerk at Haverhill North was promoted to station master Wilburton in June 1930 and was presented with a fountain pen by his colleagues before leaving for the Cambridgeshire station. John Allen was promoted from Haddenham to St Ives in May 1932 and was replaced by C. Mitson, who was promoted from Birdbrook on the ex-Colne Valley & Halstead line. His stay was short-lived for S. Green was promoted from Shepreth on the Cambridge to Royston line to Haddenham in March 1934.

Traffic Staff

Robert Waters commenced his railway career as porter at Earith Bridge in 1881 and later served at Ely and Whittlesford before gaining promotion as ticket collector at Bishop's Stortford, from where he retired in 1928.

Alfred Green, for many years signalman at Sutton, retired in October 1913. In 1914 the railway cottage at Sutton Branch Junction was occupied by Henry John Covill, signalman at the Junction signal box, who paid an annual rental of £5 4s. 0d., whilst James Newell, a ganger, occupied the cottage by Cambridge Road crossing which was rent free in return for himself and his wife opening and closing the level crossing gates for passage of all trains. Along the branch at Wilburton the four company cottages were occupied by James Yarrow, a clerk, Percy Titmarsh and Arthur Shaw, both porter-signalmen, and ganger Frederick William Lyon, all paying an annual rent of £6 10s. 0d., except Shaw who occupied the accommodation rent free in return for opening and closing the gates for all trains. James W. Wright replaced Titmarsh from 14th November, 1914. A former porter-signalman at Bluntisham, Frank Ernest Caldecoat, who had recently transferred to Fletton Road Junction signal box was killed in action on 20th July, 1918 aged 23 years. After the station masters at the intermediate stations on the branch were withdrawn in the early 1920s the station houses were occupied by traffic staff. In 1924 Bluntisham house was occupied by Joseph Harrup, goods porter, who paid a rent of £16 0s. 8d. per annum, whilst at Earith Bridge goods porter Arthur Tebbitt occupied the station house paying an annual rental of £13. In the same year the four railway cottages near Wilburton station were occupied by George Henry Skinner, clerk, John Gillett of the Civil Engineer's department, A. Shaw porter-signalman and Frederick William Lyon ganger all paying an annual rental of £9 19s. 4d. Signalman Albert O'Dell occupied the cottage at Needingworth Junction in 1924 paying an annual rental of £9 2s. 0d. T.E. Law chief goods clerk at Whittlesea started his railway career at Haddenham in May 1887 and retired on 30th September, 1933. Mr R. English porter-signalman at Haddenham died on 18th January, 1931. Mr F. Perkins, goods porter at Haddenham retired on 28th March, 1936. James Yarrow porter at Wilburton retired on 4th May, 1940. In 1924 he occupied the station house at an annual rental of £16 0s. 8d. Yarrow was replaced by Mr Marsters as porter-in-charge but owing to ill health he had to give up the position and was succeeded by T. Hills relief porter-in-charge. R. Hammett was clerk at Haddenham in the 1940s. Mr G. Gilson crossing keeper at Needingworth level crossing for 28 years retired on 29th January, 1949.

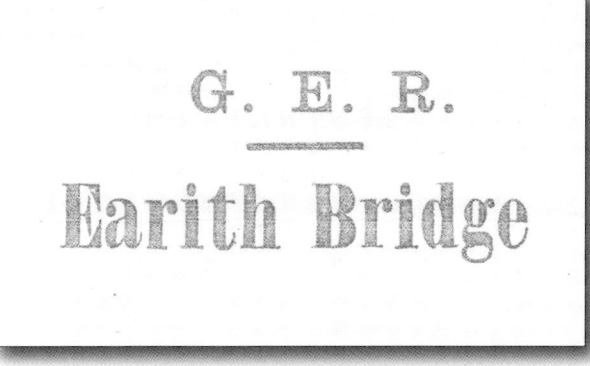

ELY, HADDENHAM, AND SUTTON BRANCH.

Single Line.

Down Trains. Week Days.

Miles from Ely.	FROM	1 Gds.	2 Parl. 1 2 3	3 Pass 1 2 3	4 A Mrkt 1 2 3	5 Pass. 1 2	6	7	8	9	10	11	12
		a.m.	a.m.	p.m.	p.m.	p.m.							
—	**Ely** ....dep	7 15	10 50	1 55	5 0	7 22	...	...	...	...	...	...	...
2¾	Stretham....................	7 25	11 0	2 5	5 10	7 31	...	...	...	...	...	...	...
4¾	Wilburton	7 35	11 8	2 13	5 18	7 38	...	...	...	...	...	...	...
6	**Haddenham**................	7 50	11 15	2 20	5 25	7 45	...	...	...	...	...	...	...
7¾	**Sutton** ....arr.	7 55	11 20	2 25	5 30	7 50	...	...	...	...	...	...	...

Goods may be worked by any of the above Trains.

A No. 4 runs on Thursdays only.

Up Trains. Week Days.

Miles from Sutton.	FROM	1 Parl 1 2 3	2 Pass. 1 2	3 A Pass. 1 2 3	4 Pass. 1 2 3	5 Gds.	6	7	8	9	10	11	12
		a.m.	p.m.	p.m.	p.m.	p.m.							
—	**Sutton** ....dep.	8 10	12 5	2 30	5 35	8 0	...	...	...	...	...	...	...
1¾	**Haddenham**................	8 17	12 12	2 37	5 42	8 10	...	...	...	...	...	...	...
3	Wilburton	8 22	12 17	2 42	5 47	8 20	...	...	...	...	...	...	...
5	Stretham....................	8 30	12 25	2 50	5 55	8 30	...	...	...	...	...	...	...
7¾	**Ely** ....arr.	8 40	12 35	3 0	6 5	8 40	...	...	...	...	...	...	...

Goods may be worked by any of the above Trains.

A No. 3 runs on Thursdays only.

The Trains on this Single Line are worked under the Train Staff and Train Ticket arrangements, as laid down in Special Order, No. 1191, of 1st April, 1866.

No Engine or Train is to be run on this Branch without a Train Staff or Train Ticket.

GER Working Timetable, October 1866.

GER Working Timetable, 1885.

ELY, SUTTON, AND ST. IVES BRANCH.—*Single Line.*

Up Trains—Week Days.

Miles from Ely.	FROM	1 A Mxd	2 B Pass.	3 C Mxd	4 B Gds.	5 D Pass.	6 E Mxd.	7 F Pass.	8 Pass.	9	10	11	12	13
		a.m.	a.m.	a.m.	a.m.	p.m.	p.m.	p.m.	p.m.					
—	**Ely** ....dep.	6 5	9 20	9 30	9 30	2 5	2 5	4 37	7 10	.....	.....	.....	.....	.....
2¼	Stretham .... ,,	6 15	9 27	9 40	*	2 11	2 14	*	7 17	...	...	...	...	...
4¼	Wilburton .... ,,	6 23	9 33	9 48	*	*	2 18	*	*	.....	.....	.....	.....	.....
6	Haddenham .... ,,	6 31	9 37	10 10	*	2 20	2 25	4 53	7 27	...	...	...	...	...
7¼	**Sutton** ....arr.	6 37	9 41	10 15	10 10	2 24	2 29	4 57	7 31	.....	.....	.....	.....	.....
	dep.	6 45	9 42	10 25	10 40	2 25	2 33	4 58	7 32	...	...	...	...	...
12¼	Earith Bridge .... ,,	6 57	9 51	10 40	*	*	2 40	5 7	7 41	.....	.....	.....	.....	.....
14¼	Bluntisham.. ....arr.	7 3	9 56	10 48	10 57	2 38	2 45	5 12	7 46	...	...	...	...	...
	dep.	7 5	9 57	10 53	11 5	2 39	2 46	5 13	7 47	.....	.....	.....	.....	.....
18	**St. Ives** ....arr.	7 15	10 5	11 5	11 15	2 47	2 55	5 21	7 55	...	...	...	...	...

A No. 1 to work Cattle and important Trucks only.
B Nos. 2 and 4 run on Mondays only.
C No. 3 does not run on Mondays.
D No. 5. Does not run on Saturdays.
E No. 6 runs on Saturdays only and conveys Passengers and Cattle only.
F No. 7 runs on Mondays and Thursdays only.

Down Trains—Week Days.

Miles from St. Ives.	FROM	1 G Pass.	2 H Eng.	3 I Pass.	4 K Pass.	5 K Pass.	6 L Gds.	7 Pass.	8 M Gds.	9	10	11	12	13
		a.m.	a.m.	a.m.	p.m.	p.m.	p.m.	p.m.	p.m.					
—	**St. Ives** ....dep.	7 30	10 15	11 30	12 47	3 0	3 55	5 30	6 50	.....	.....	.....	.....	.....
3¾	Bluntisham ....arr.	7 37	...	11 38	12 54	3 9	4 5	5 37	7 0	...	...	...	...	...
	dep.	7 38	10 23	11 39	12 55	3 11	4 15	5 38	7 5	.....	.....	.....	.....	.....
5¾	Earith Bridge .... ,,	7 43	...	11 44	1 0	3 18	4 29	5 43	*	...	...	...	...	...
10½	Sutton ....arr.	7 52	.....	11 54	1 9	3 28	4 40	5 52	7 28	.....	.....	.....	.....	.....
	dep.	7 53	10 35	11 55	1 10	3 32	5 2	5 53	7 50	...	...	...	...	...
12	Haddenham .... ,,	7 58	.....	12 1	1 15	3 40	5 17	5 58	*	.....	.....	.....	.....	.....
13¼	Wilburton .... ,,	*	...	12 5	*	3 45	5 27	*	*	...	...	...	...	...
15½	Stretham .... ,,	8 8	.....	12 11	1 25	3 52	5 37	6 8	*	.....	.....	.....	.....	.....
18	**Ely** ....arr.	8 15	10 50	12 20	1 32	4 0	5 45	6 15	8 45	...	...	...	...	...

G No. 1. Not exceeding 6 Trucks of Sheep may be worked by this Train from Haddenham on Fridays.
H No. 2 runs on Mondays only.
I No. 3 does not run on Mondays and Thursdays.
K Nos. 4 and 5 run on Mondays and Thursdays only.
L No. 6 runs from Cambridge to Peterboro'. See pages 171 and 177. Load not to exceed 20 Trucks from St. Ives.
M No. 8. To call at Jewson's Siding, near Haddenham, when required.

Chapter Seven

Timetables and Traffic

The advent of the railway in the district failed to stop the exodus of the population away from this area of the fens. The decline was gradual and reflected in the sparse train service operated between Ely and St Ives. Between 1871 and 1931 when full passenger services operated the population of Stretham declined by 19 per cent, Wilburton 14.3 per cent, Haddenham 15.6 per cent and Sutton 9.5 per cent. Even after the closure of the line to passenger traffic the decline continued although later in 1961 Wilburton showed an increase of 28.9 per cent. The population figures were:

	1861	1871	1881	1891	1901	1911	1921	1931	1951
Stretham	1,462	1,462	1,318	1,276	1,204	1,170	1,047	1,184	970
Grunty Fen	17	39	50	48	74	88	97	95	*
Wilburton	560	546	527	452	457	475	497	468	704
Haddenham	1,976	2,055	1,739	1,719	1,686	1,678	1,655	1,733	1,640
Sutton	1,731	1,717	1,525	1,433	1,420	1,531	1,476	1,553	1,499
Mepal	510	397	378	382	316	330	353	415	447
Earith	631	607	556	566	†965	†1,022	†1,006	†1,008	608
Bluntisham	720	590	529	594					587
Total	7,607	7,413	6,622	6,470	6,122	6,294	6,131	6,456	6,455

* No separate figures shown.
† Earith and Bluntisham totals combined for years 1901 to 1931.

The initial timetable for April 1866 showed three passenger trains in each direction with 30 minutes allowed for the 7¾ mile journey. The full timetable weekdays only was:

Class	1,2,3	1,2	1,2			1,2,3	1,2	1,2
	am	pm	pm			am	am	pm
Ely	dep. 10.50	1.55	7.15	Sutton	dep.	8.10	12.05	5.35
Stretham	dep. 11.00	2.05	7.25	Haddenham	dep.	8.17	12.12	5.42
Wilburton	dep. 11.08	2.13	7.33	Wilburton	dep.	8.22	12.17	5.47
Haddenham	dep. 11.15	2.20	7.40	Stretham	dep.	8.30	12.25	5.55
Sutton	arr. 11.20	2.25	7.45	Ely	arr.	8.40	12.35	6.05

An additional train ran on Thursdays only to Ely for the market, departing Sutton at 2.00 pm and returning from Ely at 5.00 pm.

By October 1866 the line was worked from Ely and the working timetable showed three passenger and one goods train in each direction, weekdays only. All passenger trains conveyed first, second, and third class passengers with the exception of the 12.05 pm Sutton to Ely and the 7.22 pm Ely to Sutton. Parliamentary fare paying passengers were conveyed by the first up train, 8.10 am ex-Sutton and the 10.05 return from Ely. 'Parliamentary' meant third class travel at 1d. per mile, which had to be provided on every line by at least one train in each direction on weekdays under the Act of 1844. An additional market train ran on Thursdays for Ely market departing Sutton at 2.30 pm and returning from Ely at 5.00 pm. Although goods trains operated across the branch departing Ely at 7.15 am and from Sutton at 8.00 pm, goods traffic could also be worked by any other services if required.

The 1870 working timetable showed the same basic service with only minor timing alterations and goods trains forming the first down service at 7.00 am ex-Ely and the last up train at 8.00 pm ex-Sutton. The 2.35 pm ex-Sutton and 4.45 pm return ex-Ely market trains ran on Thursdays only. Parliamentary fare paying passengers were conveyed on one service in each direction 8.10 am ex-Sutton and 10.45 am return from Ely. As before goods traffic could be worked by any of the passenger services.

Five years later the 1875 working timetable showed the same basic weekdays service with three passenger and one goods train in each direction, augmented by an additional passenger train each way on Thursdays only.

With the opening of the extension from Sutton to St Ives on 10th May, 1878 the following service of passenger trains ran in each direction conveying first, second and third class accommodation:

Up		*am*	*am*	*pm*	*pm*	*pm*
Ely	dep.	6.10	9.20	1.55	4.20	7.15
Stretham	dep.	6.20	9.30	*	*	*
Wilburton	dep.	6.28	9.38	*	*	*
Haddenham	dep.	6.36	9.55	2.12	4.37	7.32
Sutton	dep.	6.50	10.13	2.17	4.42	7.37
Earith Bridge	dep.	7.02	10.21	*	*	*
Bluntisham	dep.	7.10	10.38	2.32	4.57	7.52
St Ives	arr.	7.20	10.50	2.40	5.05	8.00

Down				*MThO*	
		am	*am*	*pm*	*pm*
St Ives	dep.	7.30	11.30	3.00	5.25
Bluntisham	dep.	7.38	11.39	3.11	5.34
Earith Bridge	dep.	*	11.44	3.18	5.38
Sutton	dep.	7.53	11.55	3.32	5.50
Haddenham	dep.	7.58	12.01	3.40	5.56
Wilburton	dep.	*	12.05	3.45	6.00
Stretham	dep.	*	12.11	3.52	6.06
Ely	arr.	8.15	12.20	4.00	6.15

* Calls if required. MThO Mondays & Thursdays only.

The passenger timetable for 1882 showed down trains departing St Ives at 7.30, 11.30 am MThX (Mondays & Thursdays excepted), 12.47 MThO, 3.00 MThO and 5.30 pm. The 7.30 am, 12.47 pm MThO and 5.30 pm only called at Earith Bridge, Wilburton and Stretham by request. In the up directions trains departed Ely at 6.10, 9.20 MO (Mondays only), 9.30 am MX (Mondays excepted), 2.05 MThO, 4.42 and 7.07 pm. The 9.20 am MO, 2.05 MThO, 4.42 and 7.07 pm trains only served Stretham, Wilburton and Earith Bridge by request.

The 1883 working timetable showed departures from St Ives at 7.30 Parliamentary, 10.15 MO LE (light engine), 11.50 am MThX, 12.47 MThO, 3.00 MThO, 4.00 goods, 5.30 and 6.40 pm goods. The 7.30 am train was permitted to take not exceeding six trucks of sheep from Haddenham on Fridays only, whilst the 4.00 pm goods ex-St Ives was a through working from Cambridge to

Peterborough and was limited to working 20 wagons on leaving St Ives. The 7.30 am, 12.47 pm MThO, 5.30 pm passenger trains and the 6.40 pm goods working only called at Earith Bridge, Wilburton and Stretham if required, the latter also serving Haddenham under the same conditions. Up trains departed from Ely at 6.05 mixed, 9.20 MO Parliamentary, 9.30 MX Parliamentary, 9.30 am MO goods, 2.05, 4.37 MThO and 7.10 pm. The 6.05 am mixed train was restricted to working cattle and important truck load traffic, whilst the 2.05 pm passenger train on Saturdays could work not exceeding six trucks of cattle from Ely to St Ives. The 9.20 am MO, 9.30 am MO goods, 2.05 pm, 4.37 pm MThO and 7.10 pm services called at Stretham, Wilburton and Earith Bridge only if required. In addition to the arrangements for specific trains, not more than four trucks of cattle could be worked by any passenger train on the branch except the 7.30 am from St Ives. The 1885 timetable is on page 114.

By 1886 the up service consisted of four passenger trains daily with an additional train on Mondays and Thursdays for St Ives and Ely markets. Trains departed Ely at 6.05, 9.20 MO, 9.30 am MX, 2.05 SX calling at Wilburton and Earith Bridge by request, 2.05 SO calling all stations, 4.37 pm MThO and 7.10 pm. In the down direction four trains ran weekdays only departing St Ives at 7.30, 11.30 am MThX, 12.47 MThO calling at Wilburton by request, 3.00 and 5.30 pm. Journey times for the 17 mile 55 chains journey varied from 44 to 60 minutes. The timetable for 1889 was very similar.

The working timetable for 1890 showed the following down trains from St Ives: 5.15 ECS (empty coaching stock) MO, 7.30 passenger, 11.30 am MThX passenger, 12.47 MThO passenger, 3.00 MThO passenger, 5.30 passenger and 6.35 pm goods. The 7.30 am could convey not exceeding six trucks of sheep from Haddenham on Fridays, whilst the 3.00 pm MThO on Mondays could work not exceeding 12 trucks of cattle from St Ives to Ely. A truck of milch cows destined for Gravesend could be attached to the 5.30 pm train at Bluntisham, whilst the 6.35 pm goods train called at Earith Bridge and Jewson's siding between Sutton and Haddenham, only when required. The 7.30 am MThO and 5.30 pm passenger trains only called at Wilburton when required. In the up direction trains departed Ely at 6.05 MO passenger, 9.20 passenger, 9.40 am goods, 2.05 SX (Saturdays excepted) passenger, 2.05 SO (Saturdays only) mixed, 4.37 MThO passenger and 7.10 pm passenger. The 6.05 am MO also worked cattle traffic, whilst the 9.40 am ex-Ely goods train departed Sutton at 11.20 am MThO and 12.00 noon MThX. The 2.05 pm SX passenger service only called at Wilburton and Earith Bridge if required, whilst the 2.05 pm SO mixed train conveyed passengers and cattle traffic only. The 4.37 pm ex-Ely called at Stretham and Wilburton only if required, whilst the 7.10 pm passenger, a through train to Godmanchester, also only called at Wilburton if required. As a general rule not more than four trucks of cattle could be worked by any passenger train from Ely to St Ives, except by the 7.10 pm, which was permitted to take six wagons on Wednesdays. A similar number of cattle trucks could be conveyed by passenger trains in the down direction, with the exception of the 7.30 am ex-St Ives.

In 1894 the passenger service on the branch had been reduced to three trains in each direction with an additional train each way on Mondays and Thursdays. Departures from Ely were 9.25 am, 2.05 calling at Wilburton and Earith Bridge by request, 4.05 MThO calling at Stretham and Wilburton by request and 7.10 pm. Down services departed St Ives at 7.30 calling at Wilburton if required, 11.30 am MThX, 12.47 MThO, 3.15 MThO and 5.30 pm. Journey times were now more uniform and varied between 42 and 45 minutes. The following year only minor adjustments were made (*overleaf*).

ELY, SUTTON, AND ST. IVES RAILWAY
Junction with Main Line at Ely, and with Loop Line at St. Ives.

WEEK DAYS.

			morn	noon	even.	even.					
48, 49	LONDON {	Liverpool St. dep.	5 45	11 55	2 30	5 15	...	...	...	...	...
		St. Pancras— „	—	12 5	2 35	5 8	...	...	...	...	...
	Cambridge .... „		8 16	1 30	4 6	6 40	...	...	...	...	...
	Ely — — — — arr.		8 42	1 51	4 28	7 1	...	...	...	...	...
51, 52	Norwich (Thorpe) .... dep.		7 35	11 8	2 12	5 0	...	...	...	...	...
	Wymondham — — — „		7 57	11 34	2 39	5 22	...	—	—	—	—
	Ely .... arr.		9 6	12 46	4 5	6 26	...	—	—	—	—
	ELY — — — — dep.		9 25	2 5	4 37	7 19	...	—	—	—	—
	Stretham		9 32	2 11	*	7 16	...	—	—	—	—
	Wilburton — — —		9 38	*	*	*	...	—	—	—	—
	Haddenham		9 42	2 20	4 52	7 25	...	—	—	—	—
	Sutton— — — — —		9 47	2 25	4 57	7 30	...	—	—	—	—
	Earith Bridge		9 56	*	5 6	7 39	...	—	—	—	—
	Bluntisham — — —		10 2	2 39	5 12	7 45	...	—	—	—	—
	ST. IVES .... arr.		10 10	2 47	5 20	7 53	...	—	—	—	—
62	St. Ives — — — — dep.	Mondays only	10 46 11 26	3 35	7 25	—	...	—	—	—	—
	March .... arr.		11 22 12 6	4 11	8 1	—	...	—	—	—	—
	St. Ives — — — — dep	Mondays only	10 15 11 54	2 52 4 3	6 31 8 0	—	...	—	—	—	—
	Godmanchester .... arr.		10 27 12 3	3 1 4 15	6 43 8 10	—	...	—	—	—	—
	Kettering — — — „		1 10	4 13 6 45	—	—	...	—	—	—	—
	Leicester .... „		2 7	5 32 8 12	—	—	...	—	—	—	—
63	St. Ives — — — — dep.		12 13	4 0	6 6 8 20	—	...	—	—	—	—
51, 52	Cambridge .... arr.		12 50	4 30	6 46 8 55	—	...	—	—	—	—
	LONDON { St. Pancras— „		2 63	6 13	8 35 —	—	...	—	—	—	—
	Liverpool St. „		2 50	6 8	8 25 11 3	—	...	—	—	—	—

WEEK DAYS.

			morn	morn	morn	noon		even.				
48, 49	LONDON {	Liverpool St. dep.	...	9 10	...	11 55		2 30	...	...	...	...
62		St. Pancras— „	...	9 15	—	12 5		2 35	...	...	...	...
	Cambridge .... „		...	10 50	—	1 35		4 10	...	...	...	...
	St. Ives — — — — arr.		...	11 24	—	2 8		4 43	...	...	...	...
	Leicester .... dep.			7K2	9 47	—	Mons. only	12 50	...	...	...	...
	Kettering — — — „			8 35	10 55	—		2 5	...	...	...	...
63	Godmanchester .... „		6J55	9 49	12 0	—		4 28	...	...	...	...
	St. Ives — — — — arr.	Not Mondays or Thursdays.	7J7	10 0	12 11	—		4 39	...	...	...	...
	March .... dep.		...	—	12 5	—		3 25	...	...	...	...
	St. Ives .... arr.		...	—	12 41	—		3 58	...	...	...	...
	ST. IVES .... dep.		7 30	11 30	12 47	3 15	Mondays and Thursdays only	5 27	...	...	...	...
	Bluntisham — — — —		7 38	11 38	12 55	3 23		5 35	...	...	...	...
	Earith Bridge		7 43	11 43	1 0	3 28		5 40	...	...	...	...
	Sutton— — — — —		7 53	11 53	1 10	3 38		5 50	...	...	...	...
	Haddenham		7 58	11 58	1 15	3 43		5 55	...	...	...	...
	Wilburton — — —		*	12 4	*	3 4		*	...	...	...	...
	Stretham		8 8	12 8	1 25	3 53		6 5	...	...	...	...
	ELY — — — — arr.		8 15	12 15	1 32	4 0		6 12	...	...	...	...
48, 49	Ely — — — — dep.		8 47	—	1 58	4 40	Mondays & Thursdays only	7 9	...	...	...	...
	Wymondham — — arr.		10 15	—	3 35	6 19		8 30	...	...	...	...
	Norwich (Thorpe) .... „		10 35	—	3 10	6 5		8 50	...	...	...	...
51, 52	Ely — — — — dep.		8 23	12 55	1 38	4 13		6 35	...	...	...	...
	Cambridge .... arr.		9 46	1 16	4 35			8 35	...	...	...	...
	LONDON { St. Pancras— „		10 22	2 53	4 7	6 12		8 35	...	...	...	...
	Liverpool St. „		10 13	2 50	3 58	6 8		8 25	...	...	...	...

* Will call when required to take up or set down Passengers. Passengers wishing to alight at these Stations must intimate the same to the Guard at the preceding *stopping* Station.

J From Godmanchester to St. Ives on Mondays only.

K On Wednesdays leaves Leicester at 7.30 a.m.

GER public timetable 1895.

TIMETABLES AND TRAFFIC   119

The working timetable for 1897 showed trains departing St Ives at 7.30 passenger, 7.40 MO LE, 11.30 am MThX passenger, 12.47 MThO passenger, 3.15 MThO passenger, 3.50 express cattle, 4.20 MO express cattle, 5.27 passenger and 6.15 pm goods. The 7.30 am, 12.47 pm MThO and 5.27 pm passenger trains called at Wilburton only when required, whilst the 7.40 am MO LE was permitted to work cattle traffic when necessary. The 3.50 pm express cattle from St Ives was a through train from Spitalfields via Cambridge, St Ives and Ely to Peterborough and the load was limited to 20 trucks leaving St Ives. On Mondays this train shunted at Sutton to allow the 4.20 pm MO ex-St Ives express cattle train to pass. The 4.20 pm MO express cattle train was itself a through working from Cambridge, depart 3.25 pm, to Norwich via the branch and called at Bluntisham and Sutton only. It was also permitted to leave cattle traffic at Haddenham. The 6.15 pm goods train (4.00 pm ex-Ramsey High Street) called at Earith Bridge and Jewson's siding only if required. In the up direction trains departed Ely at 6.00 MO goods, 9.25 passenger, 10.45 am goods, 2.05 passenger, 4.37 MThO passenger and 7.10 pm passenger. A carriage was attached to the 6.00 am goods train for the use of drovers, whilst the 10.45 am goods was a through train via St Ives to Ramsey High Street. The 2.05 pm passenger train only called at Wilburton and Earith Bridge if required, and on Thursdays and Saturdays was permitted to work cattle traffic from Ely to St Ives only, provided the trucks were fitted with Westinghouse brake pipes (this stipulation regarding brake pipes applies to all further references in this chapter to passenger trains conveying cattle traffic). The 4.37 pm passenger train only called at Stretham and Wilburton if required, whilst the 7.10 pm ex Ely was a thorough train to Godmanchester calling at Wilburton only if required.

The passenger timetable for 1905 showed the following services:

Down			MThX	MThO	MThO	
		am	am	pm	pm	pm
St Ives	dep.	7.30	11.35	12.50	3.15	5.18
Bluntisham	dep.	7.38	11.43	12.58	3.23	5.26
Earith Bridge	dep.	7.43	11.48	1.03	3.28	5.31
Sutton	dep.	7.53	11.58	1.13	3.38	5.40
Haddenham	dep.	7.58	12.03	1.18	3.43	5.45
Wilburton	dep.	*	12.07	1.22	3.47	*
Stretham	dep.	8.08	12.13	1.28	3.53	5.54
Ely	arr.	8.15	12.20	1.35	4.00	6.00

Up				MThO		
		am	pm	pm	pm	
Ely	dep.	9.25	2.10	4.17	7.15	
Stretham	dep.	9.32	2.16	4.23	7.21	
Wilburton	dep.	9.38	2.21	4.28	*	
Haddenham	dep.	9.42	2.25	4.32	7.30	
Sutton	dep.	9.47	2.30	4.37	7.35	
Earith Bridge	dep.	9.56	2.39	4.46	7.44	
Bluntisham	dep.	10.02	2.45	4.52	7.50	
St Ives	arr.	10.10	2.53	5.00	7.58	

* Calls if required.

In 1907 the working timetable showed four passenger MThO, three passenger MThX and one goods train in the up direction on weekdays only, with an additional express cattle train on Mondays only. The latter departed Ely at 6.00 am and omitting calls at Wilburton and Earith Bridge arrived at St Ives at 7.15 am. A carriage was attached to this train for the use of drovers. The 10.30 am goods train ex-Ely ran through to Ramsey High Street, with reversal at St Ives, whilst the 2.15 pm ex-Ely passenger train on Thursdays and Saturdays was permitted to work cattle traffic from Ely to St Ives only. The final down passenger train of the day 7.10 pm ex-Ely was a through train to Godmanchester. In the down direction the timetable showed four passenger MThO, three passenger MThX, one light engine MO, one express fruit, one express cattle MO and one goods train. The 7.40 am light engine returning from St Ives to Ely after working the up express cattle train, was permitted to take cattle wagons if required, whilst the 11.35 am MThX passenger train ex-St Ives was balanced by the 12.50 pm ex-St Ives MThO. The 3.15 pm passenger train ex-St Ives ran MThO, whilst the last passenger train of the day departed St Ives at the relatively early time of 5.18 pm. The express fruit train, 3.25 pm ex-St Ives only ran in the fruit picking season and starting from Cambridge at 2.25 pm was a through working to Peterborough. The loading of the train, which called at all stations on the branch except Earith Bridge, where the call was only if required, was limited to 20 wagons on leaving Bluntisham and was worked by two guards between Bluntisham and Ely. The express cattle train departing St Ives at 5.22 pm MO was a through train to Norwich and called only at Bluntisham and Sutton and then Haddenham and Stretham to leave cattle only. The final down working of the day was the 3.25 pm goods train from Ramsey High Street, which departed St Ives at 6.15 pm calling all stations except for Earith Bridge where the call was only if required.

The working timetable for 1908 showed the following up services departing from Ely at 6.00 express cattle MO, 9.35, 10.30 am goods to Ramsey High Street, 2.15 , 2.18 goods to Peterborough via Chatteris, 4.19 MThO and 7.10 pm passenger to Godmanchester. The 6.00 am cattle ran as a class 'B' train as it conveyed a passenger carriage for the use of drovers, whilst the 2.15 pm passenger train on Thursdays and Saturdays was permitted to work cattle traffic from Ely to St Ives. This train also conveyed a carriage truck to work fruit traffic for the north from the branch stations. The 2.18 pm goods train was a through working from Cambridge SX departing at 11.25 am. Down services departed St Ives at 7.30 , 7.40 LE MO, 11.35 am MThX, 12.50 MThO, 3.15 MThO, 5.23, 5.27 express cattle to Norwich MO and 6.15 pm goods train from Ramsey High Street. The light engine was allowed to work through cattle traffic when required whilst the 5.27 pm express cattle ran as a class 'B' train as it conveyed a carriage for the use of drovers. This train called at Haddenham and Sutton to leave cattle only.

The passenger timetable for 1910 continued to show three trains MThX and four trains MThO in each direction. Down trains departed St Ives at 7.30, 11.35 am MThX, 12.50 MThO, 3.15 MThO and 5.23 pm,whilst up services departed Ely at 9.25 am, 2.15 , 4.19 MThO and 7.10 pm. All trains called at all stations and were allowed 43 to 45 minutes for the journey.

The 1913 working timetable showed the following down services from St Ives: 7.30 passenger, 7.40 MO LE, 11.35 am MThX passenger, 12.53 MThO passenger, 3.15 MThO passenger, 5.18 passenger and 6.15 pm goods. The MO light engine was permitted to work cattle traffic if necessary, whilst the 6.15 pm goods, a through working from Ramsey High Street, depart 3.25 pm, could work brake goods and detached trucks only between Sutton and Ely. In the up direction trains departed Ely at 6.00 MO express cattle, 9.25 passenger, 10.30 am goods, 2.12 passenger, 2.18 SX goods, 4.19 MThO and 7.10 pm. The 6.10 am express cattle train conveyed a passenger carriage for the use of drovers. The 10.30 am goods train ran through to Ramsey High Street via St Ives, whilst the 2.12 pm passenger train on Thursdays and Saturdays was permitted to work cattle from Ely to St Ives. A carriage truck was also attached to this train to work fruit for the north from stations between Ely and St Ives. The 2.18 pm SX goods was a through train from Cambridge, depart 12.40 pm, to Peterborough via St Ives and March. Fruit and important traffic for destinations via the GN&GE Joint line arriving at St Ives on this train, was to be sent forward from St Ives by the 3.40 pm express fruit train from Cambridge to Whitemoor. The 7.10 pm passenger service on Thursdays and Saturdays could work cattle from Ely to St Ives.

By 1916 the up services ex-Ely were 6.00 am express cattle MO, which continued to convey a carriage for the use of drovers. Other departures were 9.46, 10.20 am goods through to Warboys, 12.40 pm MThX, 1.55 MThO, 4.25 through train to Huntingdon East, 6.08 goods to Sutton and 6.43 pm passenger through to Cambridge via St Ives. The 4.25 pm permitted to work one wagon of cattle from Ely to St Ives and also conveyed a carriage truck for fruit traffic from the branch stations for destinations in the north. The 6.43 pm to Cambridge was also allowed to work cattle between Ely and St Ives on Thursdays and Saturdays only. Trains departed St Ives at 7.38, 7.50 LE MO, 11.11 am MThX, 12.51 MThO, 3.22, 5.15 pm (3.44 pm ex-Huntingdon), 6.20 goods ex-Warboys and 7.15 pm goods Sutton to Ely. The light engine was allowed to work cattle traffic when necessary whilst the 6.20 pm goods called at stations Sutton to Stretham to detach wagons and pick up brake goods only.

After World War I the timetable for 1921 showed a reduced overall service with departures from Ely at 6.00 MO express cattle, 9.45, 10.20 am goods ex-March returning to Whitemoor via St Ives, 12.40 MThX, 2.18 MThO, 4.38 through passenger train to Huntingdon and 6.47 pm through train to Cambridge. On Thursdays and Saturdays the later train was permitted to work cattle between Ely and St Ives. Down services departed St Ives at 7.33 (a through train from Cambridge), 11.11 am MThO, 12.51 MThX, 3.22, 5.25 (through passenger train from Huntingdon), and 5.45 pm goods (through train from March).

The passenger timetable operated by the LNER in 1923 showed the following service of four trains in each direction.

				MThX	ThO	MO	
		am	am	pm	pm	pm	pm
St Ives	dep.	7.25	11.11	12.20	12.45	3.15	5.23
Bluntisham	dep.	7.33	11.19	12.28	12.53	3.23	5.31
Earith Bridge	dep.	7.39	11.24	12.33	12.58	3.28	5.36
Sutton	dep.	7.52	11.33	12.42	1.07	3.37	5.47
Haddenham	dep.	8.00	11.38	12.47	1.12	3.43	5.52
Wilburton	dep.	8.05	11.42	12.51	1.16	3.47	5.56
Stretham	dep.	8.12	11.48	12.57	1.22	3.53	6.02
Ely	arr.	8.21	11.54	1.03	1.28	3.59	6.11

				MThX	MThO	
		am	pm	pm	pm	pm
Ely	dep.	10.04	12.35	2.31	4.44	6.49
Stretham	dep.	10.11	12.42	2.38	4.51	6.56
Wilburton	dep.	10.16	12.47	2.43	4.56	7.01
Haddenham	dep.	10.20	12.51	2.47	5.00	7.05
Sutton	dep.	10.25	12.56	2.52	5.05	7.11
Earith Bridge	dep.	10.34	1.05	3.01	5.14	7.20
Bluntisham	dep.	10.40	1.11	3.07	5.20	7.26
St Ives	arr.	10.48	1.19	3.15	5.28	7.34

ELY, SUTTON AND ST. IVES.

See page			morn		morn		**WEEK DAYS.**		noon		even.			even.
35, 36	LONDON { L'pool St. dep. St. Pancras ,,		5 53	—	10 5	—	...	...	12 0	...	—	2 35	—	—	4 50
	Cambridge — — — ,,		8 12	—	11 41	—			1 25		—	4 8	—	—	6 12
	Ely .... arr.		8 36	...	12 5	...			1 44		...	4 22	...	...	6 31
38, 39	Norwich (Thorpe) — — dep.		7 25	...	10 30	...			10 30		...	1 55	...	...	5 9
	Ely .... arr.		9 23	...	12 19	...			12 19		...	3 18	...	...	6 37
	ELY — — — — — dep.		9 46	—	12 40	—			2 15		—	4 38	—	—	6 47
	Stretham .... ,,		9 52	...	12 46	...			2 24		...	4 44	...	...	6 53
	Wilburton — — — — ,,		9 57	...	12 51	...			2 29		—	4 49	...	...	6 58
	Haddenham .... ,,		10 1	...	12 55	...			2 33		...	4 53	...	...	7 2
	Sutton — — — — — ,,		10 6	...	1 0	...	Not Mondays and Thursdays.		2 38	Mondays and Thursdays only.	...	4 58	...	...	7 8
	Earith Bridge .... ,,		10 15	...	1 9	...			2 47		...	5 7	...	...	7 17
	Bluntisham — — — — ,,		10 21	...	1 15	...			2 53		—	5 13	...	...	7 23
	ST. IVES .... arr.		10 29	...	1 23	...			3 1		...	5 21	...	...	7 31
50	St. Ives — — — — dep.		10 57	...	2 3	...			3 40		...	—	...	—	7 52
	March .... arr.		11 33	...	2 39	...			4 16		...	—	...	—	8 28
51	St. Ives — — — — dep.		11 6	...	2 8	...			3 55		...	5 28	...	—	7 56
	Godmanchester .... arr.		11 16	...	2 18	...			4 5		...	5 38	...	—	8 6
50	St. Ives — — — — dep.		11 5	—	1 40	—			3 52		—	6 9	—	—	7 34
	Cambridge — — — arr.		11 38	...	2 13	...			4 25		...	6 45	...	...	8 7
	LONDON { St. Pancras ,, L'pool St.		2 7	...	5 2	...			6 10		...	8 20	...	...	10 45

B On Thursdays leaves St. Ives 4.53 and arrives March 5.23 p.m.

See page				morn		morn		**WEEK DAYS.**		morn		noon		even.	
50	LONDON { L'pool St. dep. St. Pancras ,,			—	—	8 35	—	...	...	8 35	...	12 0	—	2 35	—
	Cambridge — — — ,,			6 50	...	10 25	...			11 30		...	1 31	...	4 55	...
	St. Ives .... arr.			7 21	...	10 55	...			11 52		...	2 1	...	5 16	...
51	Godmanchester — — dep.			7 8	...	10 41	...			12 3		...	2 50	...	4 27	...
	St. Ives .... arr.			7 17	...	10 50	...			12 12		...	2 59	...	4 36	...
50	March — — — — dep.			—	—	10 27	...			10 27		...	1 0	...	3 14	—
	St. Ives .... arr.			—	—	11 2	...			11 2		...	1 36	...	3 49	—
	ST. IVES — — — — dep.			7 38	...	11 11	...	Not Mondays and Thursdays.		12 51	Mondays and Thursdays only.	...	3 22	...	5 25	—
	Bluntisham .... ,,			7 46	...	11 19	...			12 59		...	3 30	...	5 33	...
	Earith Bridge — — — ,,			7 51	...	11 24	...			1 4		...	3 35	...	5 38	...
	Sutton — — — — — ,,			8 0	...	11 33	...			1 13		...	3 44	...	5 49	...
	Haddenham — — — — ,,			8 5	...	11 38	...			1 18		...	3 49	...	5 54	...
	Wilburton .... ,,			8 9	...	11 42	...			1 22		...	3 53	...	5 58	...
	Stretham — — — — ,,			8 15	...	11 48	...			1 28		...	3 59	...	6 4	...
	ELY .... arr.			8 21	...	11 54	...			1 34		...	4 5	...	6 10	...
35, 36	Ely — — — — — dep.			8 43	...	1 53	...			1 53		...	4 30	...	7 45	—
	Norwich (Thorpe) .... arr.			10 30	...	3 34	...			3 34		...	6 3	...	9 30	...
38, 39	Ely — — — — — dep.			8 41	...	12 30	...			1 42		...	4 17	...	6 28	...
	Cambridge .... arr.			9 0	...	12 51	...			2 6		...	4 37	...	6 48	...
	LONDON { St. Pancras ,, L'pool St.			10 23	...	2 21	...			5 2		...	6 10	...	8 20	...

GER Public Timetable, 1919.

By now tickets from Stretham, Wilburton, Earith Bridge and Bluntisham stations were issued by the conductor-guard on the train.

The miners' strike of 1926 forced the LNER to make economies to conserve fuel supplies. The already meagre branch passenger service was further reduced on and from 31st May, 1926 and only two mixed trains ran in each direction departing Ely at 7.17 am and 3.15 pm and returning from St Ives at 9.45 am and 4.38 pm.

The 1927 working timetable showed a weekdays-only service of four passenger trains MThO, three passenger trains MThX and one goods train in the down direction. The initial train, the 7.17 am ex-St Ives, was a through working from Cambridge departing the university city at 6.40 am and was allowed four extra minutes between Sutton Branch Junction and Ely for recovery of time lost by exceptional circumstances. The ThO passenger train departed St Ives at 12.15 pm and the MO train 30 minutes later at 12.45 pm. The final passenger train of the day, 5.23 pm ex-St Ives, was a through train from Huntington East departing 4.24 pm and arriving at St Ives 12 minutes later. This train was allowed three extra minutes between Sutton Branch Junction and Ely for recovery of time lost by exceptional circumstances. The branch goods service departed at 3.30 pm SO with a 3 hour 25 minutes timing to Ely calling all stations and shunting at Sutton for both up and down passenger trains to pass. The SX goods service departed St Ives at 6.15 pm with a 2 hours 30 minutes timing to Ely and only served Earith Bridge, Haddenham, Wilburton and Stretham if required. This train also shunted at Sutton for the 6.49 pm Ely to St Ives and Cambridge passenger train to pass. On both goods services traffic was to be marshalled to arrive at Ely, with engine, down road traffic, up road traffic, road wagons and brake van. In the up direction the service consisted of four passenger trains MThO and three passenger trains MThX. The 4.38 pm ex-Ely was a through working to Huntingdon East, whilst the 6.49 pm from Ely was a through train to Cambridge. This latter train on Thursdays and Saturdays was permitted to work cattle traffic from Ely to St Ives if the trucks were fitted with brake pipes. Of the good services, 7.05 am MO ex-Ely worked cattle from all stations between Ely and St Ives for the market, but omitted calling at Earith Bridge and called at Bluntisham only if required. A carriage was attached to this train for the use of the drovers. The weekdays-only goods service departed Ely at 10.20 am, worked by Ely enginemen and guard, who returned with the down goods workings 3.30 pm SO and 6.15 pm SX ex-St Ives. This train was permitted an additional 35 minutes running time to St Ives on Thursdays only.

By 1928 the LNER working timetable showed the following trains in the up direction departing from Ely. The express cattle no longer ran but was replaced by a goods train departing at 7.05 am MO, although this continued to convey a carriage for drovers. Other departures from the cathedral city were 9.45, 10.20 am goods, 2.00 MThO, 4.38 passenger to Huntingdon East and 6.49 pm through passenger train to Cambridge via St Ives. The latter train was permitted to work cattle traffic. Ely enginemen and guard worked the 10.20 am goods train by this time. The first down train continued as a through service from Cambridge and departed from St Ives at 7.17 am. Other departures from the Huntingdonshire town were 12.15 ThO, 12.45 MO, 3.10 pm, 3.30 SO goods, 5.26 through train from Huntingdon East and 6.10 pm SX goods.

The final passenger timetable in 1931 was evidence of the decline of traffic with three trains in each direction with an additional working on Mondays and Thursdays only. Departures from Ely were at 9.45 am, 2.00 pm MThO, 4.38 and 6.49 pm whilst down services departed St Ives at 7.19 am, 12.15 ThO, 12.45 MO, 3.10 and 5.23 pm. Timings were extended and varied between 43 and 58 minutes.

ELY AND ST. IVES.

Single Line between Ely Dock Jc. and Needingworth Jc.
Parcels & Miscellaneous traffic & live stock at passenger train rates will also be conveyed by goods service.

Miles from St. Ives	DOWN WEEK DAYS.		1	2 Milk Pcls.	3	4 Gds.	5	6 Gds. Q	7	8	9	10
M. C.				a.m.		p.m.		p.m.				
—	St. Ives	dep.	—	7 18	—	4 10	—	—	—	—	—	—
1 71	Needingworth Junc. Ⓢ	,,	—	7 21	....	4 15	—	—	—	—	—	—
3 62	Bluntisham	arr. dep.	....	7 25 7 26	—	4 23 4 35	— —	— —	— —	— —	— —	— —
5 60	Earith Bridge	arr. dep.	....	7 30 7 32	--	4 40 4 50	— —	— —	— —	— —	— —	— —
10 16	Sutton Ⓢ	arr. dep.	....	7 40 7 45	—	5 0 5 15	—	— 6 10	— —	— —	— —	— —
11 71	Haddenham (Cambs.)	arr. dep.	....	7 48 7 50	—	5 22 5 25	—	6 20 6 55	— —	— —	— —	— —
12 79	Wilburton	arr. dep.	....	7 52 7 54	—	5 28 5 32	— —	— —	— —	— —	— —	— —
14 74	Stretham	arr. dep.	....	7 58 8 0	—	5 37 5 40	— —	— —	— —	— —	— —	— —
17 19	Ely Dock Junc. Ⓢ	,,	—	8 5	....	5 46	—	7 13	—	—	—	—
17 55	Ely	arr.	—	8 6	....	5 48	—	7 15	—	—	—	—

−2 From Cambridge at 6.42 a.m. (See page A 47.)
4 Formation leaving Sutton :—Engine, passenger van or vehicles, 3 goods road vans, brake.

Miles from Ely	UP WEEK DAYS.		1 Q Gds.	2 Q Gds. M O a.m.	3	4 Gds. a.m.	5	6 Gds. Q p.m.	7	8	9	10
M. C.												
—	Ely	dep.	—	7 5	—	9 30	....	4 0	—	—	—	—
0 36	Ely Dock Junc. Ⓢ	,,	—	7 7	—	9 32	....	4 2	—	—	—	—
2 61	Stretham	,,	....	7 20	—	9 45	—	4 25	—	—	—	—
4 56	Wilburton	,,	—	—	—	10 5	—	4 50	—	—	—	—
5 64	Haddenham (Cambs.)	arr. dep.	.... —	7 30 —	— —	10 10 10 25	.... —	4 55 5 7	— —	— —	— —	— —
7 39	Sutton Ⓢ	arr. dep.	.... —	7 41 7 50	— —	10 32 11 25	.... —	5 14 —	— —	— —	— —	— —
11 55	Earith Bridge	,,	—	—	—	11 49	—	—	—	—	—	—
13 53	Bluntisham	arr. dep.	....	* 8 10	—	11 55 12 28	—	—	—	—	—	—
15 64	Needingworth Junc. Ⓢ	,,	—	8 15	—	12 35	—	—	—	—	—	—
17 55	St. Ives	arr.	—	8 20	—	12 40	—	—	—	—	—	—

2 A carriage to be attached for use of drovers. To work cattle from stations between Ely and St. Ives.
4 Eng. to be used at St. Ives as required.
6 Stretham arr. 4.10, Wilburton arr. 4.35 p.m.

Above: LNER working Timetable 1939.

Right: LNER working timetable 1945 showing the weekdays only milk and parcels train.

ST. IVES AND ELY

Single line between Needingworth Junc. and Ely Dock Junc.

Miles from St. Ives	DOWN WEEK DAYS		1 Milk Pcls.	2	3
M. C.			a.m.		
—	St. Ives	dep.	7 21	—	....
1 71	Needingworth Junc. Ⓢ	,,	7 24	—	....
3 62	Bluntisham	arr. dep.	7 28 7 29	— —	....
5 60	Earith Bridge	arr. dep.	7 33 7 35	— —	....
10 16	Sutton Ⓢ	arr. dep.	7 43 7 49	— —	....
11 71	Haddenham (Cambs.)	arr. dep.	7 51 7 53	— —	....
12 79	Wilburton	arr. dep.	7 55 7 57	— —	....
14 74	Stretham	arr. dep.	8 1 8 3	— —	....
17 19	Ely Dock Junc. Ⓢ	,,	8 8	—	....
17 55	Ely	arr.	8 9	—	....

Parcels and Miscellaneous traffic and live stock at passenger train rates will also be conveyed by Goods Service.

After the withdrawal of passenger services two goods trains continued to serve the branch in each direction and by 1937 the freight service consisted of departures from St Ives at 7.18 am milk and parcels train (a through train from Cambridge departing at 6.42 am) and 4.10 pm goods, both calling at all stations on the branch. In the up direction trains departed Ely at 7.05 am MO and this train continued to convey a passenger carriage attached for the use of drovers, and 9.30 am goods train calling all stations on the branch. In addition, a short working from Ely to Sutton and return ran if required departing Ely at 4.00 pm calling all stations and returning from Sutton at 6.10 pm calling at Haddenham only. By 1939 the 7.05 am only ran if required whilst the other timings were unaltered.

During World War II several extra goods trains ran as required to serve various military establishments and in addition a number of services from the London Midland and Scottish Railway Midland section to East Anglia were diverted at short notice across the branch, worked as far as Ely by Kettering engine and men with LNER pilotmen. By 1944 the branch was served by one goods train in each direction, departing Ely at 9.33 am MO and 10.15 am MX and calling at all station yards with respective arrivals at St Ives at 12.40 pm MO and 1.25 pm MX. After arrival the engine was used as required for shunting the yard until returning with the 4.10 pm goods to Ely, calling at all stations, with arrival at the cathedral city at 6.15 pm. The additional 4.00 pm trip working from Ely to Sutton and the 6.10 pm return workings were suspended.

The 1946 working timetable showed the milk and parcels train departing from St Ives at 7.21 am making stops at Bluntisham and Sutton, with conditional stops at the other stations and arriving at Ely at 8.09 am. The return working was a goods train departing Ely at 9.30 am MO and 10.15 am MX and calling at all stations and arriving at St Ives at 12.40 pm MO and 1.25 pm MX. The engine was then used as required to shunt the St Ives yard before returning with the 4.10 pm goods train to Ely, arriving at 6.15 pm. The short working to Sutton had been reinstated with an engine and brake van departed Ely at 2.00 pm arriving at Sutton at 2.20 pm and returning with a goods train departing at 3.30 pm. The train called at the intermediate stations and arrived at Ely at 4.40 pm.

By 1947 the line between Earith Bridge and Sutton was temporarily closed and western end of the branch was served by a weekdays-only goods train departing St Ives at 7.45 am, arriving at Earith Bridge at 8.15 and returning at 8.36 am, with arrival at St Ives at 9.15 am. A second service, worked by the St Ives shunting engine, ran only if required departing St Ives at 4.15 and arriving at Earith Bridge at 5.23 pm, the return service running as required with no specific times quoted. Calls were made at Bluntisham in each direction. The eastern end of the branch was served by only one service, weekdays only, departing Ely at 10.15 with arrival at Sutton at 11.17 am and returning at 3.30 as a through train to Whitemoor yard, with arrival at Ely at 4.40 pm. This train conveyed important goods for Peterborough and destinations via the GN&GE Joint line. The intermediate stations were served in each direction.

By 1949 when the section from Sutton to Earith Bridge was again open the branch was served by a class 'D' goods departing Ely at 10.30 am, which called at all yards on the branch except for Earith Bridge before arriving at St Ives at 1.40 pm. On Saturdays the train departed Bluntisham 10 minutes earlier at 1.18 arriving at St Ives at 1.30 pm. In the down direction the class 'D' train departed St Ives at 4.05 pm SO and 4.10 pm SX calling at all station yards and arriving at Ely at 6.15 pm. An additional service ran SX to Sutton when an engine and brake van departed Ely at 2.00 pm, arriving Sutton at 2.20 pm and returned at 3.30 pm with goods train, calling at all stations and arriving at Ely at 4.40 pm.

The running times allowed for freight trains along the branch after World War II were:

Class	St Ives to Ely		Ely to St Ives	
	F	HJK	F	HJK
	mins	mins	mins	mins
St Ives to Bluntisham	10 (8)	13 (11)	9 (7)	11 (10)
Bluntisham to Earith Bridge	3	4	4	5
Earith Bridge to Sutton	8	11	8	12
Sutton to Haddenham	3	4	2	3
Haddenham to Wilburton	2	2	2	3
Wilburton to Stretham	3	4	4	5
Stretham to Ely	8 (6)	10 (8)	9 (7)	11 (9)

Amended times in brackets; two minutes additional starting and stopping allowance allowed on each section of line.

The June 1950 working timetable showed only one goods train in each direction across the branch. The up train running as class 'K' departed Ely at 10.30 am and called at all stations on the branch. The train cleared Needingworth Junction at 1.15 pm and arrived at St Ives yard five minutes later. The down train running as class 'F' departed St Ives at 2.15 pm and called at all stations arriving at Ely Dock Junction at 4.38 pm and Ely goods yard two minutes later. As before parcels and miscellaneous traffic and livestock at passenger train rates was conveyed by these goods services. A similar service ran in 1952.

Because of the deteriorating condition of the section between Earith Bridge and Sutton, the working timetable for 1958 showed the branch being worked from each end. The western end of the line was served by class 'F' goods trains departing St Ives at 10.00 am SO and 1.40 pm SX, the latter a through train from Histon depart 12.45 pm and returning from Earith Bridge at 11.05 am SO and 2.45 pm SX. These trains called at Bluntisham. At the eastern end of the branch, a class 'K' goods service departed Ely at 1.25 pm calling at Stretham, Wilburton and Haddenham only if required with arrival at Sutton at 2.39 pm. The return train running as class 'F' departed Sutton at 3.00 pm and calling at all station yards arrived back at Ely at 4.30 pm.

In 1961 a class 'H' train served Bluntisham, departing St Ives at 10.00 am SO and 1.30 pm SX, the latter a through train from Histon departing 12.40 pm. The return workings departed Bluntisham at 11.30 pm SO and 3.00 pm SX, and were allowed 20 to 23 minutes for the journey. One class 'K' freight in each direction, Saturdays excepted, served Stretham, Wilburton, Haddenham and Sutton departing Ely at 1.25 pm, calling at the intermediate stations by request and arriving at Sutton at 2.39 pm. The return working departed Sutton at 3.00 pm and was booked to shunt at each intermediate station before arriving at Ely at 4.30 pm. These freight services remained essentially unaltered until the section from Sutton to Ely was closed on and from 13th July, 1964 with Bluntisham to Needingworth Junction being closed on and from 5th October, 1964. However, as traffic was sporadic, for many months before actual closure trains only ran as and when required by local arrangement.

Excursions

Over the years the GER offered the inhabitants of the towns and villages cheap fares and excursions. The first excursion on Wednesday 25th July, 1866 ran from Sutton to Hunstanton with the train well filled. On 7th July, 1868 the annual excursion ran from Sutton to Hunstanton when 60 passengers joined at Sutton and 40 at Haddenham with lesser numbers from Wilburton and Stretham. At the time it was hoped to persuade the GER to run the next excursion to Yarmouth. By June 1871 the excursion fares to Hunstanton were first class 6s. 0d. and third class 3s. 0d. The following month an excursion ran to the volunteers' camp at Hunstanton from the branch stations.

The volunteer camp at Hunstanton generated another excursion from the branch in July 1874. Later in September of the same year an excursion ran from the branch stations to Great Yarmouth whilst excursion fares were offered to Ipswich at 7s. 0d. first class and 3s. 6d. third class, passengers travelling by normal service trains. At the end of June 1876 over a hundred schoolchildren from local Wesleyan chapels were taken to the branch stations by horse-drawn waggons before joining the excursion train to Hunstanton, some viewing the sea for the first time.

Monday 15th April, 1879 was very cold with a brisk northerly wind blowing. 'Sensibly the local populace stayed at home round the fireside' and no tickets were issued at any of the branch stations for the excursion to Hunstanton. Later the same year on 19th August many took advantage of the cheap fares on the excursion to Yarmouth.

For a number of years after World War II excursion trains were operated over the branch to Hunstanton and/or Yarmouth and tickets were available from the branch stations. London Midland Region class '2MT' 2-6-0 No. 46467 is working the St Ives to Heacham and Hunstanton excursion near Earith Bridge in August 1957 shortly before the section of line from Bluntisham to Sutton was closed completely. Because of the poor condition of the track and the deterioration of the Ouse viaduct, the civil engineer imposed a 15 mph speed restriction, which was later reduced to 10 mph on the section. This section of line finally closed completely on and from 6th October, 1958. No. 46467 has the narrow style of chimney fitted to later members of the class. *Dr I.C. Allen*

London Midland Region '2MT' class 2-6-0 No. 46466 awaits departure from Sutton with a Sunday excursion train to Hunstanton in 1958. The formation is of BR Mark I coaching stock, with an ex-LNER Thompson corridor vehicle second from the engine. To the left are the up platform and the up starting signal. *Dr I.C. Allen*

For some years before the turn of the century the people of Sutton and Haddenham had been pressing the GER authorities to provide a weekly three-days ticket to London and on 15th May, 1896 the *Wisbech Standard* reported that 'after several applications the new Saturday to Monday return ticket at single fare had been granted'.

An example of an excursion in the 1930s after the withdrawal of regular passenger services was the running of a special train in connection with Yarmouth Race meeting held on Wednesday and Thursday 20th and 21st September, 1933. The special train departed Histon at 6.30 am on the Wednesday combining with a section from Huntingdon to St Ives before calling at all stations via Sutton to Ely and then running non-stop, except for the engine taking water at Brandon, and via the Wensum curve thus by-passing Norwich, with arrival at Yarmouth at 10.05 am. After allowing punters a long day at the races or by the sea the special train returned by the outward route.

Typical of the excursions run in the last years of the line was the special train offered to Heacham and Hunstanton on August Bank Holiday Monday 2nd August, 1954. The train departed Bluntisham at 7.30 and called at Earith Bridge at 7.37, Sutton 7.47, Haddenham 7.52, Wilburton 7.57 and Stretham at 8.03 am, and returned from Hunstanton at 7.08 and Heacham at 7.13 pm. Return excursion fares from the branch stations were Bluntisham 11s. 9d., Earith Bridge 11s. 3d., Sutton 10s. 6d., Haddenham and Wilburton 10s. 0d., and Stretham 9s. 6d. An excursion also ran to Yarmouth.

Fares

The initial single fares charges on the branch were:

Sutton to	1st class s.	1st class d.	2nd class s.	2nd class d.	3rd class s	3rd class d.
Haddenham		5		4		3
Wilburton		8		6		5
Stretham	1	0		10		7
Ely	1	8	1	4	1	0

A letter to the *Cambridge Independent Press* published on 28th April, 1866 complained of the prohibitive third class return fare from Sutton to Ely of 2s. 0d., which represented a fifth of the average agricultural workers weekly wage in the fens at that time. The writer requested market day tickets issued at Parliamentary or half-Parliamentary rates as on other GER lines in the Ely area.

The fare table to the branch stations from Liverpool Street for 1884 shows the anomaly of charges made by the GER to places of equal distance, Ely 70 miles 33 chains and St Ives 70 miles 35 chains from London. The vast difference in fares reflected on the branch tariff where passengers were expected to travel via St Ives to obtain the lowest fare, although first and second class returns were cheaper via Ely!

	Single 1st s.	Single 1st d.	2nd s.	2nd d.	3rd s.	3rd d.	Return 1st s.	Return 1st d.	2nd s.	2nd d.	3rd s.	3rd d.
Ely	11	10	8	10	5	11½	20	0	16	0	11	11
Stretham	11	9	9	0	6	2	20	10	16	7	12	4
Wilburton	11	4	8	9	5	11	21	4	16	10	11	10
Haddenham	11	0	8	5	5	10	20	10	16	2	11	8
Sutton	10	10	8	4	5	8	20	7	15	11	11	4
Earith Bridge	9	11	7	7	5	4	19	2	14	10	10	8
Bluntisham	9	6	7	4	5	2	18	8	14	4	10	4
St Ives	8	9	6	9	4	10½	17	6	13	6	9	9

The local fares charged to and from the branch stations in 1886 were:

Ely to	1st class s.	1st class d.	3rd class s.	3rd class d.
Stretham		7		3
Wilburton		11		5
Haddenham	1	2		6
Sutton	1	5		7½
Earith Bridge	2	3	1	0
Bluntisham	2	3	1	2
St Ives	2	3	1	5
St Ives to				
Bluntisham		9		4
Earith Bridge	1	2		6
Sutton	2	1		10
Haddenham	2	3	1	0
Wilburton	2	3	1	1
Stretham	2	3	1	3
Ely	2	3	1	5

These fares remained almost unchanged until World War I.

Goods Traffic

With the advent of the railway the GER failed to gain an absolute monopoly of goods traffic and local carrier services flourished on a reduced basis until well into the 1890s. By 1879 the waggons of Nunn and Gimbert journeyed from Sutton to St Ives on Mondays whilst Gimbert ran a carrier service to Ely on Tuesdays, Thursdays and Fridays. William Amory was acting as local carrier at Haddenham travelling to Cambridge on Saturdays and St Ives on Mondays. Thomas Pant and Nightingale also went to Cambridge on Saturdays whilst Pant also travelled to Ely on Thursdays and St Ives on Mondays. However, most of the carriers provided services between the various goods yards to and from the local villages. But as late as 1883 C. Murfitt was providing a service from Sutton to Cambridge on Saturdays, whilst in 1896 Ephraim Papworth was travelling to Ely on Thursdays and St Ives on Mondays. Nathan Summit made additional runs from Stretham to Ely on Thursdays and Cambridge on Saturdays with John Weir journeying from Haddenham to Ely on Thursdays.

The initial goods traffic conveyed by the EHSR consisted of potatoes, swedes, turnips, mangold wurzels and other root crops, and wheat, hay and straw grown in great abundance in the rich fertile loam of the fens, whilst imports consisted mainly of manure for the farmers and coal for domestic and agricultural use. A.J. Pell succeeded on the death of Oliver Pell and developed five acres of land for fruit growing. Initially started as an experiment, the scheme grew gooseberries and blackcurrants but later added strawberries, apples and plums. The success soon spread and other landowners at Wilburton, Sutton and Earith commenced fruit growing in the mid-1890s.

In the periods prior to and after World War I fruit traffic increased so that during the summer months it was necessary to import outside labour as the demand for pickers increased beyond the capacity of local people. Gipsies, 'didecoys' and the poor from Cambridge, Peterborough, Huntingdon and further afield took advantage of earning money and if the demand was beyond the capacity of the normal service trains which were strengthened, then additional services ran to the branch stations at short notice. Special trains also ran after the withdrawal of passenger services to cater for fruit pickers spending a working holiday in the fens. World War I brought an immediate increase in vegetable and fruit traffic as farmers sought to increase production of food for home consumption in an effort to replace the loss of imported produce. Receipts for goods traffic at most of the stations increased by 80 per cent, although Wilburton was somewhat less.

So important was the traffic to the railway company that special trains ran in 1921 and 1922 to the *Daily Mail* 'Imperial Fruit Show' at Crystal Palace from Kings Lynn. Cheap fares were available from the branch stations in connection with the specials at Ely and many took advantage of the offer on 30th October, 1922.

The tonnage of fruit traffic conveyed along the branch was thus considerable as major development of fruit growing into the 1920s and 1930s provided a lucrative traffic from the branch stations. The seasonal loadings and types of fruit handled included gooseberries in May and June, strawberries in June and July, currants and raspberries in July, the latter continuing into August and plums from July to September. Initially in May and June, fen drays, carriers' and farmers' waggons brought the gooseberries loaded in 28 lb. and 56 lb. bags, if unripe, or 6 lb. baskets if ripe. The fruit was also sent away in 12 lb. to 24 lb. sieves. By mid-June and through July the strawberries were loaded into covered wagons, 4 lb. chips being tiered one above the other. July was far the busiest month as currants in 10 lb. chips, 12 lb. trays and 24 lb. sieves were loaded alongside tubs or chips of raspberries. As the soft fruit season waned, so plums and apples were delivered to the railway for transit to markets. By early September the plum traffic was finished, leaving the 21 lb. and 42 lb. flats and 21 lb. baskets of apples the only fruit to be dispatched, which lasted until Christmas. Unfortunately after World War II nearly all the fruit traffic quickly transferred to road transport for conveyance to markets, thus saving the double handling into and out of railway wagons.

Many of the baskets used for fruit traffic were supplied by cottage industries in Sutton. They also weaved tubular eel traps until the 1950s. In contrast to the fruit and vegetable traffic conveyed one of the largest establishments served by the branch was Drake's Forage Works at Sutton, which had its own sidings, and the firm provided regular traffic for the railway over the years. Bricks were also dispatched from the Isle of Ely Brick Works siding, between Sutton and Haddenham, and from the works at Haddenham. Considerable tonnages of timber were dispatched from Bluntisham until the traffic was withdrawn in 1964.

From the early 1920s sugar beet was grown increasingly in the fens. From October to January considerable loads were transferred from fen tumbrels and horse-drawn waggons to railway wagons at all station yards, for conveyance to the British Sugar Corporation processing factories at Ely, Wissington and Peterborough. By the late 1950s much of this traffic had transferred to road transport for direct delivery from farm to factory but until closure to goods traffic, sugar beet was still loaded at Stretham, Wilburton, Haddenham and Sutton in reasonable quantities.

Milk was regularly dispatched from all stations to dairies at St Ives and Ely in the familiar 17 gallons churns. Two consignments were sent daily during the summer months by the early morning train and then again in the late afternoon with only one consignment forwarded by the early morning train in the winter months. This area of Cambridgeshire and Huntingdon was not noted for extensive dairy farming and the relatively small amounts were quickly lost to road transport in the late 1930s, when the churns were collected from the farms for direct delivery to the dairies.

The main coal distribution depot for the area was located at Sutton where several coal merchants utilized sidings in the goods yard on the site of the old station, where Coote & Warren was the chief distributor. The merchant also had coal grounds at Haddenham, Ely and St Ives. Coal traffic was also handled at the other stations and one enterprising merchant was Thomas Fletcher, who, as well as distributing coal and coke from Stretham station to the villages of Stretham and Little Thetford, also owned the Railway Inn adjacent to the rather remote station. Coal was received from Sherwood, Newstead, Kirkley, Bestwood, Hucknall, Sheepbridge, Stanton, Shirebrook, Clipstone, Worksop and Blidworth collieries. The wagons usually travelled via Peterborough where the Stanground sidings acted as a clearing-house for loaded wagons from the collieries and empty wagons being returned. Other coal traffic was routed via the GN&GE Joint Railway via Spalding and March. In the 1920s and 1930s coke was conveyed for horticultural purposes but after World War II this commodity was taken by road.

Cattle wagons were a common feature on branch trains until the early 1950s and animals were conveyed to Cambridge, Ely, Newmarket and St Ives markets. Outgoing cattle was also regularly dispatched to Saffron Walden, Bishop's Stortford, Kings Lynn and Huntingdon markets and as already mentioned certain passenger trains were permitted to convey cattle wagons. Pigs and sheep also formed an important if lesser trade but all traffic declined with the relaxation of petrol rationing after World War II and transferred to road transport.

THE ELY & ST IVES RAILWAY

An unidentified 'J17' class 0-6-0 hauls the branch freight train between Haddenham and Sutton in the 1950s. The train is well loaded with a formation of a covered van, 13 open wagons and a goods brake van.
Author's Collection

The central tower of the magnificent Ely Cathedral is a speck on the horizon as 'J17' class 0-6-0 No. 65576 darkens the landscape whilst collecting wagons of sugar beet from the loop siding at Wilburton in the autumn of 1957. The main single line runs parallel to the siding. Goods traffic was withdrawn from the stations on the Ely to Sutton section of line on and from 13th July, 1964. In the latter years there was little traffic to collect and trains only ran as and when required.
Dr I.C. Allen

'J17' class 0-6-0 No. 65532 approaching Earith Bridge with the branch freight train in 1957. Earith Bridge was served only as required and shortly after this photograph was taken the line was abandoned between Bluntisham and Sutton because of the deteriorating condition of the River Ouse viaduct at 4 m. 55 ch. The section to Earith Bridge from the east was then used for the storage of condemned wagons, which were shunted in from the Sutton end of the line. The section was officially closed on and from 6th October, 1958. *Dr I.C. Allen*

'J17' class 0-6-0 No. 65560 negotiates the cutting through the fenland ridge on the approach to Haddenham with the branch freight train in 1958. The premises of the Isle of Ely Brick Co. which was served by a 300 ft-long siding from the main single line, was located on the down side of the railway behind the trees to the right of the photograph. *Dr I.C. Allen*

'J17' class 0-6-0 No. 65521 departing from Haddenham and negotiates the shallow cutting en route to Sutton with a train comprising a covered van and goods brake van. In the background is Haddenham Road overbridge No. 2297. *Dr I.C. Allen*

'J17' class 0-6-0 No. 65521 shunting its train consisting of a covered van, a high side open wagon loaded with coal and a former LMS goods brake van into Sutton goods yard in 1958. When the line was extended to Needingworth Junction and St Ives, the main line shown in the foreground curved sharply to take a westerly course through the new Sutton station. *Dr I.C. Allen*

TIMETABLES AND TRAFFIC

In the late 1920s and early 1930s many of the fenland roads remained unmetalled – dust tracks in summer and muddy morasses in winter. County councils undertook a rolling programme of road improvements, which involved levelling the surface before covering with granite chippings and tarmacadam. Much of this material was delivered by rail to the branch stations from where it was off-loaded and taken to site by horse and waggon. The granite and tarmacadam was then levelled by steamroller. The railway thus played a part in improving conditions for its road competitor, which ultimately led to its downfall as a public carrier.

A most unusual commodity conveyed across the branch during World War II was rubble from buildings destroyed in the London Blitz, which was offloaded at Wilburton and taken thence by road to form the foundation of the runway and buildings of the wartime airfield at Witchford. Similar loads were taken to Earith Bridge and Bluntisham for road conveyance to Mepal airfield.

The use of a tow-rope during shunting which allowed a locomotive on the main line to shunt wagons in the adjacent siding or loop road was permitted at Earith Bridge. The use of the tow-rope was also permitted at Stretham and Wilburton but only in an emergency.

Goods sheds were provided at Bluntisham, Wilburton and Haddenham, the first and last were being extensively used throughout the lifespan of the line but the shed at Wilburton, after extensive use up to World War I, gradually declined until in the 1950s and 1960s it went many months without use.

The following goods facilities were available at the branch stations:

Stretham
Loading gauge
Loading dock
Weighing machine 1 ton 2 cwt capacity
Lock-up for small packages
Cattle pen, paved
Water supply for cattle in transit

Wilburton
Loading gauge
Weighing machine 1 ton 2 cwt capacity
Goods shed with storage for 300 quarters of grain

Haddenham
Loading gauge
Loading dock
Fixed crane 1 ton capacity
Weighing machine 1 ton 1 cwt capacity
Goods shed with storage for 50, later increased to 100 quarters of grain
Lock-up for small packages
Cattle pen, paved
Water supply for animals in transit
Facilities for handling round timber and furniture vans

Sutton
Loading gauge
Loading dock
Goods shed with storage for 90 quarters of grain (later removed)
Cart weighbridge 7 tons capacity
Weighing machine 1 ton 2 cwt capacity
Weighing machine 10 cwt capacity, later 5 cwt
Lock-up for small packages
Facilities for handling round timber and furniture vans

Earith Bridge   Loading gauge
Loading dock
Weighing machine 1 ton capacity
Lock-up for small packages
Fixed crane 10 cwt capacity (removed at an early date)

Bluntisham   Loading gauge
Loading dock
2 Weighing machines, each 5 cwt capacity
Goods shed with storage for 350 quarters of grain
Lock-up for small packages
Cattle pen, paved
Water supply for animals in transit
Facilities for handling round timber and furniture vans

The latest time for receipt of animals or goods at stations for forwarding the same day was 6.00 pm. The GER employed agents, usually local carriers, to deliver goods from each station to the local community.

At the branch junction stations the following goods facilities were available

Ely   Loading gauges
Loading dock
3 x fixed cranes 1 ton 10 cwt capacity each
Goods shed with storage capacity for 25 quarters of grain
Lock-up for small packages
2 x weighing machines 1 ton 2 cwt capacity each
Weighing machine 5 cwt capacity
Truck weighbridge 20 tons capacity
Wagon turntables (access to goods shed removed by 1902)
4 paved cattle pens
Water supply for animals in transit
Facilities for handling round timber and furniture vans

The latest time for receipt of animals or goods for forwarding the same day for next day delivery was 6.30 pm. Cartage was by the GER.

St Ives   Loading gauges
Loading dock
Fixed crane 1 ton capacity
Goods shed with storage for 500 quarters of grain
Lock-up for small packages
Weighing machine 1 ton 2 cwt capacity
Cart weighbridge 7 tons capacity
13 paved cattle pens
Water supply for animals in transit
Facilities for handling round timber and furniture vans

The latest time for receipt of animals or goods for forwarding the same day for next day delivery was 6.00 pm on weekdays and 3.00 pm on Saturdays. Cartage was by the GER.

TIMETABLES AND TRAFFIC 137

In 1870 the maximum loadings of goods engines between Ely and Sutton was:

	Goods trucks Loaded		Coal trucks Loaded		
Four-wheel coupled	Down	Up	Down	Up	
Second class engines	30	30	25	25	Gross load 300 tons or 200 tons net
Third class engines	24	24	20	20	Gross load 252 tons or 160 tons net
Fourth class engines	22	22	18	18	Gross load 252 tons or 160 tons net

Later loadings for goods engines on the Ely to St Ives branch were:

	1st class engines		2nd class engines		3rd class engines	
	Down	Up	Down	Up	Down	Up
Goods trucks loaded	35	35	30	30	25	25
Coal trucks loaded	30	30	25	25	20	20

Sutton branch passenger engines, 'Little Sharpie' Nos. 7 to 25 and 'T7' class Nos. 81 to 86 working the mixed trains with three passenger coaches were not to exceed 14 trucks of coal or 17 trucks of goods. These engines when working goods only were only permitted to work 16 trucks of coal or 20 trucks of goods.

Around the turn of the century the loads for goods engines were revised as under:

	Down		Up	
Class of locomotive	Minerals	Goods	Minerals	Goods
A	49	50	49	50
B	33	47	33	47
C	30	42	30	42
D	26	37	26	37
E	24	34	24	34
F	23	33	23	33
G	21	30	21	30
H	19	27	19	27

The undermentioned locomotives regularly allocated for branch duties were classified as follows:

GER class	LNER class	Type	Classification
'Little Sharpie'	–	2-4-0	H
M15	F4	2-4-2T	D
C32	F3	2-4-2T	E
Y14	J15	0-6-0	C
Y65	F7	2-4-2T	E
T26	E4	2-4-0	B

By 1935 the wagon limits of trains on the Ely to St Ives line was 60 vehicles, although loads of this size were never handled. The full list of authorized loads then permitted was:

Ely to St Ives

Class of Locomotive	Minerals	Goods	Empties
1	32	48	60
2	36	54	60
3	40	59	60

St Ives to Ely

Class of Locomotive	Minerals	Goods	Empties
1	36	54	60
2	40	59	60
3	45	60	60

After World War II the load limits for locomotives hauling class 'J' and 'K' freight trains across the branch were:

Ely to St Ives

Class of Locomotive	Heavies	Goods	Empties
1	26	46	52
2	31	55	60
3	34	60	60
4	38	60	60

St Ives to Ely

Class of Locomotive	Heavies	Goods	Empties
1	26	46	52
2	32	57	60
3	35	60	60
4	40	60	60

A class '3' goods engine was a 'J15' and class '4', a 'J17'. The freight train loads book effective from 6th April, 1964 permitted trains of 60 wagons across the Sutton branch and the Brush type '2' diesel-electric locomotives working the branch were capable of hauling such trains of this length; they were never conveyed as the branch freight traffic was heavily in decline.

The fireman's view from the cab of 'J17' class 0-6-0 No. 65578 crossing from the loop siding to the single main line at Stretham on 28th July, 1961. The 16 ton all-steel mineral wagons occupy the 340 ft refuge siding, which ran parallel with the single main line at the western end of the yard. By this date some of the sidings at the branch stations were used for the storage of condemned or 'one journey only' wagons. *R. Powell*

Chapter Eight

Locomotives and Rolling stock

The light nature of the permanent way on the Ely to St Ives branch severely restricted the choice of motive power available to the GER to work the line. Fortunately the company had an ample supply of locomotives with light axle loading to work the services, although the following locomotives were restricted from the route: Nos. 725, 776, 778, 1000 and 1001, 1140 to 1249, 1260 to 1269, 1500 to 1571 and 1790 to 1900.

The LNER route availability permitted the following locomotives between Ely and St Ives via Sutton, tender class 'E4' and 'J15', tank 'F3', 'F4', 'F5', 'F6' and 'F7' also 'J62', 'J63', 'J65', 'J66', 'J67', 'J68', 'J69' and 'J70', with 'Y1', 'Y3', 'Y5', 'Y6' and 'Y10'. The 'J17' class 0-6-0 tender locomotives were later permitted to travel across the line, initially with a speed restriction of 25 mph throughout. Later the LNER coded the line under Route Availability 3, although the 'J17' class of RA4 was permitted. Double-heading on the branch was prohibited. Under British Railways the line continued as RA3 and after the elimination of steam from the ex-GER section the following diesel-electric locomotives were permitted to work the freight trains: BTH/Paxman type '1', later class '15' and Brush type '2', later classes '30' and '31'.

William T. Mousley, the contractor for the Sutton to Needingworth Junction extension used a Manning, Wardle 0-6-0 saddle tank locomotive *Diamond* dating from 1868 (Works No. 253) on the final stages of installation and ballasting of the permanent way. The locomotive was removed from site before the opening of the line and was still being employed by Mousley in 1896 on the construction of the Norfolk and Suffolk Joint Committee line from North Walsham to Mundesley, where she was recorded as running as a 2-4-0ST with front coupling rods removed. *Diamond* was a Manning, Wardle 'K' class engine with 12 in. x 17 in. cylinders, 3 ft 1⅜ in. driving wheels and 10 ft 9 in. wheelbase.

On 6th April, 1866 ex-Eastern Counties Railway 2-2-2 tender locomotive No. 276 hauled the inaugural train along the branch to Sutton and back for the EHSR and GER Directors. The engine had an eventful journey before reaching Sutton for it had been sent from Ely to Stratford on 5th April, to work the 3.55 pm Director's special train back to Ely but on the return journey failed at Bishop's Stortford with the firebars welded together, because of the action of bad coke. Sinclair 'Y' class 2-4-0 tender locomotive No. 360 took over the special train but on arrival at Cambridge failed with a hot leading bearing. The Directors' journey continued to Ely behind inside cylinder 2-2-2 tender locomotive No. 63. No. 276 received repairs and worked to Cambridge. On the morning of 6th April she doubled-headed with 2-2-2 tender locomotive No. 84 the 8.30 am local train to Ely to take up duties hauling the Directors' special train, the Directors' having stayed overnight at Ely. No. 276 was a member of the '274' class, also known as class 'C', designed by John Gooch and built at the Canada Works, Birkenhead, Works No. 44. No. 276 was built in July 1856 and withdrawn from service in October 1875. The leading dimensions of the '274' class were:

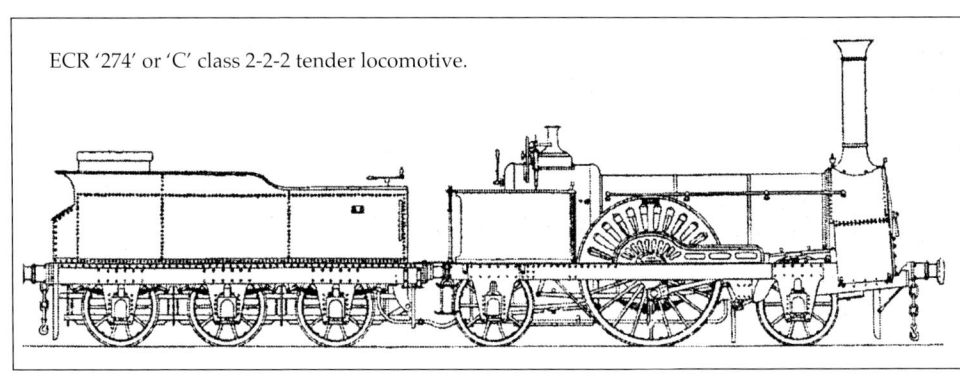

ECR '274' or 'C' class 2-2-2 tender locomotive.

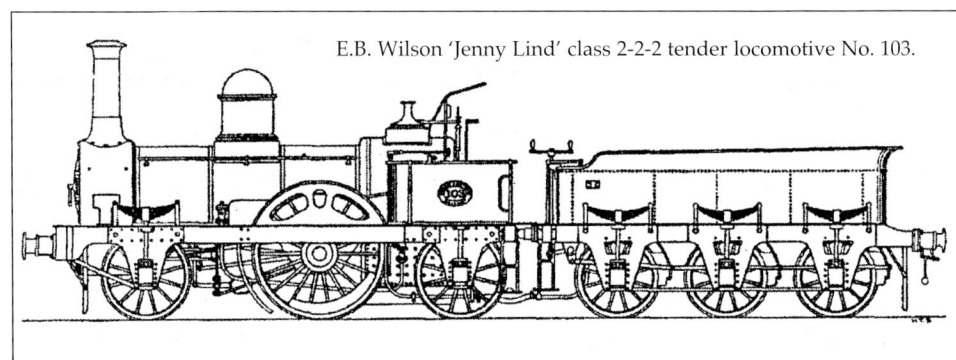

E.B. Wilson 'Jenny Lind' class 2-2-2 tender locomotive No. 103.

E.B. Wilson 'Jenny Lind' class 2-2-2 tender locomotive No. 105.

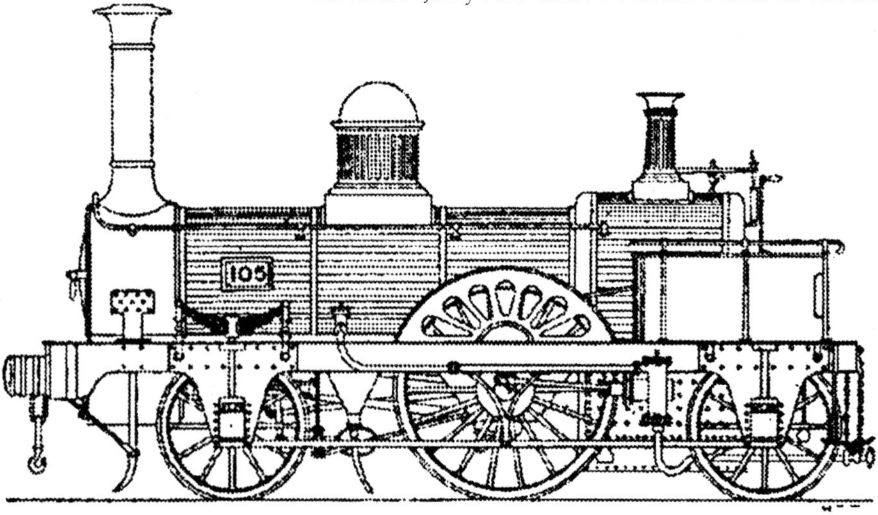

LOCOMOTIVES AND ROLLING STOCK

Cylinders		15 in. x 22 in.
Boiler	length	10 ft 6 in.
	max. diameter	3 ft 7⅛ in.
	tubes	164 x 1⅞ in.
	firebox	4 ft 2 in.
	boiler pressure	120 psi
Leading wheels		3 ft 8 in.
Driving wheels		6 ft 6 in.
Trailing wheels		3 ft 8 in.
Locomotive wheelbase		14 ft 0 in.

Train services from the public opening of the line were hauled by E.B. Wilson 'Jenny Lind' class 2-2-2 tender locomotives. The use of the 'Jenny Lind' class in the Cambridge District alternated between the Saffron Walden and Sutton branches, and Nos. 103, 105 and 107 were often outbased at Sutton for the first few months until October 1866 when the line was worked from Ely. The class had quite an eventful career for No. 103 was derailed on 20th February, 1860 when approaching Tottenham with the 7.00 am train from Cambridge, the left leading tyre on the locomotive fractured and derailed the train. Six people lost their lives in the accident including driver Rowell and fireman Cornwell. After they were relegated to branch line work No. 107 appears to have been the regular Sutton branch engine from the opening of the line to passengers but was replaced by No. 105 on 1st May, 1866. When No. 105 was required for maintenance at Cambridge on 7th May she was replaced as the Sutton branch engine by Vulcan 2-4-0 tender locomotive No. 180. However, the '103' class were soon back working the branch for No. 107 collided with a horse at an occupational crossing between Haddenham and Sutton on 16th July, 1866. The animal was killed but the locomotive and tender sustained damage that required repairs at Cambridge the following day. On 18th July George MacAllan, the Cambridge district locomotive superintendent attended a meeting at Stratford to discuss the type of branch engines required for the Sudbury, Saffron Walden and Sutton branches and presumably the '103' class were considered suitable for the Ely to Sutton line; on 31st July locomotive No. 103 and its tender arrived at Cambridge for maintenance after a stint at Sutton but the tender was immediately removed and attached to locomotive No. 107 to enable it to take up service on the Sutton branch. Unfortunately when working the 8.10 am Sutton to Ely train on 6th August, 1866 No. 107 when working tender first derailed at Ely Sutton Branch Junction. The Cambridge breakdown vans attended the derailment and the stock was soon recovered. By 10th August repairs to locomotive No. 103 were completed and the engine was reunited with its own tender enabling it to take up duties on the Sutton branch. No. 103 was built in June 1847 and No. 104 in September of the same year. Three further locomotives with slightly larger dimensions, Nos. 105, 106 and 107, were built in October, November and December 1848 respectively. The locomotives were scrapped as follows, Nos. 103 in June 1874, 104 in July 1868, 105 in November 1867, 106 in October 1869 and No. 107 in April 1869. The leading dimensions were:

Cylinders		15 in. x 20 in.
Boiler	max. length	10 ft 6½ in.
		11 ft 0 in.*
	diameter	3 ft 6 in.
	firebox	4 ft 3 in.
		4 ft 6 in.

Heating surface	tubes	124 x 2 in.	720.0 sq. ft
	tubes	148 x 2 in.*	
	firebox		80.0 sq. ft
	total		800.0 sq. ft
			1,000.0 sq. ft*
Grate area			12.7 sq. ft
Boiler pressure			120 psi
Leading wheels			4 ft 0 in.
Driving wheels			6 ft 0 in.
Trailing wheels			4 ft 0 in.
Locomotive wheelbase			14 ft 6 in.
			14 ft 7 in.*
Weight	engine		23 tons 11 cwt
	max. axle weight		10 tons 19 cwt
Tender	wheels		3 ft 6 in.

* Nos 105 to 107

Interspersed with the 'Jenny Lind' class, some of the Vulcan Foundry outside cylinder 2-4-0 '172' class tender locomotives, normally utilized on ballast workings, also handled the branch services. No. 180 worked the branch as replacement for 'Jenny Lind' No. 105. The Vulcan Foundry Co., previously Charles Tayleur and Company, constructed 10 four-coupled goods tender engines between August and December 1847 and they received Nos. 172 to 181 inclusive. Some of the locomotives, which had long boilers, Nos. 172, 174, 175, 177, 178 and 181,were rebuilt between December 1859 and March 1862, but the remaining four, Nos. 173, 176, 179 and 180. were not rebuilt and remained in original condition. No. 180 was withdrawn in March 1871 and its leading dimensions in unrebuilt form were:

Cylinders, 2 x outside	15 in. x 24 in.
Leading wheels	3 ft 6 in.
Coupled wheels	5 ft 0 in.
Locomotive wheelbase	10 ft 6 in.

The next locomotives to work the Ely to Sutton services were Sinclair's celebrated 'Y' class 2-4-0 goods engine. Between July 1859 and August 1866 one hundred and ten engines were introduced into service from a variety of makers, Neilson & Co. building Nos. 307 to 326, Robert Stephenson & Co. Nos. 327 to 341, R. & W. Hawthorn Nos. 342 to 356, Kitson & Co. Nos. 357 to 381, Vulcan Foundry Nos. 382 to 406 and Schnider et Cie of Creusot Nos. 407 to 416. Each batch had detailed differences and engine No. 327 was displayed at an exhibition held in Hyde Park, London in 1862. The engines worked all over the GER system on passenger, mixed and goods trains and those allocated to Cambridge spent considerable time on express and trip diagrams. Over the years most were rebuilt and a number were converted into 4-4-0 tender locomotives for passenger work. Scrapping of the class commenced in 1882 and after 1888 surviving engines were placed on the duplicate list by having a prefix '0' placed before the running number. No specific numbers of locomotives working on the branch are known, but the leading dimensions of the 327 to 356 batch as built were:

LOCOMOTIVES AND ROLLING STOCK 143

Cylinders			17 in. x 24 in.
Boiler	*max. outside diameter*		4 ft 0 in.
	length		11 ft 5¾ in.
	firebox		4 ft 8 in.
Heating surface	*tubes*	192 x 1⅞ in.	968.52 sq. ft
	firebox		72.36 sq. ft
	total		1,040.88 sq. ft
Grate area			13.75 sq. ft
Boiler pressure			120 psi
Leading wheels			3 ft 7 in.
Coupled wheels			6 ft 1 in.
Tender wheels			3 ft 7 in.
Engine wheelbase			15 ft 1 in.
Tender wheelbase			11 ft 5 in.
Weight in working order	*engine*		30 tons 16 cwt
	tender		21 tons 15 cwt
	total		52 tons 11 cwt
Water capacity			1,600 gallons

Interspersed with the tender classes Ely also had a small allocation of Samuel Johnson's 'T7' class 0-4-2Ts especially built for light branch traffic. Fifteen locomotives were built between 1871 and 1875, although the first three engines, Nos. 81, 82 and 83 were actually prototypes included in the class total. It is believed that Nos. 81 to 86 inclusive saw service on the branch in their declining years before withdrawal. The class was extinct by 1894 and introduction and condemnation dates were:

No.	*Date new*	*Date condemned*
81	March 1871	1892
82	March 1871	1891
83	April 1871	1892
84	June 1873	1892
85	June 1873	1893
86	September 1873	1892
13	November 1873	1891
14	December 1873	1894
11	December 1874	1893
12	December 1874	1892
15	April 1875	1894
16	April 1875	1894
17	May 1875	1893
18	May 1875	1891
19	June 1875	1894

The leading dimensions of the 'T7' class were:

Cylinders			15 in. x 22 in.
Motion			Stephenson with slide valves
Boiler	*max. outside diameter*		3 ft 10 in.
	length		9 ft 1 in.
	firebox		4 ft 4¾ in.
Heating surface	*tubes*	204 x 1½ in.	754.0 sq. ft
	firebox		76.0 sq. ft
	total		830.0 sq. ft

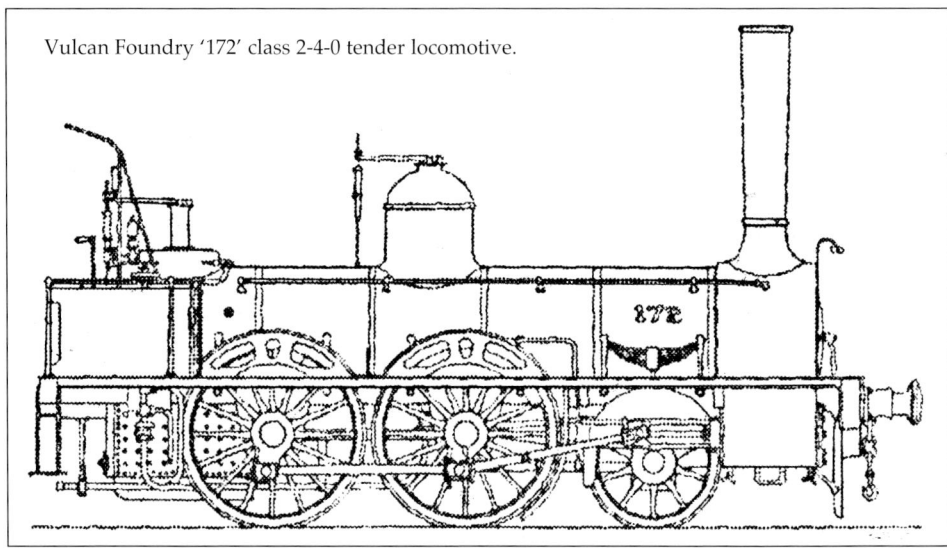

Vulcan Foundry '172' class 2-4-0 tender locomotive.

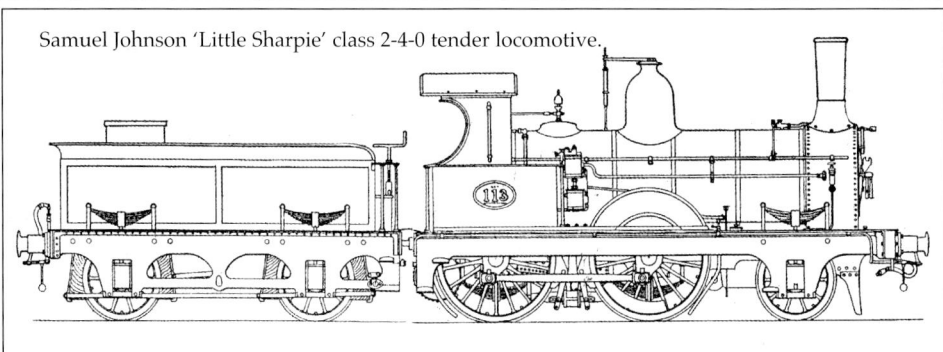

Samuel Johnson 'Little Sharpie' class 2-4-0 tender locomotive.

Samuel Johnson 'Little Sharpies' 2-4-0 worked the Ely to St Ives branch services from the early 1870s until 1907. No. 27, along with others allocated to Cambridge shed, regularly performed on the branch and this particular engine was affectionately nicknamed 'The Grunty Fen Express' by local staff and regular travellers, *Author's Collection*

LOCOMOTIVES AND ROLLING STOCK

Grate area	12.75 sq. ft
Boiler pressure	140 psi
Driving wheels	5 ft 3 in.
Trailing wheels	3 ft 7 in.
Length over buffers	23 ft 7 in.
Wheelbase	14 ft 6 in.
Weight in working order	33 tons 12 cwt
	30 tons 19 cwt*
Water capacity	750 gallons
	500 gallons*

* Nos. 81 to 83.

The last five engines also differed in that the boiler contained 148 x 1¾ in. tubes with boiler heating reduced to 636.9 sq. ft, firebox to 74.43 sq. ft giving a total of 711.12 sq. ft. The use of the 'T7' class was not without problems becasue of their limited water capacity.

From the early 1870s St Ives and Ely sheds utilized representatives of Samuel Johnson's 'No. 1' class, nicknamed 'Little Sharpies', on the branch passenger and freight trains. Thirty of the class of 40 locomotives were built by Sharp, Stewart & Co. and introduced into service between October 1867 and August 1872. Between 1889 and 1893 the whole class was rebuilt and most were then allocated to cross-country and branch line duties. The Cambridge District had a small allocation and although their booked diagrams included regular workings between Cambridge and Peterborough, Ipswich and Colchester, they were also sub-shedded at Ramsey High Street to work the branch from Somersham and at Ely and St Ives where they were used on the Ely to St Ives branch. No. 27 regularly worked from St Ives along the Sutton branch for a number of years when the service acquired the nickname of the 'Grunty Fen Express'. Several locomotives were placed on the duplicate list before withdrawal by having a '0' prefix added to their running numbers. Those known to have worked across the branch included:

GER No.	GER Duplicate No.	Date	Withdrawn
1	01	1911	1913
3			1904
27			1910
32			1901
36			1901
47			1908
48			1911
104	0104	1905	1911
106			1903
118			1903
160	0160	1901	1902
161	0161	1901	1901

The leading dimensions of the class were:

Cylinders			16 in. x 22 in.
Motion			Stephenson with slide valves
Boiler	max. dia.		4 ft 2 in.
	length		9 ft 1 in.
	firebox		4 ft 6 in.

GER 'T26' class 2-4-0, later classified 'E4' by the LNER, were regularly allocated to haul passenger services on the branch. No. 7415, in immaculate livery, was used on the line and is shown in June 1932 with stovepipe chimney, wooden cab roof and watercart tender.

Author's Collection

This poor quality image shows 'E4' class 2-4-0 No. 62784 hauling a 2-coach special near Bluntisham shortly before withdrawal of the engine in May 1955. The locomotive is fitted with a 'watercart' tender originally built for a 'P43' class 4-2-2 locomotive in 1898.

Author's Collection

LOCOMOTIVES AND ROLLING STOCK

Heating surface	tubes	223 x 1⅞ in.	881.24 sq. ft
	firebox		78.00 sq. ft
	total		959.24 sq. ft
Grate area			12.4 sq. ft
Boiler pressure			140 psi
Leading wheels			3 ft 8 in.
Coupled wheels			5 ft 8 in.
Tender wheels			3 ft 8 in.
Engine weight in working order			30 tons 15 cwt
Tender weight in working order			18 tons 6 cwt
		total weight	49 tons 1 cwt
Max. axle loading			10 tons 10 cwt
Water capacity			1,184 gallons

When the 'Little Sharpies' were withdrawn from the branch around 1907 their place on the Sutton services was taken by Holden's 'T26' class 2-4-0 locomotives, nicknamed 'Intermediates'. Originally introduced in 1891, a total of 100 were placed into service and from the turn of the century until the withdrawal of passenger services, Cambridge District 'Intermediates', sub-shedded at Ely or St Ives, worked the branch passenger and mixed trains. The LNER classified the 'T26s' to 'E4' but soon after Grouping many of the locomotives were withdrawn from service. Usually the locomotives used on the Sutton branch were in a run-down condition working out their last mileage before being sent for scrap. A representative of the class, ex-BR No. 62785, is now in the National Collection as GER No. 490. Locomotives known to have operated the branch services included:

GER No.	LNER 1924 No.	LNER 1946 No.	BR No.	Withdrawn
415	7415	–	–	June 1937
417	7417	–	–	January 1930
424	7424	–	–	January 1929
430	7430	–	–	April 1926
432	7432	–	–	July 1929
433	7433	–	–	April 1927
434	7434	–	–	December 1933
436	7436	–	–	June 1929
438	7438	–	–	May 1926
454	7454	–	–	June 1928
455	7455	–	–	March 1934
456	7456	–	–	December 1928
457	7457	–	–	June 1931
458	7458	–	–	August 1937
459	7459	–	–	March 1935
460	7460	–	–	April 1929
461	7461	–	–	September 1931
463	7463	2781	62781	January 1956
478	7478	2784	62784	May 1955
479	7479	–	–	March 1938
482	7482	–	–	September 1929
500	7500	–	–	June 1936
501	7501	–	–	October 1938
502	7502	–	–	January 1939
504	7504	–	–	November 1938

Leading dimensions of the 'E4' class were:

Cylinders	2 inside	17½ in. x 24 in.
Motion		Stephenson with slide valves
Boiler	max. diameter outside	4 ft 4 in.
	barrel length	10 ft 0 in.
Heating surface	firebox	100.9 sq. ft
	tubes 242 x 1⅝ in.	1,063.8 sq. ft
	total	1,164.7 sq. ft
Grate area		18.0 sq. ft
Boiler pressure		160 psi
Leading wheels		4 ft 0 in.
Coupled wheels		5 ft 8 in.
Tractive effort		14,700 lb.
Length over buffers (engine and tender)		48 ft 2 in.
Wheelbase		16 ft 6 in.
Weight in working order		40 tons 6 cwt
Max axle loading		14 tons 3 cwt
Tender	wheelbase	12 ft 0 in.
	wheel diameter	4 ft 1 in.
	weight in working order	30 tons 13 cwt
	water capacity	2,640 gallons
	coal capacity	5 tons

After the problems encountered with the 'T7' class it was usual, and for many years an unwritten local railway instruction, that tender locomotives only were to be rostered to the Sutton branch services because of the lack of watering facilities at intermediate stations. Tank locomotives were therefore rarely used and if so had to enter the branch with their side tanks fully topped up, with the proviso that there was to be no delay incurred en route. However, in 1909/10 S.D. Holden introduced 12 of his 'Y65' class 2-4-2 tank locomotives Nos. 1300 to 1311 into service for light branch passenger duties and for a short period Nos. 1307 and 1308 were put to work on Sutton branch services. All were built at Stratford and with their small boiler and enormous cabs they soon acquired the nickname of 'Crystal Palaces'. From all accounts the engines were not popular with footplate staff, being hardly able to haul more than a four-coach train, and were displaced elsewhere. No. 1308 subsequently became the regular engine on the neighbouring Somersham to Ramsey High Street branch. The class was later reclassified 'F7' by the LNER. Engines regularly employed between Ely and St Ives were:

GER No.	LNER 1924 No.	LNER 1942 No.	LNER 1946 No.	Withdrawn
1302	8302	–	–	May 1931
1307	8307	7596	–	June 1943
1308	8308	7597	7093	November 1948

The leading dimensions of the 'F7' class were:

Cylinders		15 in. x 22 in.
Motion		Stephenson with slide valves
Boiler	max. diameter	3 ft 11½ in.
	barrel	9 ft 1 in.
	firebox	4 ft 6 in.

LOCOMOTIVES AND ROLLING STOCK

Heating surface	tubes 199 x 1⅝ in.	797.2 sq. ft
	firebox	75.7 sq. ft
	total	872.9 sq. ft
Grate area		12.2 sq. ft
Boiler pressure		160 psi
Leading wheels		3 ft 6 in.
Driving wheels		4 ft 10 in.
Trailing wheels		3 ft 6 in.
Tractive effort		11,607 lb.
Length over buffers		30 ft 11 in.
Wheelbase		19 ft 6 in.
Weight in working order		45 tons 14 cwt
Max. axle loading		14 tons 3 cwt
Water capacity		1,000 gallons
Coal capacity		2 tons

In the event of the non-availability of a 'Y65' class locomotive occasional use was made of the GER 'M15' class 2-4-2T. Initially designed by T.W. Worsdell the first locomotive entered traffic in 1884. Three years later 40 were in service but they proved troublesome and their excessive fuel consumption, partly caused by the incorrect setting of the Joy's valve gear, led to them receiving the nickname 'Gobblers'. When James Holden became mechanical engineer of the GER he removed the Joy's valve gear and fitted the conventional Stephenson's valve gear.

In 1909/10 S.D. Holden introduced 12 of his 'Y65' class 2-4-2Ts, Nos. 1300 to 1311 inclusive, into service for light branch duties and Nos. 1307 and 1308 were put to work on the Sutton branch trains for a short period. They were unsuccessful as they were hardly able to maintain timings on the usual four-coach trains, let alone if wagons were attached to form a mixed train, and were quickly replaced. No. 1307 is shown in GER livery. After Grouping the class were reclassified 'F7' by the LNER. *Author's Collection*

150 THE ELY & ST IVES RAILWAY

Between 1903 and 1909 a further 120 locomotives were built and put to service on the London suburban lines. From 1911 to 1923 the GER rebuilt 30 locomotives with increased boiler pressure and reclassified them 'M15R'. Withdrawal of the 1884 to 1887 batch commenced in 1913 and the remainder were later scrapped by the LNER, the final locomotive being withdrawn in 1929. Some of Holden's 1903 to 1909 series were withdrawn in the same year although it was 1956 before the 'F4s' as they were reclassified by the LNER were extinct. Cambridge District had few members of the 'M15' ('F4') class allocated but those known to have worked Ely to St Ives passenger services were:

GER No.	LNER 1924 No.	LNER 1946 No.	BR No.	Withdrawn
79	7079	7187	67187	August 1955
105	7105	–	–	May 1932
174	7174	7170	–	April 1948
799	7799	–	–	March 1926

The leading dimensions of the 'F4' class were:

Cylinders	2 inside	17½ in. x 24 in.
Motion		Stephenson with slide valves
Boiler	max. diameter	4 ft 2 in.
	barrel length	10 ft 2½ in.
	firebox	5 ft 5 in.
Heating surface	tubes 227 x 1⅝ in.	1,018.0 sq. ft
	firebox	98.4 sq. ft
	total	1,116.4 sq. ft
	Grate area	15.3 sq. ft
Boiler pressure		160 psi
Leading wheels		3 ft 9 in.
Coupled wheels		5 ft 4 in.
Trailing wheels		3 ft 9 in.
Tractive effort		15,618 lb.
Length over buffers		34 ft 10 in.
Weight in working order		51 tons 11 cwt
Max. axle loading		14 tons 18 cwt
Water capacity		1,200 gallons
Coal capacity		3 tons 10 cwt

The only other tank class regularly to be used on the branch was J. Holden's 'C32' class 2-4-2 engines, later reclassified 'F3' by the LNER. In the latter years of passenger services the locomotive allocated to Huntingdon had a booked working across the branch between St Ives and Ely. A total of 50 engines were built between 1893 and 1902 at Stratford works to the design of J. Holden. They initially worked on the Liverpool Street to Bishop's Stortford semi-fast services and later ran from Liverpool Street to Southend and Southminster. Soon after the turn of the century many were displaced and sent to GER country depots. The following 'F3' locomotives, which carried an RA3 availability regularly worked across the Sutton branch:

LOCOMOTIVES AND ROLLING STOCK   151

GER No.	LNER 1924 No.	LNER 1946 No.	BR No.	Withdrawn
1044	8044	7145	–	April 1947
1061	8061	7134	–	May 1948
1062	8062	7135	–	November 1947
1063	8063	7136	–	November 1947
1066	8066	7138	–	August 1947
1085	8085	7130	–	November 1947

The principal dimensions of the 'F3' class tank locomotives were:

Cylinders	2 inside	17½ in. x 24 in.
Motion		Stephenson with slide valves
Boiler	max. diameter	4 ft 4 in.
	barrel length	10 ft 0 in.
	firebox	5 ft 5 in.
Heating surface	tubes 242 x 1⅝ in.	1,063.8 sq. ft
	firebox	100.9 sq. ft
	total	1,164.7 sq. ft
Grate area		18.0 sq. ft
Boiler pressure		160 psi
Leading wheels		4 ft 0 in.
Driving wheels		5 ft 8 in.
Trailing wheels		4 ft 0 in.
Tractive effort		14,700 lb.
Length over buffers		34 ft 10 in.
Wheelbase		23 ft 3 in.
Weight in working order		58 tons 12 cwt
Max. axle loading		15 tons 6 cwt
Water capacity		1,460 gallons
Coal capacity		3 tons 5 cwt

In the 1880s Samuel Johnson's '417' class 0-6-0 tender locomotives, regularly worked the Sutton branch goods services. Originally introduced between 1867 and 1869 and built by Neilson & Co. and the Worcester Engine Co., the 60 built were numbered 417 to 476 and initially worked main line goods trains, but on the introduction of the '477' and 'Y14' class 0-6-0 tender locomotives were relegated to pick-up freights and branch line work. The various members of the class allocated to the Cambridge District worked out their last years on the branch. The first of the class were withdrawn in 1888 and scrapping continued every year, with the exception of 1897, until 1899. The survivors after 1891 were placed on the duplicate list by having a 0 prefix added to their running number. The leading dimensions of the class were:

Cylinders	2 inside	16½ in. x 24 in.
Motion		Stephenson with slide valves
Boiler	max. diameter outside	4 ft 2 in.
	length	10 ft 0 in.
	firebox	5 ft 5 in.
Heating surface	tubes 203 x 1¾ in.	957.6 sq. ft
	firebox	94.9 sq. ft
	total	1,052.5 sq. ft

'J15' class 0-6-0 No. 65457 stands on the main single line at Stretham and awaits the shunter to alter the points to the goods yard loop siding. The 2-lever ground frame released by Annett's key attached to the Ely to Sutton train staff can be seen by the end of the platform ramp. The goods yard siding at Stretham was formed of a loop siding with a headshunt at the west end of the layout. The buffer stops of the dock road can be seen to the right of the photograph. *Dr I.C. Allen*

'J15' class 0-6-0 No. 65477 pauses at Earith Bridge station with the weekdays-only down freight working in the mid-1950s. Note the platform is constructed of timber strengthened by old rails. A covered goods van occupies the 310 ft-long yard loop siding on the up side of the main single line. *D. Lawrence*

LOCOMOTIVES AND ROLLING STOCK

Grate area		15.27 sq. ft
Boiler pressure		140 psi
Driving wheels		5 ft 3 in.
Tender wheels		3 ft 7 in.
Wheelbase	engine	15 ft 3 in.
	tender	9 ft 0 in.
Weight in working order	engine	30 tons 15 cwt
	tender	21 tons 17 cwt
	total	52 tons 12 cwt
Max. axle loading		11 tons 5 cwt
Water capacity		1,740 gallons

The next class to be associated with the Sutton branch goods workings was the '477' class 0-6-0 tender locomotives, designed by Samuel Johnson and dating from 1871 to 1873. Numbered in the series 477 to 526, the class came from a variety of builders: Beyer, Peacock; Robert Stephenson; Dübs, Nasmyth, Wilson; and the Yorkshire Engine Co. All were rebuilt between 1888 and 1895. By the time they were used on the Sutton branch, the engines had relinquished their main line goods turns and were relegated to branch line and secondary duties. Nos. 477 to 496 were placed on the duplicate list by having a prefix '0' added to the running number in 1894, whilst Nos. 497 to 506 were similarly treated in 1896. The remaining locomotive still in service were added to the duplicate list in 1899, and the survivors were withdrawn between 1897 and 1902. The principal dimensions of the class were:

Cylinders	2 inside	17 in. x 24 in.
Motion		Stephenson with slide valves
Boiler	max. diameter outside	4 ft 2 in.
	barrel length	10 ft 0 in.
	Firebox outside length	5 ft 5 in.
Heating surface	tubes 223 x 1⅝ in.	980.0 sq. ft
	firebox	94.9 sq. ft
	total	1,074.9 sq. ft
Grate area		15.27 sq. ft
Boiler pressure		140 psi
Coupled wheels		5 ft 2 in.
Tender wheels		3 ft 8 in.
Wheelbase	engine	15 ft 6 in.
	tender	12 ft 0 in.
Weight in working order	engine	32 tons 13 cwt
	tender	26 tons 5 cwt
	total	58 tons 18 cwt
Max. axle loading		12 tons 6 cwt
Water capacity		2,038 gallons

From the late 1890s the branch goods services were regularly hauled by the ubiquitous 'Y14' class 0-6-0 tender locomotives, originally introduced in 1883 to the design of T.W. Worsdell. The success of the design can be gauged by the fact that 289 were in service by the time construction of the class ceased in 1913. All except 19 of the class were constructed at Stratford works, the others being built by Sharp, Stewart & Co. They were later classified 'J15' by the LNER and their low RA1 availability made them ideal for working across the branch. Locomotives known to have worked on the line included:

'J17' class 0-6-0 No. 65517 hauling two covered wagons and a brake van along the up loop line at Sutton after shunting the goods yard in 1954. The connection from the main line to the goods yard is to the left behind the down starting signal. *Dr I.C. Allen*

Steam brake-only' J17' class 0-6-0 No. 65578 pauses at Haddenham with the Ely to Sutton goods service on 28th July, 1961. The guard and station foreman are discussing the finer points of operation before shunting commences. *R. Powell*

LOCOMOTIVES AND ROLLING STOCK 155

GER No.	LNER 1924 No.	LNER 1946 No.	BR No.	Condemned
508	7508	5428	–	August 1949
509	7509	5429	–	November 1950
510	7510	5430	65430	January 1956
511	7511	5431	65431	March 1951
520	7520	5437	–	September 1950
523	7523	5438	65438	June 1958
526	7526	5439	–	November 1951
527	7527	5354	–	February 1951
529	7529	–	–	December 1931
530	7530	5355	–	April 1951
531	7531	–	–	August 1928
532	7532	5356	65356	April 1957
535	7535	–	–	March 1936
536	–	–	–	August 1923
546	7546	5474	65474	February 1960
547	7547	5475	65475	September 1959
548	7548	5476	65476	September 1962
549	7549	5477	65477	February 1960
553	7553	5451	65451	September 1959
555	7555	5453	65453	August 1962
559	7559	5457	65457	February 1962
563	7563	5461	65461	April 1960
570	7570	5468	65468	September 1959
571	7571	5469	65469	August 1962
646	7646	5446	65446	December 1960
805	7805	–	–	April 1928
806	7806	–	–	October 1939
813	7813	5350	–	February 1951
825	7825	5352	–	May 1948
826	7826	–	–	April 1929
831	7831	–	–	November 1936
832	–	–	–	August 1923
833	7833	5359	65359	December 1955
834	7834	5360	–	November 1947
835	7835	–	–	September 1936
836	7836	5361	65361	September 1962
837	7837	5362	–	July 1951
838	7838	–	–	July 1934
839	7839	–	–	July 1936
840	7840	5363	–	August 1949
842	7842	–	–	November 1934
843	7843	5364	–	June 1949
845	7845	–	–	December 1938
847	7847	5366	65366	June 1952
848	7848	5367	–	January 1950
849	7849	5368	–	May 1948
851	7851	–	–	October 1936
856	7856	–	–	October 1936
857	7857	5374	–	November 1950
888	7888	5391	65391	December 1958
897	7897	5396	–	March 1951

GER No.	LNER 1924 No.	LNER 1946 No.	BR No.	Condemned
908	7908	5403	–	August 1947
913	7913	5406	–	April 1951
920	7920	5410	–	February 1948
921	7921	5411	–	April 1948
924	7924	5413	–	November 1950
928	7928	5417	65417	August 1956
929	7929	5418	–	March 1948
942	7942	5425	65425	October 1956

The leading dimensions of the class were:

Cylinders	2 inside	17½ in. x 24 in.
Motion		Stephenson with slide valves
Boiler	max. diameter outside	4 ft 4 in.
	barrel length	10 ft 0 in.
	firebox length outside	6 ft 0 in.
Heating surface	firebox	105.5 sq. ft
	tubes 242 x 1⅝ in.	1,063.8 sq. ft
	total	1,169.3 sq. ft
Grate area		17.9 sq. ft
Boiler pressure		160 psi
Coupled wheels		4 ft 11 in.
Tender wheels		4 ft 1 in.
Tractive effort		16,942 lb.
Length over buffers	engine and tender	47 ft 3 in.
Wheelbase	engine	16 ft 1 in.
	tender	12 ft 0 in.
	total	35 ft 2 in.
Weight in working order	engine	37 tons 2 cwt
	tender	30 tons 13 cwt
	total	67 tons 15 cwt
Max. axle load		13 tons 10 cwt
Water capacity		2,640 gallons
Coal capacity		5 tons

The introduction of eight-coupled heavy goods locomotives on the Whitemoor to Temple Mills and other former GER main line freight services from the 1930s gradually released the 'J17' class, GER 'G58', 0-6-0 tender locomotives for cross-country and branch line goods workings, The 'J17s' built to the design of J. Holden were initially introduced from 1900 as GER class 'F48' with round-topped fireboxes. A further batch of 30 engines was produced with Belpaire fireboxes as class 'G58' from 1905 to 1911. Thereafter some of the earlier locomotives were rebuilt with Belpaire fireboxes and reclassified. After Grouping the 'F48s' became LNER class 'J16' and the 'G58s' LNER class 'J17' but by 1932 all the round-topped firebox locomotives had been rebuilt with Belpaire fireboxes as class 'J17' and class 'J16' became extinct. With the easing of axle loading restrictions after World War II the LNER 'J17' class took over most of the branch workings from the 'J15s' and their additional tractive effort proved advantageous on the branch freight services, especially during the fruit and sugar beet seasons. Locomotive known to have worked between Ely and St Ives included:

LOCOMOTIVES AND ROLLING STOCK 157

GER No.	LNER 1924 No.	LNER 1946 No.	BR No.	Withdrawn
1151	8151	5501	65501	January 1958
1152	8152	5502	65502	September 1959
1153	8153	5503	65503	August 1960
1155	8155	5505	65505	November 1959
1156	8156	5506	65506	August 1960
1165	8165	5515	65515	September 1958
1167	8167	5517	65517	May 1955
1168	8168	5518	65518	September 1958
1170	8170	5520	65520	February 1961
1171	8171	5521	65521	February 1962
1172	8172	5522	65522	September 1958
1173	8173	5523	65523	May 1957
1174	8174	5524	65524	March 1955
1175	8175	5525	65525	April 1959
1176	8176	5526	65526	August 1959
1177	8177	5527	65527	April 1959
1178	8178	5528	65528	November 1961
1179	8179	5529	65529	May 1958
1180	8180	5530	65530	January 1960
1181	8181	5531	65531	April 1959
1182	8182	5532	65532	February 1962
1183	8183	5533	65533	January 1960
1185	8185	5535	65535	May 1958
1187	8187	5537	65537	January 1957
1188	8188	5538	65538	April 1959
1189	8189	5539	65539	August 1960
1190	8190	5540	65540	April 1959
1191	8191	5541	65541	September 1962
1193	8193	5543	65543	May 1955
1196	8196	5546	65546	January 1960
1197	8197	5547	65547	September 1954
1198	8198	5548	65548	March 1960
1199	8199	5549	65549	December 1960
1204	8204	5554	65554	September 1961
1205	8205	5555	65555	March 1960
1206	8206	5556	65556	March 1961
1210	8210	5560	65560	June 1962
1211	8211	5561	65561	December 1959
1213	8213	5563	65563	January 1960
1215	8215	5565	65565	April 1960
1217	8217	5567	65567	August 1962
1221	8221	5571	65571	February 1958
1223	8223	5573	65573	October 1958
1225	8225	5575	65575	February 1958
1226	8226	5576	65576	September 1962
1227	8227	5577	65577	February 1962
1228	8228	5578	65578	March 1962
1233	8233	5583	65583	February 1962
1234	8234	5584	65584	February 1960
1235	8235	5585	65585	November 1954
1236	8236	5586	65586	April 1962
1237	8237	5587	65587	December 1958
1239	8239	5589	65589	January 1961

The principal dimensions of the 'J17' class were:

Cylinders	2 inside	19 in. x 26 in.
Motion		Stephenson with slide valves
Boiler	max. diameter outside	4 ft 9 in.
	barrel length	11 ft 9 in.
	firebox outside length	7 ft 0 in.
Heating surface	firebox	117.7 sq. ft
	tubes	863.5 sq. ft
	flues	282.7 sq. ft
	total evaporative	1,263.9 sq. ft
	superheater	154.8 sq. ft
	total	1,418.7 sq. ft
Tubes		156 x 1¾ in.
Flues		18 x 5 in.
Elements		18 x 1⁵⁄₃₂ in.
Grate area		21.24 sq. ft
Boiler pressure		180 psi
Coupled wheels		4 ft 11 in.
Tender wheels		4 ft 1 in.
Tractive effort		24,340 lb.
Length over buffers	engine and tender	50 ft 6 in.
Wheelbase	engine	17 ft 8 in.
	tender	12 ft 0 in.
	total	38 ft 0 in.
Weight in working order	engine	45 tons 8 cwt
	tender	38 tons 5 cwt
	total	83 tons 13 cwt
Max axle loading		16 tons 11 cwt
Water capacity		3,500 gallons
Coal capacity		5 tons

As a result of the redistribution of locomotives between the Regions after nationalization, former GER depots on the Eastern Region received an allocation of ex-London Midland '2MT' class 2-6-0 tender locomotives. Designed by H.G. Ivatt they were initially introduced in 1946 and building continued after nationalization. In 1951 five of the class commenced their operational life in East Anglia, Nos. 46465, 46466 and 46467 at Cambridge and 46468 and 46469 at Colchester. Except for No. 46466 these locomotives had very narrow chimneys and were the first to carry this modification. Introduced as replacements for older engines, the '2MTs' were immediately put to work on the Stour and Colne Valley lines as well as the Mildenhall branch and the Cambridge to Kettering via Huntingdon East services. Being slightly superior in power to the 'J15' class 0-6-0s the class '2s' easily coped with the light mid-week trains and heavier weekend formations. With their light axle loading and well-distributed power ratio Cambridge depot regularly used them to haul the 8-coach excursion trains from Huntingdon or St Ives to Hunstanton and Yarmouth via St Ives and Ely. In January 1961 Nos. 46468 and 46469 were also transferred to Cambridge. The class was popular with footplate crews for their enclosed cab and tender design, self-cleaning smokebox and rocking grate, which aided preparation and disposal of the engines on shed.

The leading dimensions of the LMS '2MT' class were:

LOCOMOTIVES AND ROLLING STOCK

Cylinders	outside	16½ in. x 24 in.
Motion		Walschaerts valve gear
Boiler	diameter	4 ft 3 in./4 ft 8 in.
	barrel length	10 feet 9⅞ in.
	firebox outside length	5 ft 11 in.
Heating surface	firebox	101.0 sq. ft
	tubes	924.5 sq. ft
	total	1,025.5 sq ft
Superheater		134.0 sq ft
Tubes		162 x 1⅞ in.
Flues		12 x 5⅛ in.
Grate area		17.5 sq. ft
Boiler pressure		200 psi
Leading wheels		3 ft 0 in.
Coupled wheels		5 ft 0 in.
Tractive effort		18,510 lb.
Tender	coal capacity	4 tons
	water capacity	3,000 gallons
	wheel diameter	3 ft 6½ in.
Length over buffers	engine and tender	53 feet 1¾ in.
Weight in working order	engine	47 tons 2 cwt
	tender	37 tons 3 cwt
Wheelbase	engine	22 ft 3 in.
	tender	13 ft 0 in.
	total	44 ft 1 in.
Max. axle loading		13 tons 15 cwt

After unofficial closure of the section of line between Bluntisham and Sutton in 1957, the through excursion trains from St Ives to Ely and Hunstanton were curtailed but in 1958 British Railways agreed to operate a Sunday excursion from Sutton. Here class '2MT' 2-6-0 No. 46466, shunts round the empty coaching stock at Sutton before working the train back to Ely and on to the North Norfolk resort. The magnificent St Andrew's parish church can be seen in the background, giving a comparison of how far the station was from the town centre. Locomotive No. 46466 is fitted with the wide style of chimney. *Dr I.C. Allen*

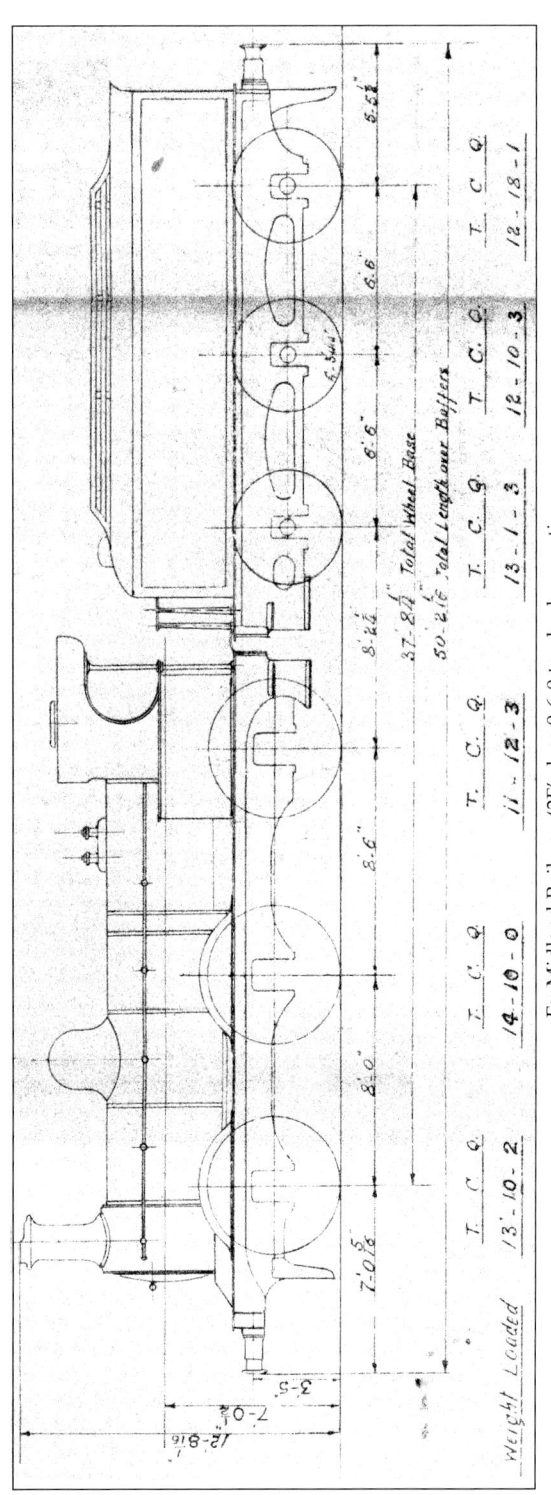

Ex-Midland Railway '2F' class 0-6-0 tender locomotive.

LOCOMOTIVES AND ROLLING STOCK 161

The LMS '2MT' tender locomotives were not the first 'foreign' steam traction to traverse the branch for during World War II when London was being bombed and at intervals until 1945, trains of essential supplies were diverted off the LMS former Midland main line at Kettering across the branch to Huntingdon and St Ives. Here because of congestion in the yards at Cambridge, the trains continued to Ely for onward working to London and some destinations in East Anglia. These trains were worked by Johnson-designed ex-Midland Railway '2F' class 0-6-0 tender locomotives dating from 1875, crewed by Kettering men with Cambridge depot providing a pilotman from St Ives to Ely and return. The engine invariably worked engine first to St Ives where after running-round its train continued tender first thence to Ely. After turning on the turntable at Ely the engine returned tender first across the branch so that it ran boiler first from St Ives to Kettering. The following locomotives were recorded on these services.

LMS No.	BR No.
2988	58162*
2990	58164*
2999	58172*
3038	58193
3039	58194
3042	58195
3090	58214
23011	58183*

* Slightly different dimensions, see below.

The leading dimensions of the '2F' class were:

Cylinders	2 inside	18 in. x 26 in.*
		18 in. x 24 in.
Motion		Stephenson with slide valves
Boiler pressure		160 psi
Coupled wheels		4 ft 11 in.*
		5 ft 3 in.
Tractive effort		19,417 lb.*
		16,786 lb.
Length over buffers		50 ft 2⅙ in.
Wheelbase	engine	16 ft 6 in.
	tender	13 ft 0 in.
	total	37 ft 8¼ in.
Weight in working order	engine	39 tons 13 cwt
	tender	38 tons 10 cwt
	total	78 tons 3 cwt
Max. axle loading		14 tons 10 cwt

With the withdrawal of steam traction in East Anglia occasional use was made of Ipswich's allocation of BR Sulzer type '2' diesel-electric locomotives Nos. D5036 to D5049, later designated class '24', on the freight trips across the branch. The leading dimensions of these Bo-Bo locomotives were:

Type	Bo-Bo
Weight in working order	75 tons

THE ELY & ST IVES RAILWAY

Tractive effort – maximum	40,000 lb.
Wheelbase	36 ft 6 in.
Wheel diameter	3 ft 9 in.
Bogie wheelbase	8 ft 6 in.
Bogie pivot centres	28 ft 0 in.
Width overall	9 ft 1⅜ in.
Length overall	50 ft 6 in.
Height overall	12 ft 8 in.
Minimum curve negotiable	4½ chains
Maximum permitted speed	75 mph
Fuel tank capacity	630 gallons
Brakes	Oerlikon type, compressed air and hand brakes on the locomotive. Vacuum brake equipment giving proportional air braking on the locomotive.
Power equipment	6-cylinder diesel engine, Sulzer '4' stroke type '6' LDA28 1160 hp at 750 rpm
Traction motors (4)	BTH type 137BY 4-pole force ventilated

The use of class '24s' was sporadic and usually Brush type '2' diesel-electric locomotives, class '31/0' and '31/1', were used on the branch goods trains and they remained the staple motive power until services were withdrawn from Ely to Sutton on 13th July, 1964 and from St Ives to Bluntisham on 5th October, 1964. The leading dimensions of the Brush type '2' locomotives were:

	Mirlees Engine	English Electric Engine
Type		A1A-A1A
Weight in working order	104 tons	106 tons
Tractive effort – maximum		42,000 lb.
Wheelbase		42 ft 10 in.
Wheel diameter		3 ft 7 in.
Bogie wheelbase		14 ft 0 in.
Bogie centres		28 ft 10 in.
Width overall		8 ft 9 in.
Length overall		56 ft 9 in.
Height overall		12 ft 7½ in.
Minimum curve negotiable		4½ chains
Maximum permitted speed		80 mph D5520-D5534 90 mph D5535-D5699, D5800-on
Fuel tank capacity		550 gallons
Brakes		Compressed air and handbrakes on the locomotive. Vacuum brake equipment giving proportional air braking on the locomotive.
Power equipment	Mirlees 12 cyl diesel engine JVs 12T 1250hp at 900 rpm	English Electric diesel engine 12SVT 1470hp at 850 rpm
Traction motors (4)		Brush DC type TM 73-68 4 pole force ventilated

The details quoted are those extant at the time the then '13/2' class operated on the Sutton and Bluntisham branches. Many alterations were subsequently made.

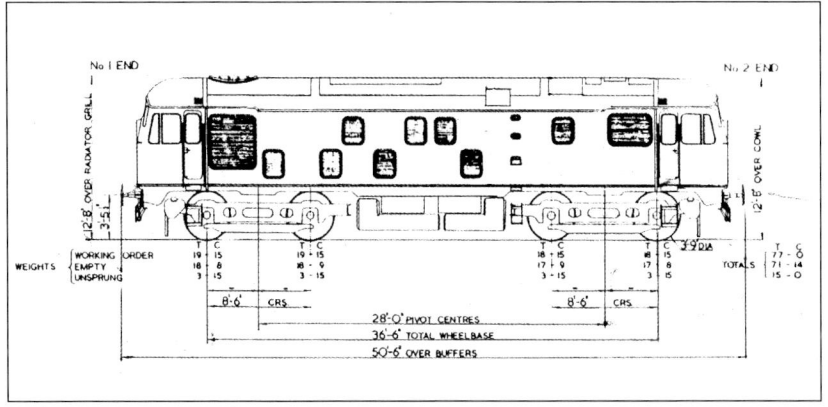

BR/Sulzer type '2' 1160 hp Bo-Bo diesel-electric locomotive, later BR class '24'.

Facilities and Footplate Staff

When the EHSR opened to traffic a locomotive was stabled overnight at Sutton where simple facilities were maintained including a coaling stage, water tank and small turntable installed at the insistence of the Board of Trade inspector and built by Simpson, the contractor, at a cost of £68 7s. 0d. Although mention was also made regarding the provision of a locomotive turntable at Thetford Corner, there is no evidence to confirm whether it was installed or not as the GER already possessed a turntable at Ely. Indeed the turntable at Sutton appears to have been little used, hence the derailment of 'Jenny Lind' locomotive No. 107 working tender first to Ely. It is believed two sets of men were outbased at Sutton, including driver Beaumont involved in the accident at Sutton Branch Junction. By October 1866 it was deemed more economical to work the line out and back from Ely and the facilities at Sutton were withdrawn and motive power staff transferred. After the line was extended the branch was worked by Cambridge, Ely and St Ives depots, the latter an outbase of Cambridge with one locomotive allocated to work the branch. From about 1910 until the withdrawal of passenger services a Huntingdon-based locomotive, usually a 'C32' class (LNER 'F3') 2-4-2T, was diagrammed to work across the branch. In BR days Cambridge shed was coded 31A.

As well as Ely and St Ives footplate staff signing route knowledge sheets for the Sutton branch, Cambridge, Peterborough, March and Huntingdon men also signed for the route in GER and early LNER days. After the withdrawal of passenger services, Ely, Cambridge and March men worked the freight services.

Locomotive water supplies were available at Ely, where a jib crane was located at the end of the down platform for down platform and down through lines, a water column on the up main platform, a jib crane at the up end of the back platform and a jib crane by the locomotive shed road for the use of engines on the turntable and shed roads. At St Ives a jib crane was located at the London end of the up platform, a jib crane at the country end of the down platform and a tank at the London end of the Huntingdon branch platform. In the early days a water supply was also available at Sutton to replenish the locomotive outbased at that depot.

In early GER days a 45 ft diameter turntable was available for turning engines at Ely. This was later increased in length to 45 ft 3 in. and then 55 ft 0 in. to accommodate longer locomotives. No turntable was available at St Ives and if locomotives required turning they were sent to Huntingdon where there was a 50 ft diameter turntable.

CAMBRIDGE DEPOT

WEEK DAYS.

No. 21.

arr. a.m.		dep. a.m.
	On Duty	5 40
	Loco	6 25 L
	Cambridge	6 40
7 12	St. Ives	7 17
8 21	Ely	9 45
10 29	St. Ives	{ 11 11 M Th. X p.m.
		12 15 Th. O
		12 45 M O
MTh.X 11 54		
Th.O 12 58	Ely	p.m.
MO 1 28		12 37 M Th. X
MTh.X 1 19		2 31 M Th. O
MTh.O 3 15	St. Ives	3 55
4 7	Huntingdon	4 24
4 36	St. Ives	5 23
6 11	Ely	6 49
7 34	St. Ives	7 51
8 25	Cambridge	L
	Loco	

First set travel home passengers M Th. X
by 1.39 p.m. ex St. Ives. M Th. O by
1.45 p.m. ex Ely.
Second set travel pass. to St. Ives. M Th X
by 11.33 a.m. ex Cambridge.
Second set travel pass. to Ely. M Th O by
11.45 a.m. ex Cambridge.
Men to be relieved on arrival 8.25 p.m.

HUNTINGDON DEPOT.

No. 1.

arr. a.m.		dep. a.m.
	On Duty	5 45
	Loco	6 30 L
	Huntingdon	6 58
7 10	St. Ives	7 20
7 32	Huntingdon	7 58
		8 30 M O
8 11	St. Ives	8 56 M X
M O 8 42	Huntingdon	8 50 M O Cattle
M X 9 8		
M O 9 5	St. Ives	9 55 G M O
10 5	Godmanch'st'r	
	Huntingdon	9 20 L M X
M X 9 23	G'dm'nch'st'r	10 25 L
10 30	Huntingdon	10 38
10 50	St. Ives	11 4
		p.m.
11 16	Huntingdon	12 5 E M O
		p.m.
12 18	St. Ives	12 40 M O
12 54	Huntingdon	1 20
1 52	St. Ives	2 6
2 18	Huntingdon	2 47
2 59	St. Ives	3 15
3 59	Ely	4 38
5 29	St. Ives	5 35
5 47	Huntingdon	5 58
6 10	St. Ives	6 24
6 38	Huntingdon	6 58
7 10	St. Ives	8 0
8 12	Huntingdon	L
	Loco	

Men change at Huntingdon 1.15 p.m.

Locomotive and enginemen's diagram Cambridge depot, 1925 showing the working over the Ely to St Ives line.

Locomotive and enginemen's workings Huntingdon East depot, 1925 showing the working over the Ely to St Ives branch.

The crew of 'J17' class 0-6-0 No. 65578 together with the guard and porter-in-charge at Sutton pose for the camera between shunting operations on 28th July, 1961. *R. Powell*

LOCOMOTIVES AND ROLLING STOCK   165

Initially the engine working the booked branch services carried no headlamp by day and one white light at the base of the chimney by night. Special trains only carried lights at night with the engine displaying a white light at the base of the chimney and another on the buffer beam, if fitted with a lamp bracket, or presumably attached to the coupling. By 1875 the headcode for ordinary trains was the same but special trains carried a white disc at the base of the chimney by day and two white lights at night. The special trains carried a white disc at the base of the chimney by day and two white lights at night. The branch headcode carried by locomotives hauling the branch trains in later GER days was a red light at the top of the smokebox by the chimney and a white light on the buffer beam. During daylight hours in place of the oil lamp a circular disc with red centre and white rim, was carried by the chimney. Special trains carried an additional white light by night or white disc by day on the buffer beam. By 1890 a red disc with white outer rim was carried at the base of the chimney by day and a red light under the chimney and a white light on the left-hand end of the buffer beam by night. Special trains then carried a red disc with white outer rim under the chimney and a white disc in the centre of the buffer beam by day, whilst at night a red lamp under the chimney and white lights on the left and right-hand ends of the buffer beam were stipulated. In 1903 the headcode for the single line was again changed to a red disc with white outer rim under the chimney during daylight hours and a red lamp under the chimney and a green lamp on the left-hand end of the buffer beam by night. From 1910 ordinary and special trains carried the same code with red disc with white outer rim or red lamp under the chimney and a green disc with white outer rim or green lamp over the left-hand end of the buffer beam. After Grouping the LNER phased out the red and green lamps and discs as a possible source of danger and replaced them with purple discs and lights. From 1925 the standard stopping passenger train code of white light or white disc at the base of the chimney was used on the Ely to St Ives branch trains and remained in use until the withdrawal of passenger services. Freight train on the branch then carried the appropriate Railway Clearing House class headcode.

The engine whistle code to be sounded by enginemen of locomotives of trains approaching Ely Sutton Branch Junction signal box was one distinct sound for the main line and three distinct sounds for the Sutton branch. At Sutton station junction, one distinct sound was made for an engine or train requiring the main single line and three distinct sounds for movements to and from the goods yard. On the approach to Needingworth Junction signal box, movements on the main line required one distinct sound and trains entering or leaving the Sutton branch made three distinct sounds.

In the event of a mishap or derailment, the Cambridge breakdown vans, later breakdown crane and vans, covered the Ely to St Ives branch, using GER No. 1A, a 10 ton capacity crane dating from 1885. When this was withdrawn Rapier 35 ton crane, LNER No. 961601 built in 1932, was utilized. Latterly Cowan's 45 ton capacity steam crane LNER 961606 (Works No. 6873), dating from 1940, later renumbered by BR to 133 and then 330133 was utilized.

Coaching Stock

The GER placed no weight or loading gauge restrictions for coaching stock on the Ely to St Ives line and conventional branch line rolling stock was used. Initially coaching stock consisted of very primitive four-wheel vehicles, with first, second and third class accommodation as well as catering for Parliamentary fare paying passengers who travelled in third class on selective trains. The first class vehicles had fully upholstered seating in compartments, whilst at the other end of the scale third class passengers were subjected to sitting on bare wooden boards. Until 1900 the coaching stock was exclusively four-wheel, provided with oil lighting and equipped with the Westinghouse brake.

During the 1860s and 1870s the stock provided was Sinclair's design for the Eastern Counties Railway with four-compartment first/second composites to diagram 33, five-compartment thirds to diagram 34, both with 24 ft body length, and a full brake van to diagram 39 with 21 ft body. The branch train usually comprised four vehicles with one composite, two full thirds and one brake van as the formation. On St Ives market day, an additional full third and composite were attached. The principal dimensions of these vehicles were:

GER diagram No.	33	34	39
	4 wheel	4 wheel	4 wheel
	Composite	Third	Full Brake
Length over body	24 ft 0 in.	24 ft 0 in.	21 ft 0 in.
Body height	6 ft 1 ¾ in.	6 ft 5 ¾ in.	6 ft 2 ½ in.
Wheelbase	13 ft 6 in.	13 ft 6 in.	12 ft 0 in.
Seating 1st class	16	–	–
3rd class	20*	50	–
Weight empty	8 tons 2 cwt	7 tons 5 cwt	7 tons 17 cwt

* Second or third class

By the late 1880s and during the 1890s, six-wheel coaches were introduced on main line services and subsequently the older stock was superseded by GER four-wheel vehicles of 26 to 27 ft body lengths which were cascaded down to work on branch and cross-country services, including Ely to St Ives. A set of three or four coaches formed of four-compartment first/third composite to diagram 216, one or two five-compartment thirds to diagram 401 and a brake/third to diagram 502, usually sufficed for most periods of the year, although if the train required strengthening an additional five-compartment third was added. Prior to abolition of second class accommodation outside the London suburban area, the composite would have provided first/second accommodation. The leading dimensions of these vehicles were:

GER Diagram No	216	401	502
	4 wheel	4 wheel	4 wheel
	Composite	Third	Brake/Third
Length over body	26 ft 0 in.	26 ft 0 ¾ in.	27 ft 0 in.
Height overall	10 ft 11 in.	10 ft 10 in.	10 ft 11 in.
Body height	6 ft 8 in.	6 ft 8 in.	6 ft 8 in.
Width over body	8 ft 0 in.	8 ft 0 in.	8 ft 0 in.
Width over guard's lookout	–	–	9 ft 0 in.
Wheelbase	15 ft 3 in.	15 ft 3 in.	15 ft 3 in.
Seating 1st class	16	–	–
3rd class	20*	50	30
Luggage	–	–	15 cwt
Weight empty	8 tons 1 cwt	8 tons 9 cwt	9 tons 5 cwt

* Second or third class

LOCOMOTIVES AND ROLLING STOCK 167

Soon after the turn of the century the four-wheel stock used on the line was replaced by six-wheel vehicles displaced from main line duties. Dating from the 1880s the vehicles were a considerable improvement over the older vehicles and were equipped with gas lighting. A three- or four-coach train formed of first/third composite with luggage accommodation to diagram 200, one or two six-compartment thirds to diagram 403 and a brake/third to diagram 511 or 514 usually sufficed for normal working. On occasions a four-wheel brake to diagram 505 may have been used in preference to the six-wheel brake/third, especially on Monday, St Ives market day, when additional produce was conveyed. The leading dimensions of these vehicles were:

GER Diagram	200	403	511	505
	6 wheel	6 wheel	6 wheel	4 wheel
	Composite	Third	Brake/Third	Brake
Length over buffers	35 ft 1½ in.	37 ft 7½ in.	35 ft 1 ½ in.	
Length over body	31 ft 6 in.	34 ft 0 in.	31 ft 6 in.	26 ft 0 in.
Height overall	10 ft 11½ in.	11 ft 3 in.	11 ft 2 in.	10 ft 11 in.
	11 ft 2½ in.			
Width over body	8 ft 0 in.	8 ft 0 in.	8 ft 0 in.	8 ft 0 in.
Width over guard's lookout	–	–	9 ft 0 in.	9 ft 3½ in.
Wheelbase	20 ft 0 in.	21 ft 0 in.	20 ft 0 in.	15 ft 3 in.
Seating 1st class	12	–	–	–
3rd class	20	60	30	–
Luggage	15 cwt	–	2 tons	3 tons
Weight empty	12 tons 15 cwt	13 tons 3 cwt	12 tons 18 cwt	8 tons 18 cwt

Increasing competition from motor bus services in the early 1920s led to the GER authorities seeking ways of making economies in the operation of its branch lines, whilst at the same time bringing improvements to the services. After investigations were carried out, it was decided to introduce conductor-guard working and at the same time provide cheaply built halts at suitable locations, in conjunction with the introduction of specially adapted rolling stock to serve the halts as well as existing stations. As part of the programme the Ely to St Ives branch was duly investigated and although no new halts were considered necessary, conductor-guard working was introduced in December 1922.

The existing rolling stock was withdrawn and replaced by specially adapted three-coach sets comprising a first/third composite, a full third and a three- or four-compartment brake/third. The coaches were gangwayed internally with a central door and drop plates at the end of each vehicle to afford the guard access between vehicles when collecting fares. The brake/third had a central gangway from the guard's compartment to the end door at the opposite end of the vehicle. The brake/third had retractable steps on each side of the vehicle, which were adapted to move out from the vehicle and inward flush with the side of the vehicle. These steps provided for use at the new halts were never used on the Ely to St Ives services. Direct access could be obtained to all coaches at the branch stations in the usual way except that only the end doors could be used as the intermediate doors were sealed off. The vehicles sufficed until the withdrawal of passenger services on 2nd February, 1931.

The carriage sets used for the conductor-guard working were converted from ordinary main line stock and appeared in the crimson livery adopted by the GER in

THE ELY & ST IVES RAILWAY

1911. In due course the LNER painted the stock in the more familiar teak or brown livery. The conductor-guard sets used on the Ely to St Ives line comprised vehicles of three types, brake/thirds to GER diagram 552 converted from main line stock diagram 514, first/ third composites to GER diagram 246 or 248 converted from main line vehicles diagrams 219, 404 and 422 and full thirds to diagram 440 converted from full thirds diagram 404. No specific numbers of coaches used on the branch are known but broad details of conversions were:

Brake/third diagram 552 Converted from main line brake/thirds built 1888-96 (diagram 514), 18 vehicles converted, four in 1922, 14 in 1923; five withdrawn 1932-3, 1 withdrawn 1937, 12 withdrawn 1940.

First/third composite, dia. 246 & 248 2 converted from composites built in 1890 and 1891 (diagram 219), converted 1922 and withdrawn 1933 and 1935, 18 converted from main line thirds built 1892 (diagram 404) and 1893-4 (diagram 422), nine converted in 1922, nine converted in 1923; two vehicles withdrawn 1932, one withdrawn 1934 and the remaining 15 withdrawn in 1940.

Full third, diagram 440 Converted from main line thirds built 1889 to 1892 (diagram 404), built 1893/4 (diagram 422), 22 vehicles converted, 10 in 1922, 12 in 1923; 6 withdrawn 1932/3, 16 withdrawn 1940.

The leading dimensions of the original vehicles and the conversions were:

GER Diagram No.	219	404	514	246
	6 wheel	6 wheel	6 wheel	6 wheel
	Composite	Third	Brake/third	Composite
Length over buffers	35 ft 1½ in.	37 ft 7½ in.	37 ft 4½ in. 37 ft 7½ in.	35 ft 1½ in.
Length over body	32 ft 0 in.	34 ft 6 in.	34 ft 6 in.	32 ft 0 in.
Height overall	11 ft 2 in.	11 ft 3 in.	11 ft 3 in.	11 ft 3¾ in.
Body height	6 ft 11 in.	7 ft 0 in.	7 ft 0 in.	6 ft 11 in.
Width over body	8 ft 0 in.	8 ft 0 in.	8 ft 0 in.	8 ft 0 in.
Width over guard's lookout	–	–	9 ft 3½ in.	–
Wheelbase	20 ft 0 in.	21 ft 0 in.	20 ft 0 in. 22 ft 6 in.	20 ft 0 in.
Seating 1st class	12	–	–	12
3rd class	20	60	30	16
Luggage	15 cwt	–	2 tons	15 cwt
Weight empty	12 tons 16 cwt	13 tons 3 cwt	12 tons 16 cwt 16 tons 14 cwt	13 tons 0 cwt
	Original dimensions converted to diagram 246/248	Original dimensions converted to diagram 246/248	Original dimensions converted to diagram 552	Converted from diagram 219, 404 or 422

GER Diagram No.	248	440	552	422
	6 wheel	6 wheel	6 wheel	6 wheel
	Composite	Third	Brake/Third	Third
Length over buffers	37 ft 4½ in.	37 ft 7½ in.	37 ft 4½ in. 37 ft 7½ in.	37 ft 7½ in.
Length over body	34 ft 6 in.	34 ft 6 in.	34 ft 6 in.	34 ft 6 in.
Height overall	11 ft 3 in.	11 ft 3 in.	11 ft 3 in.	11 ft 7 in.

LOCOMOTIVES AND ROLLING STOCK

Body height	7 ft 0 in.	7 ft 0 in.	7 ft 0 in.	7 ft 4 in.
Width over body	8 ft 0 in.	8 ft 0 in.	8 ft 0 in.	8 ft 0 in.
Width over guard's lookout	–	–	9 ft 3½ in.	–
Wheelbase	22 ft 0 in.	21 ft 0 in.	21 ft 0 in.	22 ft 6 in.
Seating 1st class	12	–	–	–
3rd class	32	43	24	60
Luggage	–	–	2 tons	–
Weight empty	13 tons 0 cwt converted from diagram 219, 404 or 422	13 tons 0 cwt converted from diagram 404 or 422	12 tons 16 cwt converted from diagram 514	18 tons 3 cwt original dimensions converted to diagrams 440, 246 and 248

Conversion of passenger carrying stock from oil to gas lighting was completed by the early 1900s and carriage charging of gas was carried out on the branch vehicles at Ely or Cambridge. For repairs and routine maintenance the coaching stock was returned to Cambridge for attention. Similarly replacement vehicles were provided by Cambridge.

After closure of the line to regular passenger traffic a few excursion trains ran from the branch stations and were formed of a variety of GER and LNER bogie corridor stock and in one instance ex-LMS corridor stock.

Wagon Stock

The wagons initially used by the GER were wooden open vehicles with side doors and fitted with dumb buffers. Where grain, straw and merchandise were susceptible to wet weather, a tarpaulin sheet was used to cover the contents of the wagon. The brake van at the tail of the train would have been a 10 ton vehicle. In the years prior to the turn of the century the GER utilized four-plank bodied, open wagons with wooden frames, dating from 1882 for the conveyance of general merchandise and minerals. From 1887, these wagons were gradually superseded by five-plank, 9 ton capacity (later 10 ton) opens, to diagram 16 with 9 ft 6 in. wheelbase and measuring 15 ft 0 in. over headstocks. Later 10 ton, five-plank open wagons to diagram 17, with a length of 15 ft over headstocks and 9 ft 0 in. wheelbase, were also used. Another variation was the use of 10 ton, seven-plank opens to diagram 55, measuring 17 ft 0 in. over headstocks and 9 ft 6 in. wheelbase for vegetable and root traffic. For fruit and perishable traffic, 10 ton ventilated vans to diagram 15 were provided, measuring 16 ft 1 in. over headstocks, with 9 ft 0 in. wheelbase and overall height of 11 ft 0¾ in. Later covered goods vans to diagram 47 were also used.

They measured 17 ft 3 in. over headstocks, had a wheelbase of 10 ft 6 in. and were 11 ft 2 in. in height. A third variation was the 10 ton capacity covered goods wagon to diagram 72, which measured 19 ft 0 in. over headstocks, whilst maintaining a 10 ft 6 in. wheelbase. The extensive cattle traffic conveyed to and from Cambridge, St Ives and Ely markets would have employed the use of three types of cattle wagons on the line. The first of 8 tons capacity was to diagram 5 and was 18 ft 7 in. over headstocks, had a 10 ft 6 in. wheelbase and was 10 ft 10¾ in. in height. The second to diagram 6 was of 9 tons capacity and measured 19 ft 0 in. over headstocks, with a 10 ft 6 in. wheelbase and overall height of 10 ft 10½ in. The third GER variant of cattle wagon to diagram 7 was of 10 tons capacity, 19 ft 3 in. over headstocks with 10 ft 6 in. wheelbase and overall height of 11 ft 2 in. At the tail of the train was usually a 20 ton four-wheel brake van to GER diagram 56 measuring 17 ft 6 in. over headstocks, a 10 ft 3 in. wheelbase and 3 ft 1 in. diameter wheels. In addition many wagons owned by other railway companies were used to deliver and collect agricultural and livestock traffic, whilst coal and coke supplies came in private owner coal wagons. These fell into two categories, those belonging to the collieries consigning the coal and merchants and coal factors wagons, which were loaded at the collieries.

After Grouping the GER wagons continued to be used, but gradually LNER standard design of wagons made an appearance. The most numerous were probably the 12 ton, five-plank opens with an 8 ft 0 in. wheelbase to code 2, and 12 ton, six-plank opens with 10 ft 0 in. wheelbase to code 91 built after 1932. Later variations included a 13 ton, seven-plank open wagon to code 162 measuring 16 ft 6 in. over headstocks and with a 9 ft 0 in. wheelbase. All were used on vegetable and sugar beet traffic. Fitted and unfitted 12 ton, 9 ft 0 in. wheelbase covered vans to code 16 conveyed perishable goods, fruit and malt and later some were designated for fruit traffic only. From 1934 12 ton capacity vans to code 171, with steel underframe and pressed corrugated steel ends, were introduced whilst at the same time the wheelbase was extended to a length of 10 ft 0 in. Specific fruit vans with both 9 ft 0 in. and 10 ft 0 in. wheelbase also saw service of the Ely to St Ives branch for malt traffic. Agricultural machinery destined for local farms were delivered on 12 ton 'Lowfit' wagons, with 10 ft wheelbase and overall length over headstocks of 17 ft 6 in. Larger machinery arrived or departed on one of the ex-GER 14 ton, 25 ft 6 in. 'Mac K2' machinery wagons to diagram 75 and later LNER builds. LNER goods brake vans provided for branch traffic included 20 ton 'Toad B' to code 34 and 'Toad E' to code 64 with 10 ft 6 in. wheelbase and measuring 22 ft 5 in. over buffers. Later 'Toad D' brake vans to code 61 with 16 ft 0 in. wheelbase and measuring 27 ft 5 in. over buffers were employed. After nationalization many of the older wooden-bodied vehicles were scrapped and much of the traffic was conveyed in the standard 16 ton all-steel mineral wagons.

In GER days the body, solebars and headstocks of the open and closed wagons were painted slate grey, whilst the ironwork below the solebar level, buffer guides, drawbar plates and couplings were black. The LNER wagon livery was grey for non-fitted wagons and covered vans, whilst vehicles fitted with automatic brakes incuding brake vans were painted red oxide, which changed to bauxite around 1940. Similar liveries were carried in BR days.

The maintenance of wagon stock used on the line was carried out by the wagon repair shops at Cambridge or by wagon repairers based at Ely and St Ives.

Appendix One

Lengths of Platforms and Sidings

Location	Distance from St Ives		Platforms Down	Loop Up	Sidings	
	m.	ch.	ft	ft	ft	ft
Bluntisham	3	62	250			150 cattle dock
						400 shed road
						220 coal
Earith Bridge	5	60	200			200 headshunt
						150 dock
						310 yard loop
Sutton	10	16	250	230	780	140 cattle dock
						680 up yard
						850 down yard
						370 yard loop
						500 forage*
						400 forage back road*
						80 forage turntable*
						150 forage shed*
Isle of Ely Brick Co. (Jewson's)						300 brickworks*
Haddenham	11	71		230		480 down reception
						50 down headshunt
						470 shed road
						400 yard
						170 dock
						130 up headshunt
						380 yard loop
						280 brickyard*
Wilburton	12	79		180		340 shed and yard
						160 headshunt
						310 refuge
Stretham	14	74		200		180 dock
						300 yard
						340 refuge

* Private sidings.

Appendix Two

Level Crossings

No.	Location	Mileage m. ch.		Local name	Status
13*	Needingworth Jn & Bluntisham	1	75		Occupation
14	Needingworth Jn & Bluntisham	2	03	Junction Crossing or Lowndes Drove	Public
15	Needingworth Jn & Bluntisham	2	13		Occupation
16	Needingworth Jn & Bluntisham	2	35	Heath Barn	Occupation
17	Needingworth Jn & Bluntisham	2	61		Occupation
18	Needingworth Jn & Bluntisham	2	77		Occupation
19	Needingworth Jn & Bluntisham	3	20	Low Wood	Occupation
20	Bluntisham & Earith Bridge	3	76	Little London	Footpath
21	Bluntisham & Earith Bridge	4	12	Islington	Occupation
22	Bluntisham & Earith Bridge	4	54	Pump House	Footpath
23	Bluntisham & Earith Bridge	4	69	Ouse Footpath	Public
24	Bluntisham & Earith Bridge	5	18	Cranes Fen	Occupation
25	Bluntisham & Earith Bridge	5	54	Hermitage Sluice	Public
26	Earith Bridge & Sutton	5	63	Hill Row Causeway	Public
27	Earith Bridge & Sutton	5	68		Footpath
28	Earith Bridge & Sutton	5	73		Footpath
29	Earith Bridge & Sutton	6	07		Occupation
30	Earith Bridge & Sutton	6	69		Occupation
31	Earith Bridge & Sutton	6	71		Occupation
32	Earith Bridge & Sutton	7	01		Occupation
33	Earith Bridge & Sutton	7	68		Occupation
34	Earith Bridge & Sutton	8	19		Occupation
35	Earith Bridge & Sutton	8	63	Rymanmoor Drove	Public
36	Earith Bridge & Sutton	9	09		Occupation
37	Earith Bridge & Sutton	9	11		Occupation
38	Earith Bridge & Sutton	9	18		Occupation
39	Earith Bridge & Sutton	9	21		Occupation
40	Earith Bridge & Sutton	9	22		Occupation
41	Earith Bridge & Sutton	9	24		Occupation
42	Earith Bridge & Sutton	9	26		Occupation
43	Earith Bridge & Sutton	9	28		Occupation
44	Earith Bridge & Sutton	9	29		Occupation
45	Earith Bridge & Sutton	9	31		Occupation
46	Earith Bridge & Sutton	9	33		Occupation
47	Earith Bridge & Sutton	9	34		Occupation
48	Earith Bridge & Sutton	9	36		Occupation
49	Earith Bridge & Sutton	9	39		Occupation
50	Earith Bridge & Sutton	9	41		Occupation
51	Earith Bridge & Sutton	9	44		Occupation
52	Earith Bridge & Sutton	9	51		Occupation
53	Earith Bridge & Sutton	9	53		Occupation
54	Earith Bridge & Sutton	9	55		Occupation
55	Earith Bridge & Sutton	9	57		Occupation
56	Earith Bridge & Sutton	9	58		Footpath

* Level Crossings Nos. 1 to 12 located on main line between St Ives and Needingworth Junction.

APPENDIX

No.	Location	Mileage m. ch.		Local name	Status
57	Earith Bridge & Sutton	9	64		Occupation
58	Earith Bridge & Sutton	9	67		Footpath
59	Earith Bridge & Sutton	10	08		Occupation
60	Earith Bridge & Sutton	10	10	Allotments	Footpath
61	Sutton & Haddenham	10	33		Occupation
62	Sutton & Haddenham	10	48		Occupation
63	Sutton & Haddenham	10	51		Occupation
64	Sutton & Haddenham	10	58		Occupation
65	Sutton & Haddenham	11	07	Milkinghill/ Bread & Cheese Lane	Footpath
66	Haddenham & Wilburton	12	33	Hedges Road	Public
67*	Haddenham & Wilburton	12	36		Occupation
68	Haddenham & Wilburton	12	62	Hawk's Nest	Occupation
69	Haddenham & Wilburton	12	77	Wilburton Station	Public
70	Wilburton & Stretham	13	20		Occupation
71	Wilburton & Stretham	13	43		Occupation
72	Wilburton & Stretham	13	54		Occupation
73	Wilburton & Stretham	13	59		Occupation
74	Wilburton & Stretham	13	69		Occupation
75	Wilburton & Stretham	13	75		Occupation
76	Wilburton & Stretham	14	01		Occupation
77	Wilburton & Stretham	14	14	Crow's Farm	Occupation
78	Wilburton & Stretham	14	28		Occupation
79	Wilburton & Stretham	14	40	Granger's/ Grunty Fen Farm	Occupation
80	Stretham & Sutton Branch Jn	14	75	Stretham Station	Public
81	Stretham & Sutton Branch Jn	15	12	Roman Road	Footpath
82	Stretham & Sutton Branch Jn	15	25	Allotments	Occupation
83	Stretham & Sutton Branch Jn	15	58	Thetford Corner	Public
84	Stretham & Sutton Branch Jn	15	60	Cambridge Road	Public
85	Stretham & Sutton Branch Jn	15	79		Footpath
86	Stretham & Sutton Branch Jn	16	50	Alderbrook Farm	Occupation

'J17' class 0-6-0 No 65565 on the Ely to St Ives daily freight trip approaching Earith Bridge just before the section of line between Sutton and Bluntisham was closed to traffic. The member of station staff holds open the gate of Hill Row Causeway level crossing No. 26, at 5 miles 63 chains from St Ives, for the train to pass. With true branch line malpractice he has not locked the gate against possible road traffic.

* Closed 12th November, 1943.
Level crossings without a name were generally referred to by number only.

Appendix Three

Bridges

No.	Location	Mileage m. ch.	Local name	Under or over	Type	Spans No.	Square span between abutments or supports ft in	Skew span between abutments or supports ft in	Width ft in	Depth of construction ft in	Distance from road or surface of water to rail ft in	Construction
2289	Needingworth Jn & Bluntisham	3 60	Bluntisham Road	Over	Public	1	26 0	34 0	25 6	3 6	18 6	Brick abutments, brick arch and parapets. Hunts County Council maintenance from 31.10.1934
2290	Bluntisham & Earith Bridge	4 28	Wadsby Folly (aka Bluntisham Fen Culvert)	Under	Stream	1	6 0	8 0	36 0	6 6	10 6	Brick abutments, brick arch, 6 ft invert
2291	Bluntisham & Earith Bridge	4 32	Bury Fen	Under	Occupation	1	10 0		14 6	1 9	16 3	Brick abutments, troughs ballasted
2292	Bluntisham & Earith Bridge	4 55	River Ouse Viaduct	Under	River	19	18 8 / 19 3 / 19 6 / 19 7 / 19 8 / 19 9 / 19 9 / 19 10 / 19 6 / 19 9 / 19 8 / 19 9 / 19 8 / 19 6 / 19 5 / 19 0 / 19 9	27 9 / 88 3 / 29 3 / 91 0 / 29 6 / 29 6 / 29 5 / 29 7 / 29 7 / 29 5 / 29 8 / 29 4 / 29 7 / 29 3 / 29 2 / 29 5 / 29 0 / 29 6				Brick abutments and piers, cylinder supports pier No. 2 for main span girders and cross girders, chaired timbers, 8 ft wide tow path
2293	Bluntisham & Earith Bridge	5 36	Earith Mill	Under	River	1	9 9	12 6	14 6	1 9	6 9	Brick abutments, running timbers in trough, steel decking
2294	Bluntisham & Earith Bridge	5 52	West River	Under	River	1	31 8	33 9	14 9	2 0	10 0	Brick abutments, cross girders, timber decking, chaired timbers, 6 ft wide towpath
2295	Earith Bridge & Sutton	8 49	South Fen (aka Powell's Fen Drain)	Under	River	1	6 9		14 6	1 9	7 9	Brick abutments, trough ballasted
2296	Sutton & Haddenham	11 08	Milkinghill (aka Black Fen Drain)	Under	Occupation	1	6 3	7 3		2 0	6 6	Brick abutments, running timbers chaired timbers, timber bearers
2297	Sutton & Haddenham	11 68	Haddenham Road	Over	Public	1	24 5	24 9	34 6	3 6	18 7	Brick abutments, wrought iron girders and jack arches. Isle of Ely County Council maintenance from 27.09.1929

Acknowledgements

The publication of this history would not have been possible without the help of many people. In particular I would like to thank the National Archives, British Railways Eastern Region, Cambridge Collection, Cambridgeshire County Record Office, Cambridge County Library, House of Lords Record Office, British Library Newspaper Library.

My thanks go to the late A.R. Cox, the late W. Fenton, R. Debenham, W. Mott, John Watling, Dave Taylor, Dave Hoser, Alan Keeler, Peter Webber, the late Canon C. Bayes, the late J.E. Kite, the late Peter Proud, the late B.D.J. Walsh, the late Dr I.C. Allen, Chris Cock, Robert Powell, also active and retired railway staff, some of whom worked on the line, and members of the GER Society.

Bibliography

General Works
Allen C.J.   *The Great Eastern Railway*
Gordon D.I.   *Regional History Railways of Great Britain - Vol. 5*
Gordon W.J.   *Our Home Railways - Vol 1*
Joby R.S.   *Forgotten Railways of East Anglia*

Periodicals
Bradshaw's Railway Manual
British Railways (Eastern Region) Magazine
Buses
Great Eastern Railway Magazine
Locomotive Carriage and Wagon Review
Locomotive Magazine
LNER Magazine
Railway Magazine
Railway Times
Railway World
Railway Year Book
Trains Illustrated

Minute Books
Eastern Counties Railway
Ely Haddenham and Sutton Railway
Ely and St Ives Railway
Great Eastern Railway
London and North Eastern Railway

Working Timetables and Appendices to Working Timetables
Great Eastern Railway
London and North Eastern Railway
British Railways Eastern Region

Newspapers
Cambridge Chronicle
Cambridge Independent Press
Cambridge Weekly News
Huntingdon Advertiser
Isle of Ely and Wisbech Advertiser
Wisbech Standard

Index

Accidents and incidents, 13, 14, 26, 28, 31, 141, 163
Acts of Parliament, 7, 9, 17, 21, 23, 26, 27, 29, 33, 101
Bluntisham, 23 *et seq.*, 28, 29, 39, 43, 44, 46, 47, 53 *et seq.*, 59, 60, 61, 63, 89, 95, 97, 101, 105, 112, 113, 115 *et seq.*, 135, 136, 162, 171, 172, 174
Bond, J.B., 33
Bond, T.P., 9, 14, 17, 19
BoT inspections, 11-2, 24-5, 28, 29, 33, 49, 95, 163
British Railways, 55, 59, 139, 147, 158, 161, 163, 165, 170
Bus competition (and replacement), 39, 47, 49, 51, 167
Cambridge, 6, 13, 17, 20, 31, 39, 43, 54, 59, 97, 111, 117 *et seq.*, 130, 141, 142, 145, 147, 150, 151, 158, 161, 163, 165, 169, 170
Camps, F., 7, 9, 17, 33
Closure to goods, 55, 59, 105, 111, 125, 126, 131, 162
Closure to passengers, 51, 105, 123
Conductor-guard working, 44, 46, 123, 167
Cropley, James, 9
Currie, G.W., 19
Drake's Forage Works, 35, 43, 73
Earith Bridge, 20, 21 *et seq.*, 26, 35, 43, 44, 46, 47, 53 *et seq.*, 60, 63, 97, 101, 105, 112, 113, 115 *et seq.*, 135, 136, 171, 172, 174
East Anglian Railway, 6, 27
Eastern Counties Railway, 6, 27, 139, 166
Ely, 6, 7, 10 *et seq.*, 15, 19, 24, 25, 26 *et seq.*, 47-8, 51, 53, 55, 89, 94, 111, 115 *et seq.*, 136, 139, 143, 145, 147, 161, 163, 169, 170
Ely & Huntingdon Railway, 6
Ely & St Ives Railway, 21, 23, 25, 26 *et seq.*, 60
Ely Dock Junction, 35, 51, 53, 89, 105, 111, 126
Ely, Haddenham & Sutton Rly, 7 *et seq.*, 16 *et seq.*, 60, 73, 83, 95, 97, 130, 139, 163
Ely Sutton Branch Junction, 13, 19, 23, 28, 31, 51, 53, 60, 89, 97, 101, 105, 113, 141, 163, 165, 173
Excursions, 53, 55, 127-8, 158
Fruit traffic, 53 *et seq.*, 130, 131, 156
Great Eastern Railway, 7 *et seq.*,16 *et seq.*, 26 *et seq.*, 45, 54, 59, 61, 95, 101, 105, 111, 127 *et seq.*, 137, 139, 142, 147, 149, 150, 156, 163 *et seq.*
Great Northern Railway, 20, 24, 27, 45
GN & GER Joint Line, 27, 59, 61, 112, 121, 125, 131

Grunty Fen, 9, 12, 53, 83, 115, 145
Haddenham, 6 *et seq.*, 16 *et seq.*, 26 *et seq.*, 39, 43, 45 *et seq.*, 53 *et seq.*, 60, 73, 83, 97, 101, 105, 112, 113, 115 *et seq.*, 135, 171, 173, 174
Haddenham, Willington & Longstanton Railway, 16, 17
Huntingdon, 27, 54, 61, 111, 121, 123, 128, 130, 131, 150, 158, 161, 163
Isle of Ely Brick Co. Sdg, *see Jewson's siding*
Jewson's siding, 27-8, 73, 105, 119, 131, 171
Locomotive loads, 137-8
LNER, 45 *et seq.*, 101, 105, 111, 121, 125, 137, 139, 147, 148, 150, 153, 156, 163, 165, 168 *et seq.*
March, 7, 20, 21, 24, 27, 55, 59, 111, 112, 121, 163
Mepal, 6, 9, 54, 63, 115, 135
Mousley, W.T. (contractor), 23, 139
Needingworth Jn, 24, 25, 27, 29, 35, 53, 55, 59, 61, 97, 101, 105, 111, 113, 126, 165, 172, 174
Opening to St Ives, 25, 116
Opening to Sutton, 12, 115, 139
Ouse, River, 6, 20 *et seq.*, 54, 63
Pell, O.C., 7, 9, 16 *et seq.*, 130
Railway (or Standard) Time, 111
St Ives, 6, 10, 16, 17, 20 *et seq.*, 27 *et seq.*, 39, 47, 49, 53, 54, 59, 61, 94, 112, 115 *et seq.*, 136, 145, 147, 158, 161, 163 *et seq.*, 169, 170
St Ives signal boxes, 33, 35, 45-6, 49, 111
Sale to GER, 31, 33
Shaw, W.H., 9
Simpson, Lightly, 9, 19
Simpson, W.S. (contractor), 9, 12, 95, 163
Sinclair, Mr (engineer), 7, 139, 142, 166
Stretham, 6, 9 *et seq.*, 20, 25, 26, 28, 29, 39, 44, 46, 47, 53, 55, 60, 83, 89, 97, 101, 105, 112, 115 *et seq.*, 131, 171, 173
Strikes, 39, 43, 45, 123
Sugar beet traffic, 53, 131, 156
Sutton, 6 *et seq.*, 16 *et seq.*, 26, 28 *et seq.*, 43, 44, 46, 47, 53 *et seq.*, 59, 60, 73, 89, 97, 101, 105, 111 *et seq.*, 115 *et seq.*, 131, 162, 163, 165, 171 *et seq.*,
Sutton, Mepal & Somersham Railway, 16
Valentine, J.S., 7, 9, 11 *et seq.*, 17, 19 *et seq.*, 33
Wilburton, 6 *et seq.*, 19, 20, 28, 29, 35, 39, 44, 46, 47, 53 *et seq.*, 60, 83, 97, 101, 105, 112, 113, 115 *et seq.*, 135, 171, 173
World War I, 39, 129, 130, 135
World War II, 54, 63, 83, 125, 131, 135, 138, 161